Lady in the Navy

Joy Bright, Yeoman (F) first class, USNR, February 1918.

Lady in the Navy

A Personal Reminiscence

by

Joy Bright Hancock
Captain, U.S. Navy (Retired)

The Naval Institute Press
Annapolis, Maryland

Printed in the United States of America

The opinions expressed are those of the author and do not
reflect the views of the Department of the Navy.

All photographs, unless otherwise credited, are official
U.S. Navy.

To the women of the United States Navy whom I admired and respected, and with whom I was privileged to serve.

Foreword

On 30 July 1972 the WAVES will have been a part of the U.S. Navy for thirty years. During that time they have served in shore stations across the United States and around the world, at sea and in the air, and have established standards for performance of duty and devotion to the service that might well be envied by other organizations with more years but fewer outstanding achievements to their credit.

Thirty years ago, when the subject of women in the Navy disturbed the traditional dignity of the Navy Department, there was, perhaps, in some quarters, as much consternation as if it had been proposed to convert battleship quarterdecks to truck gardens. Nevertheless, despite all fears and doubts, the ladies by the thousands donned uniforms and pitched in to help win a war. It is interesting to note that, thirty years later, the Navy has found it expedient to get rid of the battleships but finds it cannot get along without the WAVES.

In 1941 and 1942, there were few people in the Navy who remembered that in World War I the Navy had enlisted 10,000 women, then known as yeomen (F). One of these, Joy Bright Hancock, subsequently served for many years as a civilian employee of the Bureau of Aeronautics, where I was then Director of Training. That Bureau contended that, as women were then working in aircraft factories as civilians, they could equally well serve the Navy in many capacities connected with naval aviation. Joy Bright Hancock visited the Royal Canadian Air Force to find out how they utilized the services of women, and with her help and that of Rear Admiral John Towers, Commander Ralph A. Ofstie, and others, we presented the Bureau of Navigation with a plan on how to train and employ women in the Navy.

As might have been expected, its reception was less than enthusiastic. Even after Congress moved to establish the WAAC for the Army, there was within the Navy a feeling that there was no great need for women in uniform, although possibly a few jobs could be handled by them. The details of how a great many objections to women in service were overcome, in ensuing months, have been well told by Joy Bright Hancock and there is no need to mention them here, except to point out that there is nothing new about the slogan "Never Underestimate the Power of a Woman." The ladies had power in 1941 and 1942, chief among them being Representatives Edith Nourse Rogers and Margaret Chase Smith, who, together with Eleanor Roosevelt, pressed for the idea of women in uniform. Eventually, on 30 July 1942, President Roosevelt signed the bill which established the Women's Reserve of the Naval Reserve. Among the women officers first commissioned was the author of this book, Joy Bright Hancock.

Since that day, thousands of young women, officers and enlisted, have proudly served the Navy—some of them for a short wartime cruise, some of them through full and distinguished careers. They have been teachers, mechanics, technicians, control tower operators, photographers, draftsmen and printers, aeronautical engineers, attorneys, psychologists, aerographers and cryptanalysis experts.

It is of interest, sociologically, to note that those women who served in the armed forces were never confronted with the question of equal pay for equal performance. The standard had been set by the Navy when women were enlisted in World War I. The position of the Armed Services in this respect was and is entirely justified.

Anyone who served in the Navy during World War II or the Korean War will remember with pride the WAVES—enthusiastic, determined, helpful, and resourceful. It would have been impossible to issue enough ribbons and commendations to commend them all for their service.

Officers and enlisted, they have now become so much a part of the Navy that I doubt we could ever get along without them. I hope we never have to.

ARTHUR W. RADFORD
Admiral, U.S. Navy (Retired)

Introduction

No WAVE of the Navy knows more about the experience of women in the service than Joy Hancock, a veteran yeoman of the First World War, a civilian employee in the Bureau of Aeronautics, the widow of three naval officers, WAVE representative in the Bureau of Aeronautics in the Second World War, and from 1946 to 1953, Assistant Chief of Naval Personnel for Women.

Supplementing her personal reminiscences and observations with a wealth of documentary evidence, she tells a story which serves two valuable purposes. It is sure to rouse nostalgic memories as Second World War WAVES remember the chaotic early days of the service, and it provides them more factual material for their memories than has ever before been collected between the covers of one book. More significantly, it serves as a needed chapter in the history of the Navy and of American women. Chaos did end and 86,000 women did make a contribution to the winning of a war they sincerely believed was a necessary one. They were "Women Accepted for Volunteer Emergency Service" and the Navy did in truth accept them as colleagues, rallying from utter skepticism to possessive satisfaction. Under the leadership of Captain Hancock, they became a part of the regular Navy after the war emergency was past, accepted still as volunteers.

In the process, certain strong convictions about women were shattered. The Appendix to Captain Hancock's book lists 44 ratings held by enlisted WAVES. A single one of those ratings, that of seaman, involved women in 44 billets. In the 102 billets filled by women officers the author lists aviation, civil engineering, communications, supply corps, intelligence, legal, medical, general line, dental, engineering, and electronics. This record suggests that women showed a versatility not always associated with them. They accepted responsibility in a way which commended them to commanding officers as worthy replacements for men "released to fight at sea."

One of the difficulties encountered in the first months of WAVE history was the literal interpretation of congressional instructions to admit women only as replacements for men. I suspect this was part of the difficulty in supplying the Bureau of Aeronautics with the large numbers of women requested by them. It certainly restrained the Bureau of Naval Personnel from increasing the number of WAVES drastically until the law was finally interpreted to permit women to be assigned directly to new billets, created by the need for vast expansion of the Navy.

Every historian sees events from his own perspective and Joy Hancock's point of reference has long been the Bureau of Aeronautics. She knew it long before the war began. She suffered with its ranking officers because legislation admitting women was so long delayed. She looked across at the Bureau of Naval Personnel, charged with recruiting and training both men and women, and saw it moving with glacial slowness to accomplish what the Bureau of Aeronautics had wanted for months.

To unindoctrinated newcomers in the Bureau of Naval Personnel, however, things sometimes seemed to move at breakneck speed. Anyone familiar with the pace of the academic world must have marveled that in less than one month after legislation authorized the admission of women, the Navy had a Reserve Midshipman's School ready for business with a class ready to enter. Three specialist schools for enlisted women were ready to admit classes in little more than two months. Within six months one whole campus of Hunter College had been preempted and adapted to the needs of a recruit training school. Aviation training schools moved fast to admit women. At the end of the first year 27,000 women were on duty. The Navy taught its newcomers that it is an impressively adaptable organization.

This book is the story of a wartime adaptation of major

proportions; the invasion of a man's world by thousands of women invited to invade. The story is told by an active participant in that adaptation, an officer who served "above and beyond the call of duty," devoted both to the Navy and to the women whose capacity she never doubted.

As an autobiography it is fascinating. Captain Hancock tells of her childhood, her trips to many parts of the world, on and off the beaten track. She describes encounters with famous men and women and with anonymous enlisted women at barracks meetings. She reports dramatic moments when she christened ships, took reviews, received honors of many kinds, and experienced the satisfaction of achievement.

This is a memorable story, told by a woman memorable in naval history.

MILDRED M^CAFEE HORTON
Captain, U.S. Naval Reserve

Contents

Lady in the Navy

The next thing most like living one's life over again seems to be a recollection of that life, and to make the recollection as durable as possible by putting it down in writing.

Benjamin Franklin

WAVES of the Ship's Company render a salute of honor to the reviewing officer, Captain Joy Bright Hancock, USN, Assistant Chief of Naval Personnel for Women. *Above*, she is accompanied by Captain Frederick Wolsieffer, USN, the commanding officer of the Recruit Training Command, U.S. Naval Training Center, Bainbridge, Maryland. The occasion, the 97th Graduation Review, marked Captain Hancock's last official appearance before her retirement in June 1953.

A salute to the colors at the 97th Graduation Review, May 1953, at the U.S. Naval Training Center, Bainbridge. *Opposite*, front row, left to right: Captain Hancock, Captain Wolsieffer, and Lieutenant Commander Jean M. Stewart, USN, officer in charge of WAVE Recruit Training.

In Retrospect

$\mathcal{T}$HE reviewing officer this morning is a woman who has had a long and distinguished career in the naval service: first as an enlisted woman in World War I; later as a civilian employee in connection with editorial and research matters pertaining to naval aviation; and, finally, as a commissioned officer in key positions of great responsibility in various sections of the Navy Department in Washington, D.C.

"At the close of World War II, she was commended by the Secretary of the Navy for her outstanding performance of duty of great responsibility, that of the development, expansion, and administration of the complex and comprehensive program designed to integrate women in the naval service and to utilize their various skills effectively.

"In July of 1946, she was designated the Assistant Chief of Naval Personnel for Women, in which capacity she has served as the director of the WAVES, and, technically, as the official adviser on women's affairs in the naval service.

"This will be her last official appearance here at Bainbridge. She will be transferred to the retired list of the Navy, effective June 1, 1953....

"And now, it is with distinct honor and great pleasure that I introduce to you my esteemed friend and colleague, the Assistant Chief of Naval Personnel for Women, the First Lady of the Navy, Captain Joy Bright Hancock."

As the words of the commanding officer of the Recruit Training Command died away, I rose to perform one of my last official acts before retirement—that of reviewing officer at the recruit review and graduation exercises of the men and women at the U.S. Naval Training Center, Bainbridge, Maryland, 23 May 1953.

For me it was a day filled with emotion as well as great pride. Before me on the field, in whites, the men and women of the Navy were drawn up in company formation. The women were only a small part of the assembled recruits, of which there were well over fifteen hundred, but they were the living symbol of what we had accomplished in the program for women in the Navy: they were an integral part of the naval service.

And here was I, standing at attention before this ninety-seventh graduation review, with both the WAVE and male recruit drill teams performing in front of the reviewing stand, Captain Frederick Wolsieffer's words of praise still ringing in my ears: "...a long and distinguished career in the naval service... an enlisted woman in World War I... Assistant Chief of Naval Personnel for Women... Director of the WAVES... the First Lady of the Navy...!"

Captain Joy Bright Hancock... about to retire! Could this indeed be the same little red-headed, blue-eyed girl who had arrived on 4 May 1898, and was named Joy to offset her father's disappointment that his third child was not a boy? So much has intervened in those fifty-five years. Four wars, tremendous technological advances, make the early 1900s seem light years away and the surroundings of my youth are remembered as some backwater of a little-known civilization....

My two sisters and I were the sturdy heirs of an even sturdier generation, for our parents lived their early lives under conditions that would be regarded today as primitive. My father, William Henry Bright, was born 21 October 1863, in the first frame house erected in Sanilac County, Michigan, on the shore of Lake Huron. His parents had been living in a log cabin, and the baby might have found this humble, traditional beginning his own had not my grandfather, Henry Bright, determined that his son should make his earthly entrance in a frame house. Skilled as a master carpenter, Henry Bright built the house in time for the arrival of his son, the first of ten children, eight of whom grew to maturity.

But William Henry's time in Michigan was of no great duration, for by the time he was two years old his father and mother (Mary McClintoch Bright) had returned to Philadelphia. My grandmother found nothing congenial in the forests of Michigan and preferred the City of Brotherly Love where she had spent her early years in this country after arriving from County Tyrone, Ireland.

In Pennsylvania, my paternal grandparents bought a home in South Wark, now known as South Philadelphia, a section then inhabited by English and German artisans. The family joined and faithfully attended the Church of the Holy Apostles, taking part in all its activities and enjoying the educational and cultural advantages it offered.

The story of the family in Philadelphia was not unique. As a carpenter, Henry supported his household, which was augmented not only by birth but also by immigration. Many of the people who had known my grandmother in Ireland came and stayed with the Brights until they became accustomed to their new country, a friendly arrangement that was not unusual.

My father at an early age became a newspaper boy, a fortunate circumstance since his route was large enough to support the family during the business recession of the mid-seventies. When my grandfather became unemployed he helped his twelve-year-old son deliver the papers. Newspaper routes became a kind of family industry as the younger boys, while growing up, became assistants and later took on routes of their own.

Grandmother Bright, ambitious for her children, insisted that each of them have a trade. Thus, when young William Henry reached his fourteenth year, he was apprenticed to a machinist. But this vocation was not to his liking, and, immediately upon completing his apprenticeship four years later, at eighteen, he took a job in the office of a painting concern where he was introduced to the fundamentals of salesmanship.

A few months later, he went to work in the Philadelphia office of an attorney, one of the original members of the Holly Beach Land Company, organized to develop an island on the New Jersey coast as a resort area. This island, which later became known as "The Wildwoods," is really a sand bar, five miles long, varying in width from one to two miles. The Atlantic Ocean lies to the east and an inland waterway to the west. The sand of the beautiful, gradually sloping beach is like pulverized white sugar.

My father at his own request was sent to the island to represent his employers, and this move opened up an opportunity for him to embark in a new enterprise, and led to the acquisition of land. Dad had recognized the resort potential and the opportunity he had to grow with it. He had purchased a team of horses with which he hauled beach sand to fill the land of his employers. On his own time he started filling in additional salt and marshy land, and since little money passed hands he was usually paid for this labor in tracts of unfilled land. Later my father ventured, independently and successfully, into the business of real estate and insurance.

A further expansion of his real estate business was made possible when he teamed up with John Vance, a man who owned some moving equipment. The annual equinoctial storms and the gradual encroachment of the ocean meant the loss of houses that had been built too near the high tide mark. When it appeared certain that a house was threatened they would telegraph the owner for permission to move it. If such permission were given Vance, dad and the men of the town of Holly Beach would move the house to safety and collect a fee. If permission did not come through and the house was washed down, the lumber was carefully collected and piled on dry land. From this cache houses could be built on the newly filled lots and rented or sold.

There being no railroad to Holly Beach, my father used his horse and carriage to transport, at low tide, potential buyers from the northern tip of the island. The beaches at that time were the only surfaces that could be used as roads. Later, probably around 1885, a spur of the Pennsylvania Railroad was run to the southern part of the island and a small station and a telegraph office were erected, a development of importance to the future of the island.

My father, who was not only interested in business, but also in the community, served for many years, though himself an Episcopalian, as Sunday school superintendent of a small

Methodist church, situated facing the ocean at Taylor Avenue, which area later became the site of our home called Castlereagh.

It was, however, a community church, built later but nearby, that involved the destiny of my family, for the sister of a young evangelist conducting religious services there became my mother.

Like my father, my mother, Priscilla Buck, was one of ten children. Born in Berks County, Pennsylvania, 5 April 1872, on the family farm at Stony Run, she grew up with her four brothers and five sisters in a rural setting that had its own abundance: a large family with a multitude of tasks and the energy to match them. Since the family furnished the manpower for the cultivation of about four hundred acres, each member was committed to a schedule of "early to bed and early to rise." The chief crops were wheat, corn, hay, and potatoes with the addition, of course, of all kinds of vegetables that were canned and preserved for family use.

The dairy herd was the money crop, so the milking schedule, morning and evening for twenty to twenty-five cows, was arranged to include all the children from the time they reached eight years of age. By then they were accustomed to shouldering their share of the chores, having at the age of four or five learned to do such simple tasks as whitewashing fences and collecting eggs.

The school my mother attended with her brothers and sisters was only a mile away, but getting to Clovermill Academy in winter was not without its problems; occasionally snow drifted higher than the children themselves. Arriving at school clutching their lunch bags, the pupils were not coddled. They were expected to do their share of the work—cutting wood for the next day's fires, cleaning the blackboards, pumping pails of drinking water and, should the pump be frozen, bringing in snow to be melted.

Within limitations, English was the language of the school. The textbooks were in English and the pupils read aloud in that language, but all instruction and recitations were in Pennsylvania Dutch. A similar linguistic duality prevailed at church: the Bible was read and supplications were made in German, but the minister's sermon was preached in Pennsylvania Dutch.

But not all the time was devoted to work and worship. Barn

dances, sleigh rides, coasting and skating parties, church socials, husking bees, quilting parties, barn raisings, and wedding celebrations assured the family of a frequent change of pace.

Strangely enough, funerals were the best of all, for these occasions spelled reunion as kith and kin from miles around arrived, laden with pies, cakes, chicken dumplings, spiced hams, cider, and many other items of food and drink. The desire to excel in preparing the best culinary offerings assured rich feasts for the reunited families.

Years later, with my mother, my sisters and I, in turn, attended these reunions where we met our many cousins and the "freundschaft." On such occasions, we were initiated into the fun of "laying spoons," a practical and necessary arrangement by which one double bed could be made to accommodate five or six children if each individual lay parallel to the headboard and followed the same body contour. This arrangement, which saved space and insured warmth as the children huddled together, permitted the maximum use of blankets. The child who wouldn't "lay spoons" was swiftly brought into line by his or her parents.

At the age of fourteen, my mother went to Lansford, Pennsylvania, to help her older sister Louisa, who had three children. During the year the young Priscilla learned the rudiments of tailoring from a neighbor who had such a shop. Her skill was so pronounced that the neighbor arranged for her to go to Reading, Pennsylvania, to a dressmaking school. After a year's study, during which Priscilla lived with another married sister, she was certified a "couturiere-seamstress."

In the summer of 1891, my mother went to Wildwood, New Jersey, to visit her brother Amandus Buck and his wife Flora, both evangelists. There she met my father. At that time, she was nineteen and he twenty-nine years of age. She stayed in Wildwood throughout the following year and in December of 1892 they were married in the Dutch Reformed Church near her home at Stony Run, Pennsylvania. Thus was inaugurated a remarkable partnership in which the burdens of family and church, business and politics were light because they were shared.

During the first years of their marriage, the realty business flourished in Wildwood as the island became increasingly popular as a resort. My father no sooner built a home than he, on being made a good offer, would decide to sell it and build another. My mother scarcely became used to a new dwelling when she would be forced by the exigencies of prosperity to move to another. My father's office continued to be a part of each new home, which enabled my mother to tend office as well as tend children. His real estate and insurance transactions were something of a monopoly since he was, until 1904, the only real estate agent in town.

Early in 1898, as the nation headed toward the Spanish-American War, father wanted to enlist in the Army despite his "hostages to fortune"—two daughters and another on the way. Mother, nothing daunted, decided she could carry on the real estate business and execute the duties of city clerk, to which office my father had been elected. Her willingness to do this was never put to the test. When my father and one of his brothers went to Philadelphia to enlist, both returned crestfallen, rejected on physical grounds. The criterion for passable teeth was the ability to chew hardtack, and neither dad nor my uncle had the required number of teeth.

On 4 May 1898 I arrived on schedule. To offset my father's disappointment that I was not a boy I was named Joy. By all accounts, I was a happy child and a healthy one, with my red hair and blue eyes proclaiming a direct descendance from my English-Irish father. He took me to heart and often, holding me on his knees, would croon, "We called her Joy because she came to teach the meaning of that name. She is a girl, she's not a boy and, best of all, she is my Joy."

Though an acknowledged girl, I was the one, even after the arrival of three brothers, who cut the grass and did the gardening. I also assisted my Grandfather Bright, who lived with us, and, working with him, I learned to do many a practical task in various fields. Since he was an expert carpenter and cabinetmaker, I learned to handle tools properly before I reached my teens. I could sift unburned coals from the clinkers and ashes of the furnace. I could paint anything from houses to bicycles and bedsteads—white-enameled beds being *de rigueur* at the time. Each spring, when the family project of getting our several boarding houses ready for summer rental began, I with the others, went into action.

When I was about eight years old, my parents thought I showed some talent for drawing, so I took painting lessons. The difference between the fine and applied arts did not bother my practical mother at all. Each spring she would say, "Now Joy will enamel the beds and radiators because she can paint."

Our time after school, on holidays, or during vacations was filled, but it wasn't all work. Mother exerted every effort to accommodate our wishes for parties and never to my knowledge was a reasonable request refused.

When automobiles came on the market, our family became the proud possessor of a five-passenger Hupmobile. In those bygone days of hand cranks, dirt roads, and infrequent filling stations, punctures and flats were repaired en route. Mother was the chauffeur on the Sunday drives. My father persistently refused to learn to drive or look at the motor, a decision based upon his unhappy apprenticeship as a machinist when he was a boy. Consequently, we all learned to jack up cars, repair tires (demountable rims were to come later), patch inner tubes, mount the tires, and replace the acetylene tanks used for lighting. When our athletic teams played schools in other towns, mother could be depended upon to take at least nine in a five-passenger car, in any kind of weather, and this was long before hardtops.

Mother's talent as a "couturiere-seamstress" was put to good use. As the third girl I wore the dresses my sisters had outgrown, but my best dresses were made for me. This progressive use worked well until I was twelve, when I suddenly outgrew my second sister just at the moment I was due to inherit a georgeous red wool coat with brass buttons.

My sisters and I learned to sew doll clothes before we made household items. My introduction to this advanced field was to make pillow cases from the sturdy portions of sheets that had worn out in the center. Our reward for assignments well done was, without fail, a pat on the back. If the task was not done properly, it was done over again.

Dear to memory are the evenings at home after the chores of the house were completed. We gathered around the fireplace to listen as father read the news from the Philadelphia daily paper. Mother had the darning basket in her lap, later in the evening to be replaced by an inverted flatiron on which she would crack black walnuts sent down from the Pennsylvania farm, handing them to each of us in turn as we did our evening tasks. The girls sewed on buttons and patched underwear while the boys sharpened kitchen knives, mended clotheslines under grandfather's direction, and, on special occasions, turned the ice cream freezer.

Our social life was centered in church and school. The school in Wildwood had no gymnasium, but our church had one in the parish hall. This gym was supported in the center by upright supports so it was necessary, particularly in basketball, to conduct all play around the poles. Both girls and boys used the flying rings and the parallel bars. Because at fifteen

I was the tallest—five feet, three inches—I played center on the basketball team.

Although I never excelled in sports, I participated in them. On one occasion, I actually won a high school tennis championship, a victory which should be attributed to the temporary incapacity of my opponent, who had a sprained wrist.

Walking home after choir practice on Friday nights, we occasionally got into mischief ringing doorbells. Church was a mile from home and on Sundays we attended three services. We walked even farther to school, regardless of weather, and since we had an hour and a half for lunch, we walked or ran the distance four times a day. Automobile rides were only for Sunday afternoons. Walking was not a part of a physical fitness program, but a mode of transportation.

As a high school student, I ranked somewhere between the middle and lower sections. Had it not been for a love of history and English literature, I would have been at the bottom of the class. Mathematics was my *bête noire*. I squeaked through algebra and plane geometry. Extra-curricular activities, a term not then in use, were my chief interests. For three consecutive terms I was president of the school's athletic league and president of a high school sorority my friends and I dreamed up, Greek letters and all.

Elected class historian, I chose for the theme of my graduation address "Death." Taking Clio, the Greek Muse of history, as my expounder, I traced the tragic deaths of famous women. In attempting a dramatic presentation, I was aided by having no shyness in facing the audience, which was due to the fact that from the time we were tots we children recited at Sunday school and church, or at banquets held by the Odd Fellows or Masons. In those days local talent was the vogue. Thus, with the feeling that I had prepared a dramatic paper and with great self-confidence, I faced my, I hoped, expectant audience. All went well for the first quarter of my presentation—then the fire whistle sounded. The graduation exercises were being held on the third floor of the fire house, and immediately all members of the volunteer fire company jumped up and raced for the stairway, followed closely by practically every young man in the audience. The fire siren, located on the roof of the building, continued its deafening wail. There was nothing for me to do but sit down and wait. More men and women left the hall to make sure that it was not their house which was burning. Even my father had disappeared. But there sat mother, and a few other mothers, looking as if the only thing that really mattered was hearing my speech. I finished my presentation and returned to my seat in a properly deflated manner, but with some valuable experience gained. For this really was a prelude to taking active part in amateur theatricals, even musical revues, however deficient my ability to carry a tune. This early training combined with later public speaking courses enabled me to speak extemporaneously on many occasions in the naval service.

Early in his career, my father studied law by the clerkship method, but as the family grew and his responsibilities increased, he dropped this study although he was well versed in it. He did continue his services as a notary public and as commissioner of deeds, the latter by appointment of the governor of New Jersey.

His typewriter, one of his professional tools, was a novelty in the 1890s. Not only did father use it for drawing up wills for local residents, but he was frequently called upon to type the manuscripts of fiction writers who, with artists, constituted the local intelligentsia during the summer months. The writers would dictate their works to my father in order to send typescripts to the publishers.

My father extended his activities to banking in the first years of the twentieth century, largely because there were no banking facilities nearer than Vineland, New Jersey, some fifty miles from Wildwood. Thus, in 1900, several businessmen from Holly Beach and Wildwood met in father's office to lay plans for the establishment of the Marine National Bank. This bank opened in 1902 after the stock had been sold primarily to residents of the island. For this venture, my mother, pushing her children in a baby carriage, went from house to house selling shares in the new project. My father remained a member of the board of directors of the bank until his death in 1933.

In 1904, he was elected sheriff of Cape May County, something of an achievement since he was the first person elected to a county office who was neither a native of Cape May County nor a member of the families who had settled there in the latter part of the seventeenth century.

Since it was not possible for him to secure a deputy, he had to move to the county seat at Cape May Court House with his family in order to manage the prison. At the same time, he designated my mother as his deputy, without salary, and she actually performed all the duties of that office in his absence. Grandfather Bright, who lived with us, acted as jailor and supervised the cleaning gang while my mother directed the preparation of the prisoners' meals. This made it possible for my father to commute to the island in order to operate his real estate and insurance office.

As sheriff, dad made a remarkable record, having at one time an empty jail, this despite its reputation for good and decent treatment. Although not labeled as such, rehabilitation was dad's aim, achieved primarily through his talking with the men and seeing that their families did not suffer while they were in jail. In addition, and of equal importance, were the ministrations of my mother and grandfather. My father was honored throughout the county, and many a man kept to the straight and narrow because he would not let "Harry" Bright down.

When a man was to be released, dad often secured what would seem to be an impossible job for him. Pete was a shining example. He had been incarcerated for drunk and disorderly conduct. On the third offense dad told him it must be his last; he must straighten out for good. Dad persuaded the minister of a Wildwood church to give him a job as janitor. Pete held that job until he died. Later, when we moved back to the island, he guarded the bell rope on Friday nights so that none of our gang on the way home from choir practice at the Episcopal church would be tempted to rush in and give it a pull.

Since the jail was attached to our residence, I knew all the prisoners, particularly the trusties who did the cooking and cleaning. Quarters for the women prisoners, of whom there were few, were on the second floor. Hattie, a repeater for petty larceny but still a blithe spirit, helped in the kitchen. Whenever she returned to jail she was smiling and happy, her white teeth flashing against her dark skin. Though she was probably only eighteen or nineteen years of age, she was something of a philosopher: "My fingers are just so light I can't make them behave." Every day there was at least an hour of games after supper, and Hattie loved games—bean bag, bobbing for apples, blindman's bluff—and she was one of the best swing pushers. All of us indirectly participated in Dad's rehabilitation efforts.

Main Street has too often been maligned. Living in the small town of Cape May Court House gave me friends and experiences I shall never forget. The blacksmith's open forge fascinated me. For reciting Longfellow's "The Village Blacksmith" for him, Mr. Gabe, the village smithy, gave me the privilege of pulling down on the handle of the bellows. So frequently did I visit him that he too learned and repeated with me every word of his favorite poem.

In my mind I still see the red-hot horseshoe being plunged into a bucket of water and hammered to fit the hoof of the horse standing by. The bellows, being carefully and slowly worked, brought just the proper glow to the coals, so that the shoe could be thrust into the heat without losing its proper temper. I could not help but cringe as the shoe was finally nailed to the hoof. To this day, horses still look like dinosaurs to me, a fixation of my childhood.

Another friend in town, Mr. Champion, owned and operated single-handedly the bicycle shop. There I had my first urge to become a mechanic. In those days, tire punctures were mended by injecting a wad of rubber bands; if the tire was torn, a vulcanizing job was done with a patch. I learned to do this, as well as tighten tire chains and replace nuts and bolts as needed. Gradually I became something of a helper, and Mr. Champion stopped growling and, even without my asking, gave me jobs to perform. Possibly because I was the sheriff's daughter, these men accepted me on sufferance and kept me busy to eliminate some of my questions and chatter. But no matter, I learned how to do a great many things with my hands, and everything I learned served some useful purpose in the years ahead. My air was, I fear, vainglorious, for I could not help but brag about knowing how to do various things and showing off by doing them. I did not know the word at the time, but I was later to realize that I was a pre-cocious showoff. I think that through the years ahead this attitude remained, at least to a small degree, and forced me into action which I otherwise would have been fearful of undertaking. Both mother and dad had kindly labeled this characteristic as initiative, and ·continued to encourage independent action as well as assign tasks which, on looking back, were in many cases in the "more than juvenile" category.

One such task was assigned when I was only nine years old. A politically manipulated "run" threatened the bank which my father had organized and of which he was president. It was a sound institution but there was then no Federal Reserve System to counteract the run and securities had to be delivered to a Philadelphia bank to obtain cash. The Philadelphia institution was notified of the crisis by a telegram couched in such terms as to prevent alarm.

My father said to me, "You are going to Philadelphia this morning to carry some papers to the bank. You are to say nothing to anyone on the train about what you are carrying. You will be met at Camden." I later learned that he dared not send an employee of the bank lest the depositors surmise that the bank did not have adequate funds on hand and would therefore increase their pressure for payment. At the depot he handed me a satchel and put me in charge of the conductor for the two-hour run. At Camden I stood on the platform and looked for a Mr. Jones. To identify him I was to ask him to show me a telegram he had received from my father. I did not know what Mr. Jones looked like, perhaps because my father himself did not know. Nor did Mr. Jones know what I looked like.

One man was walking up and down and gazing at each passenger until all the travelers but me had left. The conductor stepped down from the train and asked the man, "Are you looking for Harry Bright's daughter?"

"I'm looking for his messenger," the man replied.

The conductor said, "Well, I guess this is it," and turned me over to Mr. Jones, who wiped his forehead with his handkerchief and said, "Good heavens, what will that man Bright make his children do next?"

We crossed the river by ferry and continued by streetcar, a thrilling event for me, to the bank in Philadelphia where the collateral was taken from me. I had refused up to that point to hand over the bag.

Since the next train back to Cape May Court House did not leave for several hours, I was taken to lunch by some of the ladies who worked in the bank, a high point in that day. Later, Mr. Jones took me to the train and handed the bag to me after I was seated. He too admonished me not to talk to anyone about what was in the bag.

"Well, what is in it?" I asked.

"Oh, some papers your father wants, but he doesn't want anyone to know about them."

The trip back was uneventful, and my father met me at the train. The next morning the bank opened as usual with money on hand to meet the demand. And very shortly the run was discontinued, the confidence of the depositors having been reestablished.

We often talked of this errand. Although I do not know the amount I carried in large bills, I do know that it must have been many thousands of dollars. It had never entered dad's mind to doubt my ability to carry out his orders.

Years later I learned that a messenger from the Philadelphia bank had also been on the train for the return trip, but to save my pride no one had told me. And this precaution was taken by the Philadelphia bank, not by my father.

Father being sheriff allowed me, at the age of eight, to cultivate an interest in the law, for the courthouse was just two buildings from the sheriff's residence. Since the private school I attended required my presence only in the afternoons, I would sneak into the back of the courtroom in the morning, to observe procedures as well as the conduct of my prisoner friends. The ceremonies of the court, the use of old English protocol—"Oyez, oyez, all ye who would serve as jurors, now hear ye"—the impaneling of the jurors, the solemn swearing in of witnesses, the prisoner's story, the prosecuter's statement, were the very heart of drama for me. Dad was always on hand with the prisoners and if an unsavory case came up he would send one of the court clerks to tell me to leave.

This interest in judicial procedure stayed with me. Afterwards in international law at the Foreign Service Preparatory School in Washington, and still later in correspondence courses of the Naval War College, I did well. It was, however, my sister Eloise who became a lawyer.

Upon completion of his term as sheriff in 1907, dad returned to the island where the family occupied Castlereagh, one of the first homes to have been built there. The wife of the owner had been born on the estate of Viscount Castlereagh in Ireland and their home, a copy of the family mansion, was named in memory of her birthplace. After mother and dad purchased the house there was never a discussion of changing its name.

Shortly after our return to Wildwood I experienced another occasion when my sin of pride was thoroughly counteracted. I had reached my tenth year and had a great desire to lead a parade then being planned. For this annual event the local merchants prepared floats, and the leading business and professional men were marshals.

When I broached the matter to my father, he asked, "Now why should you lead the parade?"

Not to be stumped, I said, "It would be different to have a girl leading it."

My father made no comment, but suggested that I ask the chief marshal to find out what he thought of the idea. I trudged to that office and spoke my request. He consented, albeit reluctantly, pointing out, however, that as chief marshal he must lead the parade; I would be right behind him; furthermore, I would have to get my own horse and be there on time.

When I went to a concession on the beach to see about hiring a horse there were none available, all having been rented to the marshals. But I instantly recalled seeing a nice-looking, small, brown horse that pulled the lumber wagon in town, so I went to Mr. Robbins, the owner, to ask if I might borrow his horse for the parade. He not only consented but found a saddle for me. No one questioned the fact that my knowledge of horses was that gained in the blacksmith shop of Mr. Gabe in Cape May Court House and this certainly did not include any knowledge of riding.

On the day of the parade, I presented myself at Mr. Robbins' lumber yard decked out in a white embroidered dress with a hat to match, certainly a most inappropriate costume for the occasion, but my very best summer outfit. Mr. Robbins boosted me onto the saddle and the horse walked docilely along the streets to the end of the island, a couple of miles away, where the parade was forming.

Arriving on time, I took my place behind the chief marshal, next to my Uncle John, one of the marshals. About a quarter of an hour was spent milling about and getting the floats in their proper order. Then the chief marshal gave the signal to start and the band struck up. At that instant my horse bolted.

For the next fifteen minutes, although it seemed hours, that horse ran across vacant lots, up and down streets, around corners, as I clung to the reins, my hat streaming out behind, held only by the elastic band under my chin, my long red hair floating straight out in the wind. Terrified though I was, my one thought was to stay on. The horse worked himself into a fine lather which blew back and spattered my face and clothing.

A boy of about fifteen, riding a bicycle, saw my predicament. He jumped off the bike, threw himself at the horse's head, grasped his bridle and stopped him. The young rescuer walked me back several blocks to a house with a telephone. There strangers called my home and my grandfather set off on foot to get me, and found me sitting on the steps still shaking from my experience. All he said was, "Well, Joysie, sometimes we bite off more than we can chew." With that we walked home with the horse very quietly trailing along.

I never quite lived that one down. Every time I longed to be the number one performer in some new project, a member of the family was bound to say, "Joy wants to lead another parade." And I did: the chastening did not eradicate the desire.

From the time my father came to Holly Beach in 1882, he had engaged in community affairs. At twenty years of age in 1883, he was elected a delegate to the county nominating convention, the first of many such assemblies he was to attend, there being no open primary at that time. He also began, early in life, to run for local offices. His election to the office of tax collector was followed by his election as city or borough clerk. In his youth he never became a member of the council or mayor although he ran for those offices, several times losing by two votes and in one instance by a single ballot. On occasions, he was appointed to the tax board and sat with members of the county tax board to hear appeals.

My father's political interests involved us all, and mother, a leader in the women's suffrage movements, regularly served as his campaign manager. That my father was defeated more often than he was elected was to his credit, for, an honorable man, he refused the backing of machines or bosses. As an independent, he was never open to deals, but his affiliations were basically Republican.

A delegate to the National Nominating Convention in 1912, he and twenty-eight members of the New Jersey delegation bolted the party to become Progressives with Theodore Roosevelt and Hiram Johnson, his running mate. During that campaign our parents traveled throughout the state in behalf of the ticket, dad often occupying the stage with his beloved Roosevelt, since, as a Progressive, he was running for the Congress from the Second Congressional District in New Jersey. For the Wildwood meetings, the Bright children and all their friends served as cheerleaders, a form of activity relished as much by teen-agers then as it is now.

Despite his defeat, father's satisfaction was great, for he had almost nosed out the long-term Republican incumbent from Atlantic City who was supported by a powerful political machine. It was enough for dad that he had run well, inspired by the words of Albert Beveridge in his keynote address at the convention: "We stand at Armageddon and we battle for the Lord."

The summer of 1912 stands out not only because of the stirring political events, but also because it left me in charge of the real estate and insurance office while mother and dad attended the two conventions in Chicago. I was not without experience because during past summer months my sisters and I took our turns working in the office. However, I had never had the full job to carry out. I was fourteen at the time and perhaps all would have gone quite smoothly except it was at this particular time that the insurance companies discarded the old, large, handwritten forms and substituted new, smaller, typewritten forms. Since dad's office represented some fourteen different companies, agents from each came to instruct in the new procedures and the attendant bookkeeping. I had to endure the usual throwing up of hands and the question, "Did your father leave you in charge?" after which there was the usual shaking of heads and the getting down to the business of instruction. Having learned how to deal with these new procedures I had, on dad's return, to instruct him.

In the years following 1912, dad gradually returned to the Republican party as the Progressive movement was absorbed into it. Elected in 1918 from Cape May County to the state legislature, he served for twelve years, and when president of the Senate, under New Jersey law, he was lieutenant governor. My sister Eloise, who served as his "righthand man," held the position of executive secretary for the president of the Senate and as such sat at the rostrum facing the legislature. No woman had ever held such a position but, as many of the senators agreed, she carried out her duties efficiently and Harry Bright thus demonstrated what a woman could do in such a responsible post. Mother, in her work for women's participation in government, often cited Eloise as an example of women's political capabilities.

Women of the Naval Reserve in World War I, *above*, sightseeing at the Brooklyn Navy Yard. The straw hats were regulation with the summer uniforms.

Yeomen (F) in 1917 assembling primers at a munitions factory in Bloomfield, New Jersey (*below*).

The regulation winter topcoat and blue felt hat modeled, *at right*, by a Yeoman (F) of World War I. Note the high laced shoes.

"Is there any law that says a yeoman must be a man?" Secretary of the Navy Josephus Daniels (*far right*), advocated the enlistment of women in the Naval Reserve as a wartime expediency in 1917.

Yeoman (F) in World War I

$\mathcal{I}$N the second decade of this century, the days of peace
in our world drew to a close, but along the quiet
shores of South Jersey no one dreamed that the conflict in
Europe would sweep us out of the cove of Victorian tradition
into a war that would change our lives. The resort season of
1914 and the several seasons that followed retained the familiar pattern of past summers in Wildwood, and each fall families—local and summer visitors—returned to the autumn
routines of business, home, and school.

By 1916, the tightly contested campaign of President Woodrow Wilson for reelection, challenged by Charles Evans
Hughes, was based, ironically enough, on the slogan, "He kept

us out of war." Yet little more than a month after President Wilson was again inaugurated, the United States embarked on "the war to save democracy."

While women have always contributed to any war effort, particularly as nurses, the use of extensive womanpower was not a familiar, or even welcome, concept. Women's suffrage not yet having become the law of the land, the men were firmly in command and apparently intended to stay there. But a fast-growing manpower labor shortage, existing even before the United States declared war, caused the Navy to consider a way of utilizing the services of women.

While the general citizenry was not aware in 1916 of how great was the probability of the United States being drawn into the war in Europe, the military in this country was already involved in preparations that had to be made if we were not to be caught short in an emergency. This was particularly true of the leadership of the Navy.

The Secretary of the Navy, Josephus Daniels, learned as the nation headed inevitably toward its moment of truth (despite the presidential campaign which stressed peace) that the Navy simply could not keep up with the demands for increased clerical assistance. As shore stations made their preparations for a possible showdown, they became insatiable in their demands for clerks and stenographers. But there were no appropriations and, even if there had been special funds to pay costs, the Civil Service Commission simply could not furnish the personnel required.

Secretary Daniels was later to describe his solution to the problem:

" 'Is there any law that says a yeoman must be a man?' I asked my legal advisers. The answer was that there was not, but that only men had heretofore been enlisted. The law did not contain the restrictive word 'male.'

" 'Then enroll women in the Naval Reserve as yeomen,' I said, 'and we will have the best clerical assistance the country can provide.' "

Tremendous gasps were heard, but this was an order, and it was carried out in accordance with the provisions of the Act of 29 August 1916, whereby the Naval Reserve Force was to be composed of six classes: Fleet Reserve, Naval Reserve, Naval Auxiliary Reserve, Naval Coast Defense Reserve, Volunteer Naval Reserve, and Naval Reserve Flying Corps.

In line with these provisions, the Navy Department, on 19 March 1917, authorized the enrollment of women in the Naval Coast Defense Reserve in the ratings of yeomen, electricians (radio) or "such other ratings as the Commandants considered essential to the District organization."

Thus it was possible, when the United States declared war against the Central Powers on 6 April 1917, for the Navy to expedite the recruitment of women in order to release enlisted men for active service with the Fleet. By Armistice Day, 11 November 1918, 11,275 yeomen (F) were in service. They had tackled daily and successfully an immense volume of clerical work for the Navy and carried out many highly important special duties as well.

But this is to anticipate my story. In 1917, I was attending business school in Philadelphia. My chief fear was that I would not be qualified in time for naval service. After completing the secretarial course, I took a job as a statistician, a fairly patriotic enterprise since I released a Pennsylvania National Guardsman for active duty.

As soon as possible, I explored the possibilities of enlisting in the Navy. Since Captain Elmer Wood, a retired naval officer who had lived in Cape May Court House when I was a child, had been recalled to active duty and was in charge of the Branch Hydrographic Office of the Navy in Philadelphia, I had not far to go for information. I had come to the right place, for he took me to the Philadelphia Navy Yard to introduce me to a friend of his, Captain George Cooper.

In response to Captain Wood's statement that I wanted to enlist, Captain Cooper said that, although no very formal organization had been set up to handle such a request, I should go to the Naval Home for a physical examination. If I qualified on that score, he would arrange for a test of my clerical ability.

Some consternation was clearly the reaction of the medical staff at the Naval Home when I appeared for the physical examination. But since consternation did not involve prejudice, I passed both the physical and mental tests successfully and was enlisted as a yeoman first class.

Indoctrination was not the order of the day; one simply plunged into service cold. At the Navy Clothing Depot, I was outfitted with two uniforms and told to report to the office of the Navy Superintending Constructor of the New York Shipbuilding Corporation in Camden.

The uniforms, one white and one blue, were designed to conform with those of chief petty officers (male) of the Navy. The "Norfolk jacket" boasted a sewed-on pleat running from the hem in front over each shoulder to the hem in back. A belt of the same material ran under the pleats and was buttoned in front. A white shirt was worn with a gored skirt, slightly higher than the civilian skirts of the period, that is, seven to nine inches from the ground. A sailor's black neckerchief was worn on the outside of the jacket and the shirt was open at the neck. No overcoat was prescribed, but the women were told that a cloak modeled after the officers' boat coats, in either serge or melton cloth, would be considered appropriate.

The hat was another matter, and the nearest I ever came to discovering how its design was selected came one day when I met an officer stationed at the Navy Clothing Depot in Brooklyn. He said that since the prevailing fashion for women who wished a utilitarian type of hat was known as a "sailor hat," the depot simply ordered the stock fashion. However low may be the estimate of that World War I hat, it was not out of line with the times. One advantage was that it could be readily purchased in the open market. In winter we wore it in blue felt; in summer, with the white uniform, in natural straw.

In 1918, pumps were worn only for dress. Everyday wear dictated either high-buttoned or laced shoes, worn with black or white stockings in accordance with the uniform.

No dormitory arrangements were made for the women in service; they simply lived at home and reported daily for work. Since I lived in Philadelphia with one of my mother's friends, I commuted to Camden, New Jersey, via the ferry across the Delaware River and thence a twenty-minute train ride from Camden to the New York Shipbuilding Corporation. Ferry and trains were so jam-packed with shipyard workers that it was not unusual to ride straddling the couplings. On this twenty-minute run, the men called me "Heavy Artillery," in teasing recognition of my five-feet, four inches and mere 102-pound weight.

Since I was assigned to the superintending constructor's office, one of my duties was to carry papers and plans to naval ships being built at the yard. As I walked on these errands, my friends of the daily train rides would spot me and call out cheerily, "Hello there, Heavy Artillery." This practice was discontinued when an efficiency expert following me found that the time taken out to call greetings was a comparatively costly gesture. Thereafter, a sailor took over that task.

Some of my off-duty time I spent with other yeomen (F) who were assigned to sell Liberty bonds in theaters. At Keith's Theater in Philadelphia, for example, we would go up and down the aisles during intermission to make sales.

We also participated in Liberty bond parades on Broad Street. Our training for this activity was acquired at the Navy Yard twice a week. There Marines taught us the rudiments of drill, but we learned hardly more than "forward march," "halt," and the necessity of maintaining straight lines and keeping in step. No instructions were ever given to the effect that we were not to break step for any obstacle that might be in the way, but sometimes there was sharp provocation for changing direction, as, for example, the time when we marched behind beautiful, high-spirited horses that had not been housebroken. After a particularly shabby parade performance, our instructor gave us explicit directions: "You don't kick it, you don't jump over it, you step in it."

After a year, I was a seasoned yeoman. There being no designation for women signifying their sex on the rolls, I received orders to duty aboard a combatant ship. My commanding officer, a naval constructor, had never approved of women being attached to the Navy in a military capacity, so when I presented these orders to him, he was blunt, "Carry them out." Upon reporting to the Fourth Naval District in Philadelphia, I was told in no uncertain terms that the Navy had no intention of ordering women to sea for duty on combat ships. My orders being so endorsed, I returned to my job in the superintending constructor's office. Because assignments like these were also received by other women, an "F" was placed after the rate to alert assignment officers that the yeoman was a woman.

Not long thereafter, still another order came. I was to report to the Naval Air Station, Cape May, New Jersey. As the war was ending, the Navy decided to order women to duty near their homes if at all possible. For the first two months, I commuted the ten miles by car from my home in Wildwood. When two other yeomen (F) were ordered to duty in the area, the three of us rented an apartment in the town of Cape May and set up housekeeping.

As personnel yeoman at the air station, I appeared at Mast daily with the commanding officer of the station. Upon my reading the charge, the master-at-arms would step forward, explain the situation and have the man tell his story. The captain would pronounce the sentence and I would record it. I was also the stenographer on Naval Courts and Boards. These assignments placed me in a position to be embarrassingly aware of some of the failings and misdemeanors of the men. But I was impressed by the way members of the courts would make every effort to assure that justice was done.

There was certainly no discrimination by reason of sex in the assignment of duties. On my second day at Cape May, a call came over the loud speaker, "All hands on the starboard watch, report to the hangar for sweeping down." I trooped over with the other office workers and was given a broom, learning the hard way what a huge space a dirigible hangar encompasses. While stationed in Cape May, I met my future husband. Later, I learned he had reported to the station the very day I was helping to sweep down the hangar.

Many an event made those days of duty in Cape May lively and unforgettable. Late in 1918, one of the coastal northeast storms that sweep the New Jersey coast regularly in the fall and early winter, hit the area. To transport personnel living ashore as well as to deliver material arriving by rail, the station maintained a truck. On this particular morning when the truck left for its regular six-mile run from the town to the air station, the wind was blowing a gale and a blizzard was under way.

After four miles, we could go no farther. At times, the ocean was running across the road, battering the houses between the road and the sea. There was nothing to do but start walking across the fields, heading directly into the wind, sleet, and snow which cut our faces. After the first mile, the men formed a double line abreast, and we three women fell in behind. I was nearly frozen. I had lost a rubber—there were no galoshes in those days—and my thin Navy cape kept slipping from my numb hands. The chief in charge finally told the women and men to fall in close and walk lockstep. I drew the leading chief, who was a foot taller than I, and, matching my step with his stride, I soon had my blood circulating. Upon reaching the station, we were sent to the dispensary to thaw out.

During the day, the road to the station was washed out, making it impassable even at low tide. A minesweeper was ordered to take us back via the inland waterway to Cape May. Despite the fact that the storm was still raging, we set off. Ordinarily, such a trip could be accomplished even in rough weather, since it was made through a fairly well-protected waterway. But this was no ordinary day. When engine trouble developed, the tide and wind threatened to send us out to the open sea. However, the engine ran intermittently, so we avoided that catastrophe, though we were swept beyond the breakwater. We rolled and pitched with such force that the warrant officer in charge was a worried man as he endeavored to get back to the protection of the breakwater.

I myself never got out of the galley. One of the yeomen (F) was very, very seasick. The other, scared almost to the point of hysteria, helped me nonetheless as we made coffee and egg sandwiches for the men on deck. I have never been more frightened. Not only was there the angry sea to contend with, but the hot coals continually spilling out of the galley range had to be shoveled back. A heavy lurch of the boat landed me on a crate of eggs. From then on, we had scrambled egg sandwiches.

After fighting the storm for five hours, the crew managed to get us back to the air station at ten o'clock that night. The dock was gone, carried away by an Eagle boat which had rammed it in an attempt to tie up. The boathouse had landed on the forward deck of the Eagle.

Our minesweeper finally tied up at the marine railway and we got ashore by pulling ourselves, flat on our stomachs, along the elevated, open ties. The day ended as it began: in the dispensary. After hot drinks, we three yeomen were bedded down there for the night.

Not long after the end of World War I, the Naval Air Station, Cape May, was put on nonactive status. After being mustered out of the U.S. Naval Reserve Force, I stayed on in civilian status. During the months it took to close the facility, the other Navy women departed, upon discharge, for their homes. Activity at the air station nearly came to a halt as the flying boats and blimps ceased their coastal patrols and the "O" type submarines departed.

I frequently worked with personnel from District Headquarters who came, during the following months, to check inventories, secure buildings, and remove or dispose of material. As the only woman left on the station and one of the few employees, I spent most of my time either climbing through storerooms and hangars with the visiting officers trying to locate inventoried items or typing innumerable lists. This work was daily and dreary, a far cry from the excitement of the wartime coastal patrols.

The early fall of 1919, however, was enlivened by the arrival of the NC-4 flying boat. Newspapers and magazines for the preceding weeks had been filled with accounts of the first transatlantic flight so successfully carried out in May. Of the three flying boats starting out, only the NC-4 under the command of Commander Albert Cushing Read, USN, completed the flight via the Azores and Lisbon to Plymouth, England.

Upon its triumphant return to the United States, the NC-4 was flown, in the interests of recruiting, all over the country, its itinerary dictated by the availability of a body of water on which to land. Finally, it was due at Cape May for some repairs.

Watching it land, I noted with amazement that one wing float was reinforced by a piece of two-by-four. A short while later, Commander Read came to the administration building. While he stood at my office door, I waited to hear some significant word from the first aerial conqueror of the Atlantic. He strode directly to the officer-of-the-day's desk and asked, "Where's the head?" If wisdom is the act of asking the right question to obtain the right answer, who shall deny its significance?

As I look back to World War I, I need to stress the fact that the accomplishments of the more than 10,000 women who served as yeomen (F) were not limited to purely clerical duties. They served ably as translators, draftsmen, fingerprint experts, camouflage designers, and recruiters. Five of them, connected with the Bureau of Medicine and Surgery, served with naval hospital units in France; and one found her place in the operations of the Office of Naval Intelligence in Puerto Rico. Old records reveal that a few yeomen (F) were stationed at Guam, the Panama Canal Zone, and Hawaii.

Once all of the women had been released from active duty, on 31 July 1919 Secretary Daniels sent the following message: "It is with deep gratitude for the splendid service rendered by yeomen (F) during our national emergency that I convey to them the sincere appreciation of the Navy Department for their patriotic cooperation."

Since they had enlisted for four years, yeomen (F) continued to be listed on the rolls of the Navy in an inactive status until the expiration of the enlistment, terminated by a full discharge. They were included in provisions for military preference in securing Civil Service ratings and were allowed the usual veteran's rating advantage of five percent. All subsequent benefits for World War I veterans included the women.

The author, *above*, ready for a flight in a Navy plane with
Lieutenant Ralph A. Ofstie, Navy test pilot. Joy Hancock
learned to fly in the 1920s to conquer her fear of it—the remedy
worked. In 1928, while a student in Paris, she places a wreath
on the Tomb of the Unknown Soldier (*right*).

Between the Wars

$\mathcal{I}$F naval activity at Cape May subsided, the pace of my
own life did not. Peace brought with it a new excitement—my engagement to Lieutenant Charles Gray Little,
United States Naval Reserve Force. Thus a good part of 1919
and 1920 was devoted, on my part, to preparing to be married
when he returned from his assignment in Europe.

Lieutenant Little had arrived in the United States from
France in March 1919 to become executive officer of Airship
C-5 which was preparing, for what proved to be an ill-fated
attempt, to fly ahead of the big NC flying boats on their
transatlantic flight scheduled for the spring of 1919. He flew
the C-5 twelve hundred miles from Montauk Point, New York,

to Nova Scotia, where the final checks and preparations were made. But despite an auspicious start, the C-5 never had a chance to make the Atlantic crossing. During a severe wind storm before a takeoff from Nova Scotia, the C-5 broke away from her moorings and the men handling her. At that time, Lieutenant Little was aboard, attempting to secure the log and other ship's papers. After the ship broke loose and started a fast ascent, he fell through the bottom of the control car which had been broken by repeated pounding on the ground. The fall broke his leg, but he had managed to secure the ship's papers. The C-5, blown seaward, was never seen again.

After his recovery, Lieutenant Little returned to Cape May as the executive officer of the station. It was at this time that I first met him, although I had heard much—and read more— about him and the C-5 venture. Never shall I forget his arrival in a gray Packard roadster, a dashingly tall, blond young man with a New England accent, still using crutches. I already knew his official background, for as personnel yeoman the files were open to me.

He was a Harvard man, class of 1917, but in May on the verge of graduation that year, he enlisted in the Navy as a quartermaster first class. He was given training in flying lighter-than-air craft at the Goodyear Rubber Company school at Wingfoot Lake, Ohio. By November 1917, he had received his naval aviator's wings, his commission as an ensign, and orders to overseas duty at the French dirigible station at Rochefort for additional training. In June 1918, he went to the U.S. Naval Air Station at Paimboeuf for dirigible patrol and convoy duty. By September 1918, when he was twenty-three years of age, he had become chief pilot at the U.S. Naval Air Station, Guipavas, France. While there he was part of the patrol that guarded the ship carrying President Wilson to the Peace Conference in March 1919 at Versailles. For his outstanding work during the war as commanding officer of dirigibles in the European war zone, he was awarded the Navy Cross.

Lieutenant Little's assignment to Cape May was of no great duration, for he was designated a member of the crew of the Navy's first rigid airship, an assignment that would take him again overseas. The United States government had purchased the R-38 (U.S. designation ZR-2) from England, and the contract included an agreement on the part of the British to train an American crew to fly it. Since it appeared that the training would take only a few months, we decided to be married upon his return. However, upon arriving in England, he found that although the training would be brief, the completion of the R-38 and its trials would probably take more than a year. Thus, in the fall of 1920, after voting in the presidential election for the first time, I sailed for England, accompanied by my mother and my sister Eloise, in the first *Mauritania*, headed for an exciting and romantic experience, complete with a wedding in a twelfth-century church in Elloughton-Brough, Yorkshire.

Commander Louis Maxfield, the prospective commanding officer of the ZR-2, gave me away; Eloise served as my one attendant, and Flight Lieutenant Archibald H. Wann, Royal Air Force, was the best man. At the wedding reception at the Maxfields' house, I met all the officers of the airship detachment and their wives. They were my close associates in the months to follow.

After a honeymoon in London, Paris, and Biarritz, we returned to Yorkshire to become "paying guests" at the Elloughton-Brough vicarage, a fortunate circumstance since there were few houses in the shire which could be rented. The vicarage family consisted of the Reverend Sidney Soady, his wife Emily, and their two daughters, Grace and Violet, and it was through them I was introduced to English home life. Grace, taking me under her wing, saw to it that I was properly indoctrinated in British social customs—calls, luncheons, and teas.

The vicar was a remarkable person, one of the most patient men and the kindest I have ever known. At twenty-one years of age, I thought him very elderly, but as I look back now, I realize he was only in his mid-fifties. Having won his Cambridge Blue in cricket, he was, of course, captain of the local team. I spent hours watching the play and learning the language of the game, but I never reached the point where there was enough action to satisfy me.

I learned to play golf and soon discovered why hiking and bicycling were a national pastime as well as the local means of transportation. It was just too cold to stay in the house or to stand still. Only one house in the area had central heating; all others depended on one small grate, fired by one lump, or at the most two lumps, of soft coal at a time. Frequently the uncomplaining vicar would come from his study with dried blood on his right hand where, while writing, his ever-present chilblains had cracked open. Many a time I sat down to meals in Charles' huge raccoon coat, a welcome relic of his days at Harvard.

A few days after my arrival, Grace took me to the stores

in Hull and insisted that I must have "woolies." I refused. But a week later I begged her to buy them for me, and I wore them after cutting the "knicker" legs off above the knee. Such woolen underwear brought back vividly the recollections of the embarrassment I suffered as a child because my long white underdrawers were always in lumps on the back of my skinny legs under coarse-ribbed black stockings.

England after World War I was poor indeed, and many comforts I had always taken for granted were unavailable or unknown there, or else too expensive to purchase. But if the British minded, they did not show it. Nourishing food was scarce, and what there was was too expensive to buy in any quantity. Fuel of any kind was practically nonexistent. The old expression, "carrying coals to Newcastle," was the grim truth; that is exactly what was happening. Coal from the United States was delivered there and, after the needs of industry had been met, was rationed to the population.

Before the war, the roads in Elloughton-Brough had been lighted. The lights, turned off during World War I because of the Zeppelin raids, were still off because of the lack of electricity. It was no easy task at times to walk or cycle the two-mile road from the railroad station to the vicarage with only a small cycle lamp to disclose the potholes. It was even more difficult to make it home after a dinner party for which everyone had to wear dinner clothes and high-heeled shoes never meant for walking. I learned fast what a shoe bag was really intended for; it carried your dress pumps after you shifted to heavy shoes for the walk home.

But these drawbacks vanished in the spring and summer when tennis and golf could be played as late as ten or eleven o'clock at night. Whatever I had learned in geography had not prepared me for the fact that the British Isles were as far north as Labrador.

I quickly entered into the local social life, which orbited about the church, the community, and the U.S. naval families scattered throughout the countryside from Howden to Hull. Getting the Americans together socially involved arrangements for railroad transportation, since there seemed to be neither private cars nor taxis available. Even if there had been, there was no gasoline.

The long, spring days were filled with activities, none of them vital or spectacular but, nevertheless, they were entertaining and in many ways educational since they helped me to understand how the people of a country, other than my own, thought and acted. I attended steeplechases, watched cricket and polo games, became an assistant in Girl Guides, and joined the local theatrical group. The productions we put on were ambitious; most of them were absolute steals from shows currently running in London, but this did not seem to bother anyone charged with writing and producing them. In this way, I became acquainted with many of the area's residents, but I never felt I really knew them, and I am certain they felt I was as strange as a man from Mars. Even in the closeness of living at the vicarage, there never grew a cordiality or camaraderie that we in the United States seem to develop naturally. There was always an atmosphere of eyebrows being lifted over some spontaneity, a lack of warmth for or interest in the other person, an air of superficiality (possibly not a sense of superiority, but approaching it).

This did not disturb me too much, although at times I longed to talk with someone who could and would laugh at things I found amusing, who would express an unqualified opinion on a matter under discussion, who would not be horrified at inconsequential happenings. For example, I recounted an incident of a train ride during which I discovered that the young man who shared a compartment with me was a professional Rugby player. Our conversation had been animated and interesting. But when I related this story at the vicarage during dinner that evening, the family was almost speechless. Eyebrows went up, and the only remark was, "You spoke to this young man?" In those days, a young lady in England did not speak to anyone unless properly introduced, and one was introduced only to the "proper sort" of people.

One of my activities which proved something of an ordeal for the Soady family was my unladylike predilection for taking things apart. I convinced them I could also put things together after repairing some furniture, such as an old, wooden knife-sharpening machine. But there was dismay when I was discovered taking the vicar's bicycle apart. Of course, members of the family had no way of knowing that at the age of seven or eight I had assisted Mr. Champion in his bicycle shop in Cape May Court House. But the bicycle project was a great success. With it cleaned, a chain repaired and a puncture fixed, the vicar rode off proudly to the railroad station in his top hat and morning clothes to entrain for his quarterly visit to the Archbishop of York.

When the airship training program and our finances permitted, Charles and I made trips to London for a weekend of dancing, theater, and hot baths. Our delights were simple yet marvelous in our eye: to be warm, to ride in a taxi, and to dine at the Savoy. At times like these, we found this living in a foreign country idyllic.

Back in the Howden—Elloughton-Brough locale, the intensive training continued in the R-34 rigid airship which had made a successful transatlantic flight the year before (1920). On one routine training flight, the R-34 suffered a relatively minor material failure which, unfortunately, was greatly aggravated by high winds. I saw her pass over the vicarage on her way from the North Sea to the Howden base and realized that she was late for her landing schedule. While all appeared serene, she was even then struggling to get back to her field. This she finally did, but the high winds made it impossible to maneuver her into the hangar. This was before, the days of the mooring mast, so hundreds of men on the lines held her for ten hours but could not entirely prevent her from pounding the ground when the gusts were severe. Her buoyancy depended on the hydrogen in her cells, and any breaking of her aluminum girders could create a spark. Since the wind did not abate, there was nothing left to do but to machine-gun her cells. We were witnesses of that sad sight the next morning: the proud ship was a total wreck. But we were thankful there had been no loss of life. An even sadder sight was that of the very young British lieutenant standing silently, deep pain etched on his face, watching his first command being destroyed.

This tragic loss did not appear to shake anyone's faith in the ZR-2 which was rapidly being completed at the Royal Air Force station at Bedford, where Charles and I visited it before my departure to the United States. What a beautiful sight she was. The crew had been selected from the American group which had completed training. Charles, as one of those selected, was ecstatic. The men not selected for the transatlantic trip returned to the United States on the government transport, USS *Somme* to train an American ground-handling crew at the Naval Air Station, Lakehurst. I came home on the same ship to rent a house nearby in order to be on hand to greet the ZR-2 when she arrived in the United States. I landed in June 1921, rented a house, bought an automobile, and settled down to await the completion of the trial flights of the airship.

The ZR-2's last trial on August 24 was fatal. During strenuous speed and turning maneuvers over the Humber River at Hull, her structure was fractured near the tail section. A spark from the break ignited the hydrogen and a mighty explosion plunged her into the river. Of the fifty-two persons aboard, only one American and five British survived. My husband was not one of them. He was alive when he was taken from the wreckage, but he died before reaching a hospital. The captain of the ship, Lieutenant A. H. Wann, RAF, our best man, although critically injured, was one of the survivors.

In recollection, the months which followed seem formless. Still many things had to be done and life had to be lived. In impressive ceremonies, the bodies of the American crew were returned to the United States by a British destroyer, HMS *Dauntless*. In New York Harbor and at the Brooklyn Navy Yard, many honors were paid.

Deep as was my sorrow, I welcomed the return, even though slow, of a sense of reality and the renewal of the desire to do something. Before leaving the Naval Air Station, Cape May, at the time of my departure for England, I had qualified for Civil Service employment. I therefore applied for a job in aeronautics in the Navy Department in Washington, D.C. Admiral W. A. Moffett, the first chief of the Bureau of Aeronautics, was greatly interested in the future of rigid airships. (He was later to lose his life in the crash of the airship, USS *Akron*.) Thus, in March 1922, I became an employee of the new bureau, but since Congress had not yet approved an appropriation for it, I was temporarily paid by the Bureau of Supplies and Accounts. My rating was that of messenger, and my salary was $1,200 per year.

My work, however, was not limited by that rating, for I was assigned to the Personnel Division to set up the first files of naval aviators, an occupation that swiftly acquainted me with every naval aviator on active duty.

But because my deep interest remained in the field of lighter-than-air operations, I requested, in August 1923, a transfer to Naval Air Station, Lakehurst, where the ZR-1 was nearing completion. The crew for this ship was being trained by those Americans who had returned from England before the crash of the ZR-2. The ZR-1 was built at the Naval Aircraft Factory in Philadelphia, but its parts were assembled at Lakehurst under the supervision of Commander Ralph D. Weyerbacher, USN.

I was assigned to Commander Weyerbacher's office, where I learned more of the language of airship construction and watched the final assembly of the ship as the gas cells and engines were installed.

To eliminate the danger of fire, the United States inflated

its rigid airships with helium, rather than hydrogen, since helium is a natural, inert, nonflammable gas. To meet this new requirement, a helium repurification and storage plant was built at Lakehurst. Again, at my request, I was transferred to that operation as a clerk in the office of the officer-in-charge, Lieutenant Zeno Wick.

Since only a few U.S. Navy men had been trained in England to man the new rigid airship, the Navy set up qualifications and called for volunteers. A highly desirable qualification was that of submarine experience because of the great similarity in the handling of submarines and rigid airships.

The presence of those men who responded to this call was a real catalyst. They enlivened both the official and social life of the air station, located as it was in the heart of New Jersey's desolate pine belt many miles from urban activities. Lieutenant Commander Lewis Hancock, a former submariner, was one of the new trainees who, upon completion of the instruction period, became the executive officer of the ZR-1. A Texan and a Naval Academy graduate of the class of 1910, he was known to all as "John." After graduating from the Academy, he received submarine training and in 1913 was ordered to that duty.

During World War I, he commanded the AL-4 and was part of the first submarine squadron to cross the Atlantic. Of this exploit he once said, "During the entire crossing, all we did was break down, repair while under way, shoot out of the top of a huge wave and fall smackingly in the trough." Nevertheless, he received a letter of commendation from the Secretary of the Navy for his handling and subsequent saving of the AL-4 after a loss of control during a submerged patrol. His still greater honor, the Navy Cross, was awarded "for distinguished service, in command of AL-4, which, under his command, made contact with the enemy and on one occasion attempted the dangerous feat of diving at a submerged enemy submarine to ram her."

After World War I, he served in surface ships. His general background produced the qualifications that caused him to be selected for lighter-than-air training and ordered to Lakehurst.

When the ZR-1 was completed in September 1923, she was christened by Mrs. Denby, the wife of the Secretary of the Navy. In ceremonies held in the huge hangar at Lakehurst, Mrs. Denby pulled the line which released one hundred white pigeons from the nose of the ship and said, "I christen thee *Shenandoah*." The commissioning followed immediately. How proud we all were as we watched the huge ship being walked from the hangar and then saw her rise smoothly from the ground to sail away, her silver casing glistening in the sun.

Not many days later, I resigned my job on the air station and in June 1924 I married "John" Hancock at a quiet wedding at the home of my parents in Wildwood and took up the role of Navy wife.

Living in the atmosphere of airship training and operations was not new to me. I endured occasions of tension as did all those involved in airships, particularly when a ship was several hours overdue in returning to base, or when the wind reached such a velocity that she could not immediately be taken safely into the hangar. Sometimes a ship might circle the field for five, six, even seven hours, waiting for more favorable landing conditions. You just waited, kept your fingers crossed—and prayed. Such care had to be taken. The ZR-1 was the only airship we had; her loss could mean the end of the rigid airship program.

In addition to making the use of helium instead of hydrogen mandatory, still another development by the United States was the mooring mast. This device cut the number of the ground-handling crew from several hundred to approximately ten, and reduced the long hours of waiting and attendant tension. Three- and four-day flights became routine. The new crew qualified, and all hands settled down to operations schedules.

Then came the word that the ZR-3, later christened the USS *Los Angeles* by Mrs. Calvin Coolidge, was ready for her flight from Friedrichshafen, Germany, to Lakehurst. The U.S. Navy's contract included the instructional services of Anton Heinen, a former Zeppelin captain who was already a part of the training program at Lakehurst. The station looked forward to healthy competition between the two airships.

When the ZR-3 arrived at Lakehurst manned by a German crew, she was, of course, inflated with hydrogen. All precautions had been taken. The hundreds of Navy men who would handle her wore sneakers so as not to generate a spark. (The ZR-3 was not yet equipped to be moored at the mast.) The USS *Shenandoah* was taken out of the hangar and moored at a safe distance. When the ZR-3 landed, she was walked immediately to her berth in the hangar for deflation. Imagine our amazement when the German crew members disembarked shod in *hobnail boots*. Fortunately, no sparks occurred, but from that day forward the airship was inflated with helium.

The two airships fired the imagination and interest of the

public, and the newspapers covered their operations in depth. For the *Shenandoah*, a flight of approximately a week or ten days to the West Coast was scheduled. The airship would try out the new mast and hangar at Sunnyvale and en route fly over the principal cities and state fairs. All went smoothly until the night of September 3, 1925. That night the *Shenandoah* was caught near Ava, Ohio, in a terrific storm that had not been forecast. In the turbulence, her tail section broke off, and the main frame, thus weakened, could no longer support the control car in which my husband was riding. The car tore loose and plummeted to the ground, killing all occupants. The tail and forward sections were free-ballooned to earth by the survivors, but the ship was a total wreck.

So again I faced the death of one I loved. Again I had to adjust to living under drastically changed circumstances. It so happened that illness afforded me time to think things through. For nearly a year, I was in a hospital while doctors sought to locate an infection which had caused a paralysis. When I was finally discharged, I had recovered sufficiently to take a cruise around the world with my sister Eloise.

For six months we traveled aboard the British ship *Transylvania* from New York, through the Panama Canal, to Hawaii, and the countries of Asia. In those days, a cruise ship had no other mission than to accomplish a leisurely voyage for the pleasure of its passengers. Shore excursions sometimes lasted for several weeks. For example, in India we left the ship in Bombay, traveled over land to Calcutta, visiting New Delhi, Benares, Agra and many lesser known towns and villages, rejoining our ship in Calcutta.

This trip was my introduction to filth, disease, famine, dust and heat as well as indescribable beauty, for Asia is a continent of overwhelming contrasts. The Taj Mahal sparkled in the brilliant sun, its lacy architecture reflected in the lily-spotted pool. Outside the guarded gates, men, women and children stretched out their hands and begged for food. I saw hundreds of children with enormous dark eyes, the faces of old men, and pitifully thin legs and arms marred by open sores. They beat on their bloated stomachs to make sounds like a bongo drum and called out, "Bak-sheesh, please, lady, bak-sheesh."

Every country introduced me to strange and unbelievable sights, most of which, linked with religious rites or taboos, centered around the shrines, pagodas, and temples. For six months, my sister and I glimpsed the heights and depths of human existence, often found side by side. The extreme poverty millions endured seemed to be regarded by the wealthy as a way of life which in no way concerned them.

From the Orient, we went on to Europe where we left the cruise and took up residence in Paris with the firm intention of learning French. We also enrolled in the Paris branch of the Parson New York School of Fine and Applied Arts. En route to Europe from the Orient, we had visited Egypt and, while in Cairo, I met an old Navy friend at Shepheard's Hotel, who introduced me to another naval officer, Lieutenant Ralph Ofstie. The two were on a weekend leave from their ship which was moored near Alexandria. For three days, we had a gay and happy time. Twenty-eight years later I married Ralph Ofstie when he had become a vice admiral and I had retired as a captain from my second active duty tour in the Navy.

Foreign travel, which let me see firsthand the different ways of life of many peoples, made me decide to try for a career in our State Department. In 1928, the Consular Service and the Diplomatic Service had merged under the title of the U.S. Foreign Service and women had been declared eligible. With this in mind, I returned to the United States and enrolled in the Crawford Foreign Service School in Georgetown to prepare for the entrance examinations. After two years of study and two sets of written examinations, both of which I passed with marks qualifying me for oral examinations, I failed the latter. This was a bitter blow to my pride, but I never regretted the amount of time and energy I had expended.

While attending the Crawford School, I took flying lessons at the Henry Berliner Flying School on the Virginia side of the Potomac. I wanted to learn to fly, not because it was the smart thing to do in the 1920s, but because I was afraid of anything that flew. The majority of my friends were involved in aviation, and all too often one of them would be killed in a crash. But despite accidents and fatalities, commercial flights were fast becoming the new and accepted means of transportation. I reasoned that if I learned to fly, I might conquer my fear of it. The remedy worked and, although I did not go beyond getting my student pilot's license, I did conquer the fear.

Actually, my greatest interest was the ground course where I learned to assemble and disassemble airplane engines, the adult equivalent of my childhood pleasure in bicycle repair. My success in the engine maintenance course stood me in good stead when, in 1942, the feasibility of training WAVES as aviation machinist mates was in question. I knew they could do the work. And they did.

After my second unsuccessful attempt to enter the State Department, I requested reinstatement in the Navy's Bureau of Aeronautics. Since I now had a personal background in flying, additional formal education, and new knowledge gained through extensive travel and living abroad, I hoped to get a better position than I had had before, and my hope was realized. I was placed in charge of the bureau's General Information Section, a position which allowed me freedom to exercise imagination and judgment. Being in touch daily with the various news media representatives made this one of the most interesting periods of my working life.

I frequently cooperated with magazine editors to produce special naval aviation issues and prepared rough drafts of articles, semi-technical in nature, for the authors. Securing clear and appropriate illustrations was also part of the game. I learned how publications were put together and deadlines met. Public relations representatives of the aircraft industry were daily visitors to my office since each wanted his company kept to the fore in all news releases.

Among the young reporters on aviation were many who were later to become famous in this field as it grew to maturity. One of the reporters who became a firm friend was Ernie Pyle. The rivalry of these writers was matched by their camaraderie and, because I was considered to be a part of the new industry, I was without question included.

In 1922 during my service in the Bureau of Aeronautics, I was the first editor of the bureau's *News Letter*. As head of General Information, I was again its editor but in a much better position to help it grow toward the publication which forty years later, became the monthly *Naval Aviation News*.

For three years, my days were filled with a sense of accomplishment, but suddenly I longed to explore something different. Possibly it was a combination of a rainy Saturday afternoon and the purchase of a book at the corner drugstore which modified my direction for a time. After spending a weekend reading and rereading Robert Casey's *Four Faces of Siva*, I put in my resignation Monday morning and bought a round-the-world ticket on the old Dollar Line. I had decided to go to Cambodia and see for myself the fabulous remains of the lost kingdom of the Khmers in the jungles.

Several times during this trip, I feared my ambition had exceeded my judgment. In Singapore, the travel agencies refused to book me beyond Bangkok, vowing that they could not and would not take the responsibility of enabling a young, white woman to travel alone in certain areas. I refused to accept their decision and proceeded by ship to Penang. There, with great misgivings, I watched my ship pull out of port. It was not a new sensation; I had experienced it before in other countries, but here it was different. I had felt I was on speaking terms with India, China, and Japan long before I visited them, but now I was preparing to go into the jungles of Cambodia, of which I knew nothing. On the other hand, I was more than 15,000 miles from home, either to the east or west, and I was only a few days from my goal—the Angkor Vat. There was only one thing to do: proceed.

Exploring Penang was an adventure, from the mansions of the rich Chinese to the unbelievably crowded native quarters. Everyone climbs the mountain of Penang, and I was no exception. Finally, in the beautiful, though tiny, white sand beaches, I waited for the twice-weekly train to Bangkok.

This twenty-eight hour ride through Siam in terrific, moist heat revealed a succession of rice fields where the water buffalo wallowed in the thick blue mud of irrigation ditches to shield their hides from the blistering sun. Then, suddenly, the train would plunge into dense jungle overgrown with wild banana trees. The intense fertility of the land was signaled by the almost sickening smell of the infinite variety of waxy plants and the sound of hundreds of gibbering monkeys.

Out of all this, Bangkok suddenly appeared, a beautiful modern city in many ways, but its very modernity was incongruous in contrast to the fabulous porcelain temples with their perpetually tinkling bells, the emerald Buddha, the white elephants in the stables of the palace, and the Klungs. Along miles and miles of canals was revealed a unique way of life. My keenest recollection, beyond that of the children splashing in the water and the merchants peddling their wares in their tiny shell boats, was the smiling faces of the people as they peered from the doors of their palm huts built on stilts.

Finally, my transportation to Aranya Pradesa was arranged, and I boarded a train which operated on narrow-gauge tracks. It left the station in Bangkok at sunrise, and I felt I was leaving the last outpost of civilization, a feeling certainly justified by events. We proceeded at twenty-five miles per hour. No greater speed was allowed because the intense heat often would buckle the rails and send a train into the mud of the paddy fields. The trip took thirteen hours, instead of the purported nine, because a small bridge had been burned and a section of the tracks torn up. "Bandits" was the explanation. While we awaited repairs by a crew, which was carried at all times on the train, the thermometer registered, at midday, 120 degrees Fahrenheit.

I arrived at Aranya Pradesa too late to proceed to Siem Reap, according to the French official who had arrived from Poipet. He seemed to find something wrong with my passport for entry into Cambodia, but he promised to return it to me at the frontier the following morning and meanwhile helped me to secure an automobile and driver to take me on my way.

The night spent at the rest house was a sleepless one for me. Wild dogs howling in the jungle were answered by those chained to the house supports of the villagers; twelve-and fourteen-inch hammerhead lizards scurried up the walls and across the ceiling; and innumerable squeaking bats and the myriad humming insects added their noise to the night. My pallet with its encircling net seemed to offer small protection against these nocturnal creatures.

At dawn, I started the 160-kilometer trek to Siem Reap. Two native lads sat in the front seat in a most impassive manner, a stance which they maintained throughout the trip. We traveled at breakneck speed, considering the condition of the road, over miles of plains with giant ant hills, or through jungles which seemed to press in on both sides and overhead. But the threat of dire consequences if we broke down or if bandits waylaid us did not materialize. Passing through Siem Reap, we went another ten kilometers to "the bungalow," a rest house operated by the French government for their road engineers. Since this was not the season for road building, the manager, an obese but pleasant Frenchman, and I were the sole occupants. But the bungalow was only a half mile from Angkor Vat. The manager willingly helped me to secure a guide who, in turn, hired the necessary elephant on which I would make my explorations of the area.

The sights I saw, the unbelievable way of life of the natives, the fascinating stories of the past the guide told me, the heat and humidity of the jungle and the revealed glories of an ancient civilization, the lost kingdom of the Khmers, were worth my struggles to reach Angkor Vat. I contracted no tropical diseases. I was not prostrated by the heat as had been predicted. On the contrary, I had satisfied my initial desire to see this place for myself. Life for me was richer because of this journey.

After an uneventful trip back to Singapore, I continued my trip around the world, making an extensive stay in Europe, and then returning to Washington. In March 1934, I summoned courage and asked to be reinstated in the Bureau of Aeronautics. Again I was accepted and placed in charge of the Editorial Research Section, where I remained until 1942.

Left to right (*above*): Admiral DeWitt C. Ramsey, Bureau
of Aeronautics; Admiral Audrey Fitch, Bureau of Aeronautics;
Lieutenant Commander Joy Bright Hancock, Women's
Representative for Women in Naval Aviation; Admiral Arthur
W. Radford, Director of Naval Aviation Training in 1944. Admiral
Radford was an enthusiastic advocate of women in the Navy.
  Prior to her enrollment in the Women's Reserve of the
U.S. Navy in 1942, Joy Bright Hancock (*opposite*), worked as
a civilian in the Bureau of Aeronautics as head of
Editorial Research.

Pre–World War II Legislation

IN every war, the belligerents have summoned the common people to support the professional fighters in their armies and navies. Back of the armed forces have always stood the reserves, the home guard composed of men and women, young and old.

Such a force supported the Trojans as well as the Greeks. The Goths, Vandals, Huns, and Magyars brought their families with them when they moved against imperial Rome. In the Middle Ages, women and girls defended the beleaguered cities of France and the Lowlands when the men were away on military duty. War was a major industry at that time and everyone worked at it.

In the United States, the mothers, wives, and daughters were not idle during the skirmishes with the Indians. World War I had called thousands of women into the war effort. And World War II was to be no exception, but it took far more time than it should have to achieve the legislation which added womanpower to the strength of manpower.

And it needn't have taken so long. The legislative history underlying the creation of the Women's Reserve illustrates the folly of administrators tying the hands of their successors by gratuitously freezing into a statute their notion of military policy. Had the word *male* been omitted from the Naval Reserve Act of 1938, six to nine months might have been saved in setting up the Women's Reserve to meet the crisis of war.

Under the Act of 29 August 1916, the word *male* was not used to designate those eligible for admission to the United States Naval Reserve Force. That act simply opened the force to "citizens of the United States on terms to be further fixed by regulations." When the need for women in the Navy arose in World War I, they were taken in under the 1916 Act even though that legislation contained certain ambiguities which daunted many a faint-hearted interpreter. But certainly, it did not deter Secretary of the Navy Josephus Daniels. Despite the obvious lessons of this precedent, those who drafted the Naval Reserve Act of 1925 made either a slip—or perhaps a calculated effort to keep women in their place—and limited the Naval Reserve to "male citizens of the United States."

The change did not pass unnoticed at the time it was made. The Navy women of World War I, designated Yeomen (F), appeared before the Senate Naval Affairs Committee to protest the change, arguing that it was an unmerited slur upon the services rendered by women in the Navy. Senator Tasker L. Oddie, of Nevada, was sufficiently impressed to move on the floor of the senate that the word *male* be stricken from the bill. But Senator Wadsworth of New York countered this move by asserting that such a change involved far-reaching, even unknown, implications. He then asked why the provisions should not be made equally for all other branches of the armed services, a proposition, he obviously felt, to be a demonstration of the absurdity of Senator Oddie's proposal. Unwilling to delay the passage of the bill over a point on which he received no support from his colleagues, Senator Oddie withdrew the amendment. There was no discussion in the House. Later, the terms of the 1925 act were carried over into the 1938 act.

The Bureau of Aeronautics, in 1941, requested the Bureau

of Navigation—soon to become the Bureau of Naval Personnel—to set up a program and obtain necessary legislation which would permit women to become members of the Naval Reserve. This request was met with singular disinterest, the Bureau of Navigation stating flatly that since no need for women was visualized, no legislation would be requested. So, for the moment, the Bureau of Aeronautics was stymied in its legislative proposal. However, it was so convinced of the logic of its thinking and of its request that studies and estimates of aviation manpower needs, later substantiated by the Navy's overall estimates, for the immediate years ahead, were continued. All of these studies and estimates dictated the employment of womanpower. Further, these studies encompassed such factors as the types of duties the women would be expected to perform and the methods to be established for their training, and were based largely on what the women in Great Britain and Canada were doing and what civilian women employed by the U.S. aircraft and related industries had been trained to do successfully.

Much of this knowledge was contributed by Rear Admiral John H. Towers, Rear Admiral A. B. Cook, Captain A. W. Radford, and Commander Ralph A. Ofstie, the last named having, upon the declaration of war, returned from duty in London as naval attaché. For additional information concerning the administration, housing, and recreation of women in the service, I was sent to Canada to visit the various stations of the Royal Canadian Air Force, and to prepare a detailed report. The bureau then drew up their comprehensive plan for presentation to the Bureau of Personnel for implementation as soon as permissive legislation would be available. This plan included the number of women desired for naval aviation, the types of work which would be assigned to them, and the training which would be given to qualify them for the work. But patience was indeed needed, and it was not until the Navy's 1941 estimate of the manpower it needed to fulfill the requirements of its ships and bases in time of war was conveyed to the War Manpower Commission that it became alarmingly clear that there would not be enough men available to match the Navy's stated needs. To secure enough men for the Fleet and forward bases it would be necessary to release the men from the shore establishment within the United States. How then could the shore establishment of the United States continue to function?

There was an easy answer, but one unacceptable to many an admiral. Dean Virginia Gildersleeve of Barnard College later wrote, "Now if the Navy could possibly have used dogs or ducks or monkeys, certain of the older admirals would probably have greatly preferred them." Women? There must be some other way to solve the growing manpower problem. Twenty-some years separated the high-ranking planners from World War I when the Navy had successfully used 10,000 women in its reserve. Flag officers of 1941 seemed to have no knowledge of that fact; junior officers had never hear of yeomen (F).

In the fall of 1941, the introduction of H.R. 4906 creating a Women's Auxiliary Army Corps (WAAC), prompted the first official consideration for a similar program for the Navy. Pressure was rising as civilians called regarding the possibilities of women serving in the Navy. Prompted by calls from several members of the Congress, the head of the Naval Reserve Division in the Bureau of Navigation, in October 1941, reluctantly explored the details of the Army plan after firmly expressing the opinion that such a plan was not needed for the Navy. His summation was to the effect that any duties which women could perform would be largely of a clerical nature or in the communications field, and would properly be done by civil service personnel. Since the Civil Service Commission provided the means of procuring such personnel it would be entirely unnecessary to create a special establishment in the Navy for this purpose.

But this was certainly not the end of the matter. On 9 December 1941, Representative Edith Nourse Rogers, sponsor of the WAAC bill, telephoned the chief of the Bureau of Navigation, then Rear Admiral Chester W. Nimitz, and pointedly asked whether the Navy was interested in the passage of a bill which would enable the Navy to use women along the lines of the bill proposed for the Army.

Admiral Nimitz's reaction was cautious: "I advised Mrs. Rogers that at the present time I saw no great need for such a bill, but at the same time I told her that there were undoubtedly some positions that could be filled by members of such a corps." He thereupon suggested that Mrs. Rogers formally request the views of the Secretary of the Navy. On 12 December 1941, Nimitz ordered that the various bureaus and offices of the Navy furnish their views to the Bureau of Personnel, since he anticipated the necessity of having to render an official opinion to the Congress.

The action of Mrs. Rogers really started a fire. The creation of a women's reserve was taken up by the Navy because its leaders feared that if they did not move, Mrs. Rogers and thers on the Hill would, and the Navy would be entangled in legislation of a character it could not administer. This ear, rather than any firm conviction as to the need of women, moved them to action, reluctant though it was. A survey was s good as any other measure to indicate interest and yet elay decision.

The response of the bureaus and offices reflected general indifference as well as scant imagination or open-mindedness regarding the possible use of women as replacements or substitutes for men. With three exceptions, they failed to foresee the coming shortage of military manpower and civilian employees. Their lack of enthusiasm stemmed, I believe, from a ear that a change would take place. It was much simpler to ay "no," rather than "yes," particularly when "yes" would mean doing a job that could be avoided.

These statements spelled out the disinterest:

Office of the Judge Advocate General: "No use for the services of Women's Auxiliary is seen at this time."

Bureau of Medicine and Surgery: "Do not visualize a need."

Bureau of Supplies and Accounts: "It does not appear that the establishment of a Women's Auxiliary Corps would be esirable."

Bureau of Yards and Docks: "Such a corps is unnecessary o assist this bureau in carrying out its functions."

Bureau of Ships: "As clerks, typists and stenogs," thought "probable" but deemed such use was precluded because it would invade the province of Civil Service.

Bureau of Ordnance: "Based upon the experience of other ations in this war, it is entirely possible that combatant aval service (limited to zones of interior and continental 'aval Districts) may be desirable in the case of women." However, noting that a corps, such as that proposed for the WAAC, designated duty as noncombatant, the Bureau of Ordnance believed that all such jobs could well be filled by Civil ervice employees.

The Assistant Secretary of the Navy saw no place for a omen's corps and reported that "we have encountered no ifficulty in enrolling women under Civil Service procedures or any types of positions."

But for the enthusiastic support of the Chief of Naval Operations and the Bureau of Aeronautics, the response of the Navy Department would have been wholly negative. Noting he educational and social changes which had taken place etween the two wartime periods of service, BuAer visualized much broader scope of activity for women in the Navy than had been involved in World War I and indicated the firm belief that they could be employed in a wide variety of technical and skilled positions. Furthermore, the Bureau of Aeronautics made further suggestions of policy which anticipated most of the major aspects of the subsequent organization of the Women's Reserve.

As a woman who had served in World War I and had, by 1941, served for many years as a civilian employee in the Bureau of Aeronautics, I was given the task of working with responsible officers in that bureau to draft another letter to the Bureau of Personnel, not only in support of the requested Reserve, but also outlining specifically the types of employment visualized and the numbers of women needed in the aeronautical organization of the Navy. This letter was dated 1 January 1942, and was hand-carried to the Bureau of Personnel. Informal information had reached BuAer that the results of the survey requested in Admiral Nimitz's letter of 12 December 1941 were being studied and it was felt that the BuAer letter containing specifics would strengthen the entire picture.

Prior to Admiral Nimitz's letter requesting the views of all bureaus in the Navy Department, the Bureau of Personnel had turned a deaf ear to the affirmative views expressed by the Chief of Naval Operations and the Bureau of Aeronautics. CNO had submitted the mounting need for communication personnel who must be under strict military discipline and control. The only way to meet the need of men trained in communication in the Fleet would be to build up a Women's Reserve to fill the billets ashore vacated by these men and to meet expanding needs. Thus this part of the Navy recommended that such a program be begun "without delay."

BuPers itself had made no serious survey of the extent to which it would be possible to use a Women's Reserve. Its officer division suggested the use of three commissioned personnel. In all fairness, I must point out that one man in BuPers displayed foresight and imagination. The chief clerk filed a memorandum in which he made a prophecy that would be amply fulfilled: a Women's Reserve would be vitally needed because of a tightening labor supply and nonavailability of Civil Service personnel.

With introduction of legislation authorizing the WAAC (Women's Auxiliary Army Corps), the number of congressional inquiries regarding the Navy's intentions increased daily. Despite the negative or generally indifferent replies to the 12 December letter and despite the overwhelming, built-in conservatism of the Bureau of Personnel, that bureau did, on 2 January 1942, recommend to the Secretary of the Navy that Congress be asked to authorize the creation of a women's organization.

Though cautiously phrased, the recommendation demonstrated greater foresight than had been exhibited by most of the bureaus in their response to queries as to the value of such a service: "While the number of billets in which personnel of a Women's Auxiliary Corps should be used appears limited at this time, it would be visualized that the need for the employment of women in the shore establishment of the Navy in specialized duties will be more apparent as the war progresses. It is considered that legislation should be requested which will permit such employment under rules prescribed by the Secretary of the Navy."

For reasons of security, flexibility in assignment to duty and control of conditions of work, as well as the convenience of having the women within the scope of all applicable legislation, the Secretary of the Navy desired as far as possible to blanket the women into the existing Reserve legislation. In fact, the Secretary of the Navy preferred to have no women's organization at all rather than accept an "auxiliary corps" like the WAAC.

The Navy, therefore, first proposed simply to add to the Naval Reserve Act of 1938 an additional title as follows:

Title V, Sect. 501. A Women's Auxiliary Reserve is hereby established which shall be a branch of the Naval Reserve and shall be administered under the same provisions in all respects (except as may be necessary to adapt provisions to the Women's Auxiliary Reserve) as those contained in this Act or which may hereafter be enacted with respect to the Volunteer Reserve. Appointments and enlistments in the Women's Auxiliary Reserve shall be made only in time of war and for periods to expire not later than six months after the termination of war.

Although called "auxiliary," such an organization would clearly have been a full-fledged part of the Naval Reserve. This bill was submitted 2 February 1942 to the Director of the Budget, whose responsibility it was to serve as a clearing house for all proposed legislation to insure that it be consistent with executive policy.

Thereupon ensued another of the long, frustrating delays, for the Bureau of the Budget on 19 February replied: "The enactment of the proposed legislation in the form submitted would not be in accord with the program of the President."

However, there would not be, it was further noted, any objection to the Navy's submitting legislation "on the same basis as the legislation which had been cleared for the establishment of a Women's Army Auxiliary Corps." The following month, the Bureau of Personnel asked the Judge Advocate General to ask the Bureau of the Budget to reconsider its judgment, and the Chief of Naval Operations made a similar recommendation.

The continual prodding by the Bureau of Aeronautics did nothing to hasten the fulfillment of its desire that a presentation be made of proposed legislation to the Congress. By now desperate, BuAer decided to make an under-the-table effort, and turned for aid to a long-time friend of naval aviation.

Some background is needed here. The well-known Dr. Margaret Chung of San Francisco had for many years been keenly interested in the Navy, particularly in naval aviation. Throughout the war years, her cordial hospitality to naval aviators and later, submariners, whom she claimed as "sons," had earned her the name of Mom Chung. Out of this warm relationship had grown an informal organization known as "the sons of Mom Chung."

Dr. Chung, seeking some direct way in which she might contribute to the war effort, came to the Bureau of Aeronautics to inquire if and when the necessary legislation would be passed, so that she might join the service. One of her "sons," Lieutenant Commander Irving McQuiston, described the foot-dragging process the Bureau of Aeronautics had to contend with in proposing legislation and pointed out that no legislation had been sent to the Congress for consideration.

Dr. Chung was not at a loss for a solution. She suggested that she herself would go to Representative Melvin Maas of Minnesota, one of her "sons," and ask him to introduce legislation without reference to the Navy. This she did, and Representative Maas immediately reacted by asking the Office of the Judge Advocate of the Navy for a copy of the legislation to be proposed by the Navy.

On 16 March 1942, as requested by Representative Maas, a copy of the legislation to be proposed by the Navy and which was still being passed back and forth between the Bureau of the Budget, Judge Advocate General, and the Bureau of Personnel, was forwarded. Two days later, 18 March 1942, Representative Maas introduced his own bill, H.R. 6807. He requested Senator Raymond E. Willis to introduce an identical bill. This was done as S. 2388, dated 19 March 1942. These bills simply read:

Title V—Women's Auxiliary Reserve:

Section 501. A Women's Auxiliary Reserve is hereby established which shall be administered under the same provision in all respects (except as may be necessary to adopt said provisions to the Women's Auxiliary Reserve) as those contained in this Act or which may be hereafter enacted with respect to the Volunteer Reserve. Appointments and enlistments in the Women's Auxiliary Reserve shall be made only in time of war and for periods to expire not later than six months after termination of the war.

This, of course, was not the final permissive legislation, but it certainly served to start the fires under the Navy Department's weak efforts. From that time forward, the legislative battle was on.

The Judge Advocate General, in forwarding the Navy's proposed legislation, was still cautious. He pointed out that it was not to be regarded in any sense as an approval of enrolling women in the Navy. "This work has been undertaken as an informal matter only and is not to be construed as an indication of the opinion of the Navy Department or of this office regarding the merits of the measure." This notation was probably intended to forestall any critical suggestion that the Navy might have circumvented proper channels in proposing legislation which the Bureau of the Budget had disapproved.

The reception of Representative Maas' bill in the House Naval Affairs Committee was favorable and it was sent with approval to the Senate Naval Affairs Committee. There the bill met with strong opposition, chiefly because its terms did not parallel those of the WAAC legislation. Without surrendering this point, the Bureau of Personnel designed a substitute bill which was aimed at conciliating opposition by meeting the various objections raised by the committee. Various compromises had to be made to secure the blessing of the Senate Naval Affairs Committee, including the limitations as to the areas where women of the Navy could serve and their employment in naval aircraft. Later, these restrictions were overcome by appropriate legislation.

When the final request for permissive legislation was received by the Congress, another hue and cry of protest was raised. Senator David. I. Walsh of Massachusetts, the chairman of the powerful Senate Naval Affairs Committee, and several other chivalrous gentlemen were sure that a woman's place was in the home and that to permit women to become members of the armed forces would destroy their femininity and future standings as "good mothers." This point of view was held in spite of the fact that women by the thousands were already manning the assembly lines in war production plants and that Civil Service workers in Washington were, in the majority, composed of women.

The recommendations which would make naval legislation parallel to that establishing the WAAC were sent to President Roosevelt on 25 May. The President informed Senator Walsh and the Secretary of the Navy of his approval. The Navy asked the President to reconsider.

And right here, "the fine Italian hand" of a woman handled a delicate matter. On 30 May 1942, Dean Harriet Elliott of the University of North Carolina wrote Mrs. Roosevelt to explain the need for legislation as requested by the Navy and to ask the First Lady's help in getting presidential approval. In her reply, Mrs. Roosevelt wrote, "I showed your letter about the organization of the Women's Reserve of the Navy to the President." Thus it came about on 16 June that the Secretary of the Navy informed the Chief of the Bureau of Naval Personnel that the President "has given me *carte blanche* to go ahead and organize the Women's Reserve along the lines I think best." He also suggested that "we now press this matter to as swift an enactment as we can."

The final bill, Public Law 689, was reported favorably by the Senate Committee on 24 June, passed by the Senate, approved in its new form by the House of Representatives and sent to the President on 21 July. It was signed 30 July 1942.

Rear Admiral Randall Jacobs, USN, Chief of the Bureau of Naval Personnel in 1942 (*above*), reviews the first WAVE uniform, as Lieutenant Commander Mildred McAfee, USNR, the first Director of the Women's Reserve, presents her staff. Left to right: Lieutenant Elizabeth Reynard, Lieutenant Jean T. Palmer, Lieutenant (jg) Virginia Carlin, Lieutenant (jg) Marian Enright, and Ensign Dorothy Foster.

Joy Bright Hancock is sworn into the Naval Reserve by Rear Admiral John Sidney McCain, USN, Chief of the Bureau of Aeronautics, 23 October 1942 (*above*).

The only WAVES eligible to wear the World War I Victory Ribbon—Lieutenant Commander Joy Bright Hancock and Lieutenant Eunice White (*opposite*).

Beginning
Organization

$\mathcal{T}$ HEN faced with the need of making a decision regarding what its stand on legislation would be, the Chief of Personnel, Rear Admiral Randall Jacobs, and his advisers followed a course frequently pursued when seeking aid and advice in the recruiting of men. They turned to the educational field.

Virginia C. Gildersleeve, Dean of Barnard College, was invited to contribute her views and make recommendations on the subject of a possible Women's Reserve. One of her first steps was to nominate Professor Elizabeth Reynard as a consultant and as her assistant. Miss Reynard had for several months been investigating throughout the country the types of work that might be done by women. Professor Reynard— later Lieutenant Reynard—brought to the program a wealth of energy and imagination combined with logical recommendations, particularly in the field of training.

Dean Gildersleeve was asked to recommend names for and assist in the formation of an advisory council of women. This she did and the impressive membership, including several college presidents, deans, and civic leaders, was representative of the various sections of the country.

Serving with Dean Gildersleeve, who was chairman, were Miss Meta Glass, president of Sweet Briar College; Miss Ada Comstock, president of Radcliffe; Dean Harriet Elliott from the University of North Carolina; Dean Alice Lloyd, University of Michigan; Mrs. Malbone Graham, a noted lecturer from the West Coast; and Mrs. Thomas Gates, wife of the president of the University of Pennsylvania. Later, when Dean Elliott resigned, Alice Baldwin, dean of women at Duke University, took her place. Dr. Lillian Gilbreth had, in consultation with Dean Gildersleeve and Miss Glass, aided in designing a basic structure for the administration of women in the Navy. However, Dr. Gilbreth could not continue to serve since that would have meant there would be two representatives from the New York area, herself and Dean Gildersleeve.

In the formation of the council and in its subsequent workings, Lieutenant Albert Hartenstein, USNR, was an untiring and valuable adviser and assistant.

One of the notable acts of this council was its selection of Miss Mildred McAfee, the president of Wellesley College, as director of the WAVES. Dean Gildersleeve, at the request of Rear Admiral Jacobs, accepted the task of persuading the reluctant Wellesley trustees to release the vivacious, able president for service in the Navy. The judgment of the council was magnificently upheld by the outstanding job Miss McAfee performed. She brought not only prestige to the entire program, but also her gift for getting along with people, even with certain recalcitrants, salty officers who ultimately came to see the great service women could perform. Since the highest rank or grade that could be held by a woman, in accordance with legislation as finally enacted, was that of lieutenant commander, Miss McAfee was commissioned in that rank as the first director of the WAVES. She was the first woman officer ever sworn into the Reserve of the Navy, for at that time women in the Nurse Corps of the Navy held only "temporary" rank.

To Elizabeth Reynard the WAVES owe their distinguished

acronym. In 1942, when the planning for the Women's Reserve began, the question of a short and catchy name was posed, in the interest of publicity and recruiting. On a train, during one of the frequent trips that took her from Washington to New York—she was on loan from Barnard College—Miss Reynard addressed herself to the problem. Explaining shortly thereafter to Dean Gildersleeve how she hit on the name, she said, "I realized that there were two letters which had to be in it: W for women and V for volunteer, because the Navy wants to make it clear that this is a voluntary service and not a drafted service. So I played with those two letters and the idea of the sea and finally came up with 'Women Appointed for Volunteer Emergency Service'—WAVES. [Later, when it was realized that *Appointed* applied only to officers, *Accepted* was the word substituted.] I figured the word *Emergency* would comfort the older admirals because it implies that we're only a temporary crisis and won't be around for keeps."

The first estimates of the number of women who would be needed by the Navy were, as already indicated, far too low. The Bureau of Aeronautics at the very start of the program informed the Bureau of Personnel that it would need some 20,000 WAVES in the aeronautical organization. Upon receiving this information the Bureau of Personnel advised BuAer by letter:

"The Bureau has not made provisions for enlisting or training such a large complement of enlisted women but will proceed to plan in that direction.

"The specialist personnel for whom requests were received will be sought at once and referred to the Bureau of Aeronautics as soon as properly qualified candidates can be procured and trained in indoctrination schools. The details of such training will be discussed with the officer assigned to be the liaison officer between the Bureau of Aeronautics and the Bureau of Personnel in connection with the Women's Reserve.

"The Bureau of Personnel will welcome additional information from Bureau of Aeronautics as to the schools which are now training enlisted and officer personnel which could be available for the training of women."

Actually, the initial thinking and planning of the Bureau of Personnal estimated a grand total of 10,000 and those were to be in clerical ratings. The Bureau of Aeronautics' estimate had a beneficial effect in that it caused BuPers hastily to raise its figure to 75,000 enlisted women and 12,000 officers.

Initially there was an apparent need for at least a small group of women to assist in getting the program underway, to aid in recruiting, training, and administration. As a result, on 5 August 1942, Elizabeth Reynard was commissioned as a lieutenant, and on 7 August 1942 Elizabeth Borland Crandall, Virginia Carlin, and Dorothy Foster received their commissions as lieutenant, lieutenant (jg) and ensign, respectively. Lieutenant Crandall was ordered to Northampton, where the school for training women officers was being established. Lieutenant (jg) Carlin and Ensign Foster were assigned to Lieutenant Commander McAfee as assistants. Four days later, eleven more officers were commissioned and assigned to duty at the main recruiting offices in the various naval districts. They were:

Lieutenant Harriet Felton Parker, Boston.
Lieutenant Mildred L. McFall, Charleston.
Lieutenant Mary Daily, Chicago.
Lieutenant (jg) Frances Elizabeth Shoup, Los Angeles.
Lieutenant Serepta Bowman Terletzky, Miami.
Lieutenant Katherine L. Luna, New Orleans.
Lieutenant Mary Grace Cheney, New York City.
Lieutenant Margaret C. Disert, Philadelphia.
Lieutenant Tova L. Petersen, San Francisco.
Lieutenant (jg) Jane Bogue, Seattle.
Ensign Elizabeth R. Leighton, Washington.

One other name was added to the list of the so-called "unindoctrinated" and that was mine. It was not until 23 October 1942 that the requested physical waiver was approved and my oath of office was administered by Admiral John S. McCain.

Once in service and many weeks behind those who were the first to enroll, it was considered that my World War I experience and my years of work as a civilian in the Navy Department would be accepted in lieu of formal indoctrination training. With the aid of the Naval Clothing Depot, I was able to procure one uniform, but no hat and no overcoat. To overcome the lack of the last two items I wore a civilian overcoat, in spite of the warm weather, and a civilian hat to work, having been assigned immediately to the Bureau of Aeronautics, where I arrived early and left late. It was during these two weeks that the first output of officers from the Midshipmen School at Northampton started to report to Washington for duty. However, I think that none of those reporting to BuAer knew that I was "out of uniform."

My job was Women's Representative to the Chief of the

Bureau of Aeronautics and to the Deputy Chief of Naval Operations (Air), and as such was liaison officer with the office of Lieutenant Commander Mildred McAfee in the Bureau of Personnel. From this time on there was no need to use various schemes to find out what was going on. Miss McAfee very early let me know that I was her representative in naval aviation, that all matters there were of great interest to her, and that she was aware of the great amount of advance work I had done as a civilian.

But I was nearly blocked from this service. Once the WAVE legislation had passed, I discovered I was too old to enlist, as the top age level for enlisted WAVES was thirty-five. I would have to apply for a commission, but I did not have a college degree. While I had more than the equivalent in credits, they failed to meet the requirements for a degree. But I had allies. So great was the insistence on the part of the Bureau of Aeronautics that special consideration be given in my case that it was arranged for me to have a personal conference with Miss McAfee. This took place with Miss Reynard and Lieutenant Albert Hartenstein, an adviser for the Advisory Council and the Women's Reserve, also being present.

A few days later, an official letter notified me that the educational waiver was granted and directed me to to to the Office of Naval Officer Procurement in Washington, D.C., for a physical examination. Knowing I was below the weight standards and remembering the many tales of the men in World War I, I stopped en route and consumed all the bananas I could hold and drank bottles of cola. The latter was ill-advised, for when I was told to bend down and touch my toes, disaster almost overtook me. The bananas didn't help anyway, for I was declared thirty-three pounds underweight.

But that wasn't the worst of it. The examining physician endorsed my letter with the notation: "Disqualified by reason of thirty-three pounds underweight and a history of gastroenterostomy." In those days, the latter was enough to disqualify one either for entry or retention in the service. That was a dark day.

I returned to the Bureau of Aeronautics with the news of my failure. But my many lifelong friends were not without resources. That very day I found myself before a bevy of flight surgeons in the Navy's Bureau of Medicine and Surgery. I was X-rayed, interrogated and examined. The result was that this impressive but informal board wrote a recommendation of approval on the grounds that the weight standards did not take into full consideration the changing physique of a woman over the years and that it was the opinion of those making the reexamination that the second defect noted had been cured by surgery.

These findings were sent to the Bureau of Naval Personnel, but it was not until 19 October 1942 that I was declared a successful candidate. My oath was administered by Rear Admiral John S. McCain, Chief of the Bureau of Aeronautics, on 23 October 1942.

But in the following days of ceaseless activity in my capacity as Women's Reserve representative, there were moments of elation. One day I was called by an aide of Admiral Ernest J. King, Chief of Naval Operations, asking me to come to his office. Having worked directly for Admiral King when I was civilian head of press and public relations at the time he was Chief of the Bureau of Aeronautics, I knew his high standards, expressed in the phrase, "Deeds, not words," and I as well as others found myself stirred by awe in facing him. But beneath his habitually stern mien, there was the human touch, certainly evident on this occasion.

In his office, he greeted me with these words, "Weren't you an enlisted woman in the Navy in World War I?"

When I answered affirmatively, he asked, "Why aren't you wearing your World War I service ribbon on your uniform?"

I explained that I had wanted to but that I did not know whether or not I had such authorization and had felt some hesitation in trying to find out. (At that time, I was the only woman in naval service who had also served in World War I. Later, Lieutenant Eunice White, another World War I veteran, was enrolled.)

Admiral King then said, "Well, you are eligible to wear the ribbon and I have one for you." He proceeded to pin it on the pocket flap of my jacket. Then he concluded the little ceremony with a smile and a handshake.

Leaving his office, I walked down the corridor of the old Navy building on Constitution Avenue and saw an elderly admiral coming toward me, apparently one of the retired officers recalled to active duty.

Coming opposite me, he said, "Young lady."

I acknowledged the salutation, "Yes, Admiral."

"Are you a WAVE?"

"Yes, Admiral."

"Then there is one thing you ladies must learn. You do not wear decorations unless you have earned them."

"But, Admiral," I said, "I did earn this ribbon. I was in

World War I, and Admiral King has just pinned this ribbon on my uniform."

A bit taken aback, he recovered sufficiently to pat my arm and say, "Well, there are only a few of us left."

Time and again on inspection trips, I repeated this story to the delight of the enlisted WAVES. My prior service as yeoman in World War I brought me close to the enlisted women in World War II, for on many occasions when problems were under discussion, the girls would say, "You understand because you too were enlisted."

Admittedly a great many officers were ready to resist what they apparently regarded as a feminine invasion of an area sacred to manhood, the Navy. While animosity was veiled, it was lurking within and waiting to be expressed if the opportunity presented itself. Such opposition was not long in coming.

At the outset, the Bureau of Naval Personnel established the Office of the Director of the Women's Reserve as an integral part of its general operating division, but the responsibility of the director was not clearly defined nor were the lines of authority made clear. The incumbent, Lieutenant Commander McAfee, was simply told that she was to "run" the Women's Reserve and that she could go directly to the Chief of the Bureau of Naval Personnel for answers to her questions. Unfortunately, this decision was not made known to the operating divisions of the bureau.

Of necessity, the Office of the Director of the Women's Reserve quickly expanded to include various aides: an assistant director, a public relations officer, and two special assistants, as well as Women's Reserve officers assigned to duty in the bureau divisions of Officer's Orders, Enlisted Orders, Training, and Recruiting, and whose additional function was to maintain liaison between those key activities and the director of the WAVES. As a result of this arrangement, the original group of women, all unfamiliar with the Navy and its methods of operation, was initiating a program that would cut across every established activity of the bureau—recruiting, training, personnel assignment and, particularly, planning. Not visualizing the use of existing schools for both men and women, separate schools for the training of women in the clerical, communications, and storekeeper fields of work were set up in leased facilities, manned for the most part by recently commissioned women officers whose knowledge of the Navy's functioning was obtained during their short time of indoctrination at Smith College, Northampton,

Massachusetts, the officer training school for the Women's Reserve.

The director plunged at once into the maelstrom of details the new program involved. Her initiative was encouraged by bureau officials, who in the beginning were only too relieved to have "the women's viewpoint" on such matters as recruiting, housing, training, etc., of the Women's Reserve. But their interest was not focused intensely on these problems since the bureau was being reorganized and their preoccupation with this matter precluded any concentrated concern for what was quantatively a minor program.

Small wonder, then, that with this casual handling of the creation of the new office, Miss McAfee and her staff shortly ran into a substantial amount of friction. This was clearly no fault of hers. No attempt had been made by the Bureau of Personnel to fit the Women's Reserve into the patterns and traditions of the existing organization of the Navy. The damaging consequences of this failure ran deep and were to be a continuing source of difficulty during the first fifteen months of the program.

No one realizes more clearly than I, who have served in both a civilian and a military capacity in the Navy for many years, the inevitability of conflicts when a new program is inaugurated. It is easy to look back now and see how much better if... or if... or if.... What an ordeal it must have been for Miss McAfee to be told to "run" the Women's Reserve within an organization the language of which she did not know and the workings of which she was unfamiliar.

Miss McAfee and her staff officers entered the Navy knowing no more of it in general than any group of intelligent laymen, and naturally they knew even less of the Bureau of Naval Personnel. Yet no indoctrination was given them, no experienced officer of the regular Navy was assigned to advise them. Had such reasonable steps been taken, they would probably not only have precluded certain mistakes but would also have hastened the adoption of appropriate policies.

What must have been of initial value to Miss McAfee upon her accepting the directorship of the WAVES turned out to be an irritant: her ready access to the Chief of the Bureau of Naval Personnel. Operating division heads, who enjoyed no such channel of communications, appeared to me to react uncharitably to what they regarded as special privilege. In consequence, the Women's Reserve became, in a sense, separated from the divisions. Thus, when Miss McAfee's assistants sought to initiate or at least anticipate the stages of major policies and implement them, they met with rebuffs or lack of cooperation. This issue, which grew to sizable proportions, involved the question of how much authority Miss McAfee had in determining matters of policy: training, discipline, housing standards, etc.

Finally, this problem had to be met head-on. A directive was issued 16 September 1942, stating that the Director of the Women's Reserve should have the authority and the duty to take the initiative in formulating "major policies governing the activities of the Women's Reserve and ...the coordination of the work in the operating divisions of the bureau in connection with the Women's Reserve."

However noble the intent on the part of its authors in the Bureau of Naval Personnel, the directive did not solve the problem but extended the controversy and led ultimately to the issuance of Bureau Organization Series #27 of 7 May 1943. This document made Miss McAfee a special assistant to the Chief of the Bureau. In substance, this left Miss McAfee's office the function of policy and put her in the chain of command so that all papers on matters affecting the Women's Reserve must bear her initials before going to the Chief of the Bureau of Personnel or the various division heads.

On paper, it looked good, but in action it simply caused enormous delays since any policy statement had to be returned to the originating desks if the Women's Reserve found some feature unsatisfactory. Since "the women's point of view" had not been previously solicited, refusals to initial were inevitable. Such an arrangement ran counter to principles of good management.

Management advisers therefore recommended that the head of the Women's Reserve be the director of her program under Manpower, Policies Section, of the Bureau of Naval Personnel. They pointed out that not only did the existing setup violate sound management doctrine, but it also negated legislation which had established the Women's Reserve as an integral part of the naval establishment.

The Chief of the Bureau of Naval Personnel, Admiral Randall Jacobs, rejected this recommendation and told Miss McAfee to bring to him whatever problems arose, great or small. He undoubtedly believed that such an arrangement would enhance the dignity and prestige of the Women's Reserve. He probably also thought that a lieutenant commander in an organization in which she was so outranked by so many men should have the support of flag rank.

Actually, with the creation of a Planning Division in the

Bureau of Personnel, the separateness of the Women's Reserve should have been obliterated, for it was to this division that all other divisions of the bureau channeled their proposals and ironed out their differences before submitting a program to the bureau chief. However, since the Women's Reserve still had direct access to him, the feeling of distrust spread and aroused resentment in the Planning Division. But time and concessions on both sides eventually diminished friction.

All this interdepartmental and interbureau discord probably accounts for the unsatisfactory situation which arose because of the noncompilation of the needed policies for the administration of the Women's Reserve. The commanding officers of the field activities were confused by conflicting directives. Frequently, while on my many inspection trips, situations were encountered that were not covered by any policy and the only thing to do was to make a decision based on common sense.

It was in less than a year that limitations contained in the original legislation for the Women's Reserve were found to be real stumbling blocks and weaknesses in attempts to administer the program successfully. The need for additional and corrective legislation became more and more apparent. However, the feeling still persisted in some quarters of the Navy that the war would be of short duration and, therefore, existing legislation and policies regarding women were adequate. Nevertheless, request was finally made that certain changes be made by the Congress. Representative Melvin Maas, on 20 January 1942, introduced H.R. 1364 to remove the limitations which Bureau of Personnel had come to regard as undesirable, such as the statutory limitations on rank and on foreign service. The House refused to approve the bill and some weeks later H.R. 2859 was substituted, with the portion concerning overseas service omitted. Overseas assignment permission was not granted until 27 September 1944, under Public Law 441.

While H.R. 1364 had been pending in the Congress, the WAVES were informed of its content via the *Wave News Letter*. The policy regarding transfers for women had always been, in my mind, one of the best examples of saying "no" that could be conjured up: "Although technically a transfer from one station to another may be requested at any time by application through the chain of command, such application is not encouraged because it is a major asset to the Navy to have the majority remain in billets to which they were first assigned. The WAVES are in the Navy to do the job which the Navy needs to have done. The Women's Reserve is a service—not a career—and but for the need for such service there would be no Women's Reserve." My own reaction to this was that certain problems did actually exist because of initially incorrect assignments in that it could readily be seen that initial classification and assignment could and did result in many cases in the nonutilization of a woman's talents to the most efficient degree. The round pegs that appeared in the square holes necessitated using the more commonsense method, which was reassignment. Certainly a definite transfer policy was needed. Many technically trained women were being used in jobs such as conducting bond sales or recreation programs when their engineering knowledge, for example, could, if used, have proved more valuable to the war effort. Also, after several years of doing one particular type of work, such as, for example, communications, with its attendant irregularities of living occasioned by the need for "watches," it was desirable that a transfer to another type of duty be considered as a health factor.

Public Law 441 also clarified the matter of whether or not members of the Women's Reserve were eligible for allowance for dependents. The wording of the original Act of Congress establishing the Women's Reserve had been interpreted to not entitle WAVES to this allowance.

It was a mere three weeks—25 November 1943—after the passage of P.L. 441, that the changes permitted were put into effect. The change regarding promotions and the limitations on rank for the women was a drastic one. Until that time all women had been given the grade of ensign or lieutenant(jg), mostly ensign, regardless of age. It had become impossible to handle promotions on a fair basis with only 35 senior grade lieutenants allowed, most of which allowance was already filled. It now became possible to make certain commitments, as was done for male officers, based on age, experience and background of the applicant. Age limits were established for women: that is, ensign, 20 through 33; lieutenants (jg), 34 through 41; and lieutenants, 42 through 49. Further, it was possible to stipulate that after reporting for active duty all women officers would be eligible for promotion to ranks through the grade of lieutenant on the same basis as men of the Naval Reserve.

A quiet but needed shift in the function of the Director of the Women's Reserve gradually took place after the passage of Public Law 441. As the work of the director became increasingly that of an "inspector general," it was apparent by the end of 1944 that this was a meaningful and workable arrangement. However, this shift in function was not achieved without a few pitfalls. At first, as a sort of inspector general, Captain McAfee (her rank increased from lieutenant commander under P.L. 441) was to receive all over-all information from the bureaus, districts, stations, training schools, etc., regarding WAVES. Because the commanding officers at these activities were so engrossed with the administration of the tremendous war personnel program, a woman officer in each activity was designated to submit reports of their activities directly to Captain McAfee's office. This was supposed to decentralize most of the work of her office. It was a heretofore unheard-of procedure in the Navy and almost immediately the Commandants and others rose in wrath. The Bureau of Personnel formally and informally assured the worried Commandants and Air Command Directors that the matter was in hand. By letter of 19 October 1943, the provision for direct reports by the Women Representatives in the field, bureaus etc., were abolished.

So by trial and error, or perhaps because of it, the experiences of the first fifteen months, though frustrating, were fruitful. The two remaining years of war continued the polishing operations, and the soundness of the policies developed by the WAVE administration was proved by the fact that so many of them are retained to this day.

The establishment of periodic conferences in Washington of the Women's Representatives was an immeasurable aid to the entire program, for these conferences solved many a question or problem. The understanding and cooperation between field activities and the Bureau of Personnel, as well as between naval districts and air commands, where some overlapping of function and responsibilities seemed inevitable, made traditional contentions less ominous and small irritations minimal.

At the conference in 1944, the WR's from the field were thoroughly at ease as they talked about their areas of responsibility and influence. Each name of those attending brings back to me clearly, after more than a quarter of a century, the appearance and characteristics of these women as each one presented to the group the possible conflicts over policy that might have arisen in "her district" and what her efforts had been to explain the women's policy to "the admiral." Because these names have brought back such vivid and interesting memories, I list them here:

Lieutenant Helen M. Woodruff, First Naval District (Boston)
Lieutenant Commander Elizabeth B. Crandall, Third Naval District (New York)
Lieutenant Bessie L. Miller, Fourth Naval District (Philadelphia)
Lieutenant Grace C. Dimelow, Fifth Naval District (Norfolk)
Lieutenant Kathryn Dougherty, Sixth Naval District (Charleston)
Lieutenant Virginia R. Sweeney, Seventh Naval District (Miami)
Lieutenant Serepta B. Terletzky, Eighth Naval District (New Orleans)
Lieutenant Commander Nancy W. Forsman, Ninth Naval District (Great Lakes)
Lieutenant Commander Edith P. Merritt, Eleventh Naval District (San Diego)
Lieutenant Commander Doris T. Westcott, Twelfth Naval District (San Francisco)
Lieutenant Commander Mary Daily, Thirteenth Naval District (Seattle)
Lieutenant Commander Eleanor Durette, Potomac River Naval Command (Washington, D.C.)
Lieutenant Edith L. Stallings, Naval Air Operation Training Command (Jacksonville)
Lieutenant Miriam A. Shelden, Naval Air Primary Training Command (Olathe, Kansas)
Lieutenant Minerva Lewis, Naval Air Technical Training Command (Norman, Oklahoma)
Lieutenant Bess A. Dunn, Naval Air Intermediate Training Command (Corpus Christi, Texas)

In addition, there were the WR's of the various bureaus in Washington with whom I had sometimes daily contact.

At such conferences, I came to realize fully that the program for women was growing impressively. I knew too that the work and effectiveness of the women at naval air activities were matched in performance and uniqueness of work assignments by the women at remote and little-heard-of activities, and at the large, city-based, shore establishment of the Navy as well. For example, at the Armed Guard Centers in the United States, the WAVES were close to war activities, for from these centers, the men set out to man the guns on cargo ships, tankers and transports, thus providing armed protection for merchant ships participating in invasions and carrying materials and men to the combat areas. The WAVES' responsibilities generally involved keeping pay records of the crews, disbursing which continued around the clock, issuing clothing and small stores to the men (including survivors), keeping service records and orders current, and maintaining mail, recreation, medical records, and work in the station hospital and sick bay laboratory.

At the Naval Supply Depot, San Pedro, the WAVES helped keep supplies moving to their destination. One WAVE ensign gained a working knowledge of stevedoring operations in order to have on hand at all times adequate operating stock of stevedoring gear, such as wire rope, turnbuckles, clips, shackles, and lumber. She signed inspection reports on material and service received and certified invoices for services rendered, including those of derrick, barge and crane, as well as for stevedoring, wharfage, docking, and truck tonnage. Every third Sunday she stood her regular duty, and at that time she was responsible for the operations of the station which included checking ship movements in the harbor, coordinating the movement of equipment to the dock with the scheduled loading of ships, and the general security of the area.

The WAVES were making their way fast, learning as they worked and honestly contributing significantly to the war effort.

The mission of the Navy's Midshipmen Training School, Smith College, Northampton, Massachusetts, was to turn young civilian women into Women's Reserve officers in the short period of two months. *Top,* an indoctrination class at Northampton. As soon as one class graduated, new recruits would arrive to take their place (*above, left*). At Northampton, as at Hunter College, where the enlisted women trained, physical fitness was a regular part of the curriculum. *Above, right,* a physical education class at Hunter enjoys an out-of-doors session in the summer of 1943. In short order, the WAVE officers were performing smartly on the drill field (*opposite*).

Officer Training at Northampton

𝕴N preparing the ground for the training of the WAVES, the Civilian Advisory Council, practically all of whom had had wide experience as educators of young women, recommended that officers and enlisted training should be given on campuses where possible, since this environment would confer the dignity and prestige of academic communities and would have immediately available the necessary classroom, housing, feeding, and recreation facilities as well.

The initial planning for training was based largely on proposed strength figures, which in turn derived from a survey made by BuPers of the number of billets in the shore establishment that could be filled by women. The result of this survey indicated that approximately 1,200 officers and 8,200 enlisted men held billets that could be filled by women. A number of colleges were surveyed by Elizabeth Reynard and those findings were studied by the Council. Smith College at Northampton, Massachusetts, was selected for the officer training, those facilities later augmented by Mount Holyoke College in nearby South Hadley.

The prerequisites for the selection of officers were high physical and moral standards, a baccalaureate degree from an accredited college or university, or at least two years of collegiate training with no less than two years of active business or professional experience. A two-month course of study was recommended in naval traditions and customs; organization and administrative procedures; military drill; and physical education. This recommendation followed, in general, the format that was in operation for male naval reserve officer candidates.

At Smith College, Northrup, Gillett, and Capon House dormitories were available; for lectures and classrooms, Faunce Hall and a part of Seelye Hall; the use of the John M. Green auditorium when needed; and the gymnasium and playing field were to be shared by the Navy and Smith.

To supplement the facilities for messing and housing, the City of Northampton procured Northampton Hotel (Wiggins Tavern), making available housing for 500 trainees and the messing of the entire group of trainees and staff.

On 27 June 1942, Lieutenant Elizabeth Reynard submitted her survey of Smith College facilities to the Bureau of Personnel and the Advisory Council. The establishment of the officers' training school at Northampton was satisfactory to the bureau and on 1 July 1942, the Smith College Board of Trustees also approved. On 15 July 1942, the contract was signed. This was indeed a remarkable show of speed, for the legislation authorizing WAVES was not signed into law until fifteen days later. It was a necessary speedup, however, for the first women officer trainees were scheduled to report for training on 28 August 1942.

The 120 women who began their active military career on that date had been selected for their exceptional qualifications to form the nucleus around which the WAVE program would be built. Among them were specialists in such technical fields as engineering, radio, and meteorology. They received probationary commissions and were designated W-V(P). So important was it to the program to get them into actual administrative billets that they received only one month of indoctrination training.

Captain H. W. Underwood, USN (Retired), who had been recalled to active duty, was issued orders to serve as commanding officer of the Naval Reserve Midshipmen's School, 13 August 1942, fifteen days before the reporting of the first trainees.

From the beginning the school operated with the full cooperation of the Bureau of Personnel, but at the same time there was a high degree of independence apropriate to a project essentially experimental in nature. Captain Underwood, as commanding officer, was confronted by formidable obstacles. First, Northampton was unready to receive the trainees; second, the outline of courses and textbooks did not arrive. Both obstacles were overcome by Captain Underwood's intelligent administration and the tremendous enthusiasm, good humor, and serious purpose which then, and through subsequent years, characterized the trainees. Without fear of denial, I can state that the morale prevailing at the school was unsurpassed anywhere in the naval establishment. Every officer candidate was determined to prove that she was equal to the extremely high standard of effort and accomplishment demanded by the staff and to the opportunity for service to her country. It was a totally different life for these women. Though I was not one of this number I have known hundreds, yes, even thousands of WAVES who found in the service a new appreciation of the value of discipline. They learned to obey without question, to muster as quickly as any ready seaman, and proceeded as smartly as their brother trainees to accustom themselves to the protocol and lingo of Navy life.

The officer complement for staffing the school at Northampton was set at 52. At first, the staff was drawn from line officers of the Navy, active, reserve, or retired, but as quickly as possible women officers came in to replace the men. The first executive officer, from October 1942 until May 1943, was Lieutenant Commander William A. Bullis, USNR, who was assisted by Lieutenant Elizabeth B. Crandall, on leave from her position as assistant dean of women at Leland Stanford University. Miss Crandall also served as adviser to the commanding officer, her duties being analagous to that of a dean of women to the president of a university. She represented the executive officer in dealing with WAVES in regard to such matters as uniforms, inspection of quarters, etc., and, in general, coordinated and supervised the WAVE performance at the school.

The mission of the Naval Reserve Midshipmen's School was at once simple and vast. The task was to convert civilian women, widely varying in age and experience, in the short period of two months, into military persons with military habits of thought and behavior; and to equip them with sufficient knowledge of fundamental traditions and procedures so that they could effectually replace male officers in general duty billets on shore stations. The regimental phase of the training was designed to inculcate sound principles of military character and leadership.

Indoctrination curricula remained basically unchanged throughout the period of the school's operation: Organization; Personnel; Naval History and Law; Ships and Aircraft (Recognition); Naval Communications and Correspondence. Realizing that in two months a completely trained naval officer could not be turned out, the aim was to teach the basic fundamentals of life and work in the naval service with emphasis on administrative procedures (in which field the women would for the most part operate). Even within these limitations the amount of ground that had to be covered was formidable. However, since all trainees were of college level with experience in absorbing and retaining facts, they were able, with a few exceptions, to digest the mountain of minutiae presented in the five courses of instruction.

On 30 September 1942, looking extremely shipshape as WAVE officers in their new uniforms, 119 graduates fell into formation for the final review. Twenty-four remained at Northampton to fill staff billets, where they understudied the male instructors, and learned ways of the Navy in order to qualify as a relief.

The official opening date of the school, however, was 6 October 1942, when 776 apprentice seamen, enlisted in class V-9, reported for training. (V-9 was a designator for women officer candidates selected by procurement officers as potential officer material.) With the third class of trainees, the expedient of probationary commissions on a large scale was discontinued and thereafter all trainees reported as apprentice seamen and underwent two months of indoctrination before receiving their commissions.

In May 1943 a change in the administrative structure of the school took place. The billet of Executive Officer was eliminated and the Executive Officer WR was redesignated Officer in Charge of Midshipmen. By this time WR officers had assumed a large share of administrative responsibility on the staff and most of the instructional billets were filled by the women. It was logical, therefore, that the greatest share of executive administration, after the commanding officer, should be allocated to a woman officer.

Lieutenant Crandall served in this capacity until August 1943, when she was ordered to the staff of the Commandant Third Naval District, New York City. She was then relieved by Lieutenant Margaret Disert.

During the thirty months the school was in existence—it closed 26 December 1944—it graduated 9,479 general duty officers plus 1,043 communicators, 771 of whom were Mount Holyoke trained and 272 Northampton.

With the strength goals for womanpower enlarged, based on surveys relative to the numbers that could be assigned to communication duties, it became evident that additional space would be needed to train the women, after Indoctrination, for communication watch officer duties. Arrangements were, therefore, made with Mount Holyoke College to take care of any overflow from Northampton. This contract provided for the Navy's use of Rockefeller Hall for housing 320 trainees plus a Women's Reserve staff; Eastman Hall for executive offices; Skinner Hall and Science Lecture Hall for classrooms. The Navy was to share, with the college, the gymnasium and playing field, the Chapel and the Student Alumnae Hall.

Reorganization of instruction at the Midshipmen's School, Northampton, resulted in the concentration of indoctrination at that place and the establishment of communications as a specialized officer training school at Mount Holyoke. It was a separate unit from the Midshipmen's School and was designated Naval Training School, Communications. The officer in charge was Lieutenant Commander L. R. Reiter, USN (Retired), later relieved by Lieutenant Commander Harry Wohl, USNR. It was, however, under the command of Captain Underwood. Thus it became, as other schools for officers were, a place for specialized training after commissioning.

At Holyoke the women were trained for two months. The curriculum included Naval Communications, Radio Room Procedures, Code and Cipher Instructions, Typing, and Fundamentals in Radio. In March 1944, the communications training was returned to Northampton.

Late in 1942 and early in 1943, when the Coast Guard and the Marine Corps were inducting women reservists, the school at Northampton provided the training of officers for those few months. Twelve WAVES from the 16 December 1942 class resigned their commissions in the Navy to accept commissions in the Coast Guard and form a nucleus of the SPAR organization. In this group was Dorothy Stratton, who had resigned, at the special request of the Commandant of the Coast Guard, to become the Director, SPARS. Similarly, a short time later, nineteen WAVES were selected to form the initial units of officers for the Marine Corps Women's Reserve. After June 1943, SPARS were indoctrinated at the U.S. Coast Guard Academy, New London, Connecticut, while the Marine women went to their own training center at New River, North Carolina.

On 3 July 1943, the first group of enlisted WAVES reported to Northampton for officer training. Upon recommendation of their commanding officers, outstanding WAVES of marked intelligence and ability who had served at least six months in the ranks could make application for officer training. It was felt that in addition to meeting the qualification standards which were set, their experience, gained through their enlisted service, would provide a familiarity with naval procedures invaluable to an officer.

For those many women who received their naval indoctrination at Northampton, "Judge" Underwood and his wife Frances became lifelong friends and fondest memories.

The initial thinking regarding the services of women officers in the Navy had not been truly geared to visualizing the various specialities, under the cognizance of the various bureaus—technical and material—and offices of the Navy Department, where these women would be serving. But it rapidly became evident that this situation needed immediate attention, again prompted by the realization and the necessity that the women, if properly trained, could and must be expected to do the work.

First to meet this contingency was the Supply Corps. The Supply Corps School was located at the Graduate School of Business Administration, Harvard University, and this school also trained the male officers of the Supply Corps. Living accommodations for women were set up in Briggs Hall, Radcliffe College; beginning January 1943, women candidates were selected from the graduating classes at Northampton. The three-months' course was broken down into eight weeks of disbursing and transportation and five weeks of supply. The requirements for the specialized training were a bachelor's degree, higher than average grades, and a major in mathematics, commerce, business administration, economics, or allied subjects. By April 1943, approximately 300 women had been designated as officers in the Supply Corps of the Navy. Practically every type of business experience was represented by these women, including agricultural economists, statisticians, textile analysts, dieticians, buyers, transportation reservationists, accountants, office managers, bankers, and market research analysts. From Puget Sound in the northwest to Jacksonville in the southwest, these women officers were represented in every phase of supply work. They handled storage problems, stock maintenance, shipping, transportation, and purchasing. At supply depots they were concerned particularly with the control and maintenance of the flow of materials, which consisted of anything from airplane motors to submarine parts. As assistant supply officers they were found in purchase, voucher and ordnance sections of Navy yards. Many of those who had had civilian experience in the dietetic field or in restaurant management were placed as commissary officers at naval stations, at first to aid in the preparation of daily menus and later to assume full responsibility in the feeding of naval personnel. All were trained in Navy subsistence methods.

Of the women officers who were placed in disbursing billets, more than thirty were sent to as many colleges and universities as disbursing officers with complete responsibility for the disbursing of Navy funds in connection with the V-12 program (naval summer program for male college students). These WAVES personally disbursed the money to the students on pay day. Those officers assigned to the Bureau of Supplies and Accounts in Washington filled a variety of positions. They handled emergency purchases of material, procured radio and emergency supplies, worked in transportation of officers' household effects, in the salvage conservation program, and scheduling the conversion and distribution of damaged battle equipment. A former executive secretary for an engineering firm placed orders for several million dollars worth of supplies for advance bases. Three, with former dietitic experience, reviewed and revised the famous *Navy Cook Book*. Another, a former cost accountant, assisted in the analysis of lumber contracts; another was responsible for publishing a catalogue on aviation instruments, as well as for the assignment of stock numbers.

The Bureau of Ordnance, in the original surveys made, had indicated that the services of women were not needed. However, by early 1943, it was necessary to face up to the reality that they must put the women to work or eventually their activities would suffer in the extreme because of lack of manpower, and the effectiveness and efficiency of the Fleet would be curtailed.

The ordnance schools established for men were opened to women on 25 September 1943. In the general ordnance school were studied the intricacies of torpedoes, mines, or bombs; the design, manufacture, and use of all naval ordnance, and observation of machine production shops. All these came within the approximate five weeks' course. In addition, the course covered the characteristics of various metals and their suitability for ordnance purposes. They learned about the construction and operation of various types of breech mechanisms and the general functions and structure of naval gun mounts. Other subjects included the history and development of modern fire control, the marking and stowage of naval projectiles, and a study of depth charges and projectors, machine guns, torpedoes, mines, and aviation ordnance.

The chemical warfare course included study of all types of gas warfare, its uses and effects. The women received instruction also about the various chemical agents, the methods of protection and decontamination, and how to identify different types of gases.

The course of training in aviation ordnance, of three months' duration, was given at the Naval Air Station, Jacksonville, Florida. This consisted of the study of all types of ordnance equipment used in airplanes, from machine guns to aerial torpedoes. Like the men in the class, the WAVES fired the guns on the range from moving platforms at moving targets. A typical day's schedule might include a class in boresighting, gun disassembling, oiling and reassembly, and studying the cycle of operation of the 30-caliber machine guns.

With the "ordnance indoctrination" plus the naval indoctrination received at Northampton, the women officers were considered ready to go to work in the Bureau of Ordnance and its field activities. For example, in the ordnance stock office of the Washington Navy Yard, six women officers handled the distribution of spare parts for technical ordnance equipment. Their duties included scheduling the delivery of equipment and setting up stock allowances. In the ordnance optical shop, a WAVE officer with civilian experience was an inspector of mica insulation for vacuum tubes in radio equipment and of optical materials, including range finders and telescopes.

Bids for contracts for certain types of fire control equipment for underwater ordnance came to the desk of Ensign Virginia M. Dente, a former mathematician. She was responsible for making contracts and seeing them through until the materials were actually shipped to vessels under construction and in commission. Lieutenant Lydia L. Allen, former librarian of the explosive and research laboratory of the du Pont Company, was a natural for the ammunition section of the Bureau of Ordnance. She became the liaison officer between manufacturers of smokeless powder and the bureau, and was concerned with the acceptance of manufactured powder and explosives as well as assisting in estimating the amounts of powder and explosives needed to meet fleet requirements and in expediting the delivery of vital materials to the plants under contract. A WAVE ensign, trained in architecture and design in civilian life, was engaged in drafting and design at the wind tunnel at the Naval Gun Factory, where her work included testing of model planes.

The Bureau of Ships, responsible for the design, maintenance, construction, and repair of naval vessels, was one of the bureaus which pondered seriously over the possibilities of utilizing the services of women. However, with the tremendous shipbuilding program and the nonavailability of men, the only source of help visible on the horizon was women. Another gate was opened and WAVES were requested and ordered to duty there. By the fall of 1943, there were 350 WAVES on duty in that bureau in Washington, and many hundreds more were in the bureau's field activities.

Rear Admiral E. L. Cochrane was, in 1943, chief of the bureau, and under his direction the WAVES were placed in skilled billets based on their experience in civilian life and subsequent training by the Navy. One interesting innovation in the bureau was the establishment of the "flying squad" which was a group of WAVES assigned for short periods of time to various sections of the bureau where there were emergency deadlines to meet. Simultaneously, enlisted WAVES were working as radio draftsmen, yeomen, statisticians, IBM operators, and many other types of work.

The women officers fitted into both technical and administrative billets. In the technical field, a group was given training at Harvard University for five months and then on to Massachusetts Institute of Technology for advanced training. In the meantime, civilian backgrounds of many permitted immediate placement. For example, an ensign with a master's degree in astronomy was assigned to the division working on

the development and improvement of optical systems for nav
igational equipment, checking their design for practicabilit
and adaptability for quantity production. Another, with a B:
degree in business administration, took charge of the record
of radio equipment for advance bases. Another became liaiso
officer between the Maritime Commission and the Bureau c
Ships in matters concerning the construction of frigate:
A former X-ray technician studied the X-rays of steel to b
used in Navy equipment, picking out any flaws which showe
up on the plates.

And so the placement and utilization picture started to gro
rapidly within the first year. Although the manpower shor
age, developing as critical early in the war, dictated to a si
able extent the acceptance of women in the Navy, I feel th:
their acceptance was more truly based on their fine effor
in early assignments to duties of responsibility. In these typ(
of assignments they were able to demonstrate their wort
They were called "eager beavers" by the men, and that
exactly what they were. Where they were given responsibili
somewhat in accordance with their ability they left no sto
unturned to learn the job quickly and carry it out efficientl
Never have I encountered a finer "can do" attitude. And ho
it delighted my heart, when on my regular visits to the acti
ities, to listen to the commanding officer relating with gre
pride what his WAVES were doing and how they were doi
it. The only politic reply to that was to say how encouragi
it was to find a commanding officer who recognized their p
tential usefulness and had shown great foresight in givi
them responsibilities.

The Navy's medical service offered a clearcut example
the unwisdom of the original legislative limitations, demc
strated by the extreme difficulty encountered in attempts
sign up women doctors. Certainly the availability of only t
lowest ranks to women who had already proved themselv
in their profession could but be construed as a slight to th(
standing in that profession.

The Bureau of Medicine and Surgery got busy and t
result was that in the spring of 1943 legislation was obtain
authorizing the Surgeon General of the Navy to enroll wom
doctors in the Navy Medical Corps on the same terms as m:
doctors. [Public Law 38, 78th Congress, 1st Session.] BuP(
did not regard, as sound policy, that women in one branch
the Navy should enjoy favored opportunities. Discussion arc

o the effect that BuPers had been shortsighted in drawing up he initial legislation, and that the limitations requested were he paramount features rather than a broad picture under which any limitation thought necessary could be imposed administratively. That type of discussion was of water over the dam, and Public Law 38, sponsored by BuMed, proved to be a splendid precedent in BuPer's efforts to secure legislation to permit higher rank for women in other categories, such as Line and Supply.

By February 1944, more than 140 women officers, assigned to medical activities of the Navy, had been classified as W-V(S)(H). The letter H designated those officers who were qualified by education and experience in given medical specialties as distinguished from personnel in the Medical Corps or the Hospital Corps. Fifty of these officers were bacteriologists, and the next largest number served as occupational therapists, physiotherapists, and psychologists. Other medical specialists included that of laboratory technician, medical illustrator, medical researcher, industrial hygienist, hospital librarian, parisitologist, X-ray technician, medical journalist, blood plasma technician, and dental hygienist.

Ensign Marie Kohoe, *top left*, was one of nine officers of the Women's Reserve to complete a nine-months' meteorological course at the University of California, Los Angeles, in 1943. Air navigation instructors were in short supply early that year, and Lieutenant Sue King was one of the first WAVE officers to qualify. She is shown at *top, right*, checking instruments at the navigator's station in a plane prior to takeoff. WAVE officers under indoctrination training in ship and aircraft recognition, *above*, examine the identifying features of an F4U Corsair.

The Director of the Women's Reserve, Captain Mildred McAfee, *opposite*, chats with Captain Joseph Bolger, USN, commanding officer of the Naval Air Experimental Station, Philadelphia, while on an inspection tour in 1944.

WAVE Officers in Naval Aviation

$\mathcal{D}$URING World War II, as more and more naval activities ashore were forced to relinquish trained personnel to the Fleet, the cry, "Send us WAVES!" was heard in the land. Facilities that once had placed some of their fields of work on the "cannot-use-the-services-of" list were ready to amend the restriction and sent in formal requests for WAVES to be trained. Womanpower was coming into its own.

Naval aviation was in the forefront of this trend. Of the approximately 2,000 women officers assigned to naval aviation, some 600 were given specialized training in aviation subjects. In addition, approximately 300 women officers underwent training in other specialized aviation subjects in schools located at their respective air stations. These included courses dealing with the duties of officers in the fields of air combat intelligence, air transport, aircraft recognition, navigation instruction, etc. The remaining officers were placed in regular billets in personnel, administration, supplies, publications, recreation, welfare, and others, jobs which had normally been held by male officers.

On 11 November 1942, the Bureau of Aeronautics requested women officers then attending the officer indoctrination schools at Northampton and Mount Holyoke be selected for enrollment in the nine-month meteorology course at the Massachusetts Institute of Technology. Thus, on 4 January 1943, the selected WAVE officers meeting the qualifications reported in Cambridge and became participants in the course already set up to train men as aerologists.

Less than a month after the original request, on 3 December 1942, the Bureau of Aeronautics requested an additional 25 officers for a similar course to be given at the University of California in Los Angeles. These requests were followed by still another on 1 March 1943, this time for 50 officers. Just as the first women aerologists were being graduated from M.I.T., still another group of women officers began, on 7 September 1943, a nine-month aerological engineering course at the University of Chicago.

The requirements for these courses specified that the candidate should be between 21 and 35 years of age and a college graduate with courses which had included differential and integral calculus and a year of physics. Previous training in meteorology was desirable but not essential. Since those who graduated would eventually be completely in charge of aerological operations at various stations and facilities, emotional stability, qualities of leadership, and sound judgment were the personal qualities most desired. It was also stressed that the candidates should be volunteers.

The first women aerologists in the Navy, graduating 4 September 1943 from the Massachusetts Institute of Technology, were Lieutenants (junior grade) Mary Elizabeth Brown, Mary Estelle Ellinwood, Rosana J. Robuck, and Henrietta P. Terry; Ensigns Rachel A. Beard, Evelyn H. Beaulieu, Zelda Carof, Margaret M. Finnigan, Katherine M. Hale, Helena C. Hendrickson, Laura H. Henry, Kathryn L. Howe, Marguerite F. Hunold, Loretta Mersey, Margaret Newman, Evelyn Parrick, Martha E. C. Perrill, Dorothy A. Schmitt, Rosalyn J. Smith, Audry M. Stier, Esther M. Turnbull, Florence W. van Straten and Margaret E. Worden.

To introduce these WAVES to actual operations, the Bureau of Aeronautics assigned all graduates of the aerological course to a month's duty at a large heavier-than-air station and another month at a lighter-than-air station before they proceeded to their permanent assignments. This program continued in effect until 25 May 1944, when the Bureau of Aeronautics notified the Bureau of Personnel that the desired number of women officers, 113, had been trained for the billets available in the United States. Accordingly, the training was discontinued 14 August 1944, the graduation date of the last class given at the University of California.

Early in 1943, the Bureau of Aeronautics faced a critical loss of civilian navigation instructors in its preflight schools. College professors were being called up by selective service, and colleges and universities had to replace these drafted instructors, in many cases, with those civilians teaching navigation in Navy schools. Thus, at the very time pilot training programs were being expanded, the Navy was running out of instructors in aerial navigation.

At an aviation training conference in March 1943, when this critical situation was being discussed, I asked—as I usually did on the slightest provocation—if it might not be practicable to train women officers as air navigation instructors, particularly when we had many officers who had formerly been teachers. To determine the feasibility of acting upon this suggestion, Captain Radford inaugurated a study to discover the availability of women who could meet the qualifications for navigation instructors.

The qualifications were not dissimilar to those for aerological engineers: The candidates should not be over 35, have a college degree, and training in mathematics through trigonometry. Women who had a background in civil aviation as ground instructors, pilots, or technicians would make ideal candidates. Those with engineering or drafting experience would be considered, since such training gave evidence of an analytical mind. A keen, inquiring mind with good powers of visualization was also an asset. My remark that we had many women with good teaching backgrounds was not just ignored, it was contradicted. Attached to the statement of qualification was a notation to the effect that "a teaching background is not considered particularly helpful and long teaching experience is not desired if the other qualifications can be met." The request was sent to the Midshipmen School on 9 May 1943, where approximately 30 women students met the qualifications.

A month earlier, I had gone to the Navigation Traini
School at Annapolis to confer with the commanding offic
on the practicability of setting up a course there. He fir
recommended a separate school for women officers. Howeve
when I informed him of the Navy's success in combining tl
enlisted women's training with that of the men, he agree
that the training of women officers should also be coeduc
tional.

Accordingly, I went to the Naval Aviation Training Scho
already in operation at the Hollywood Beach Hotel, Holl
wood, Florida, to arrange for the instruction of women. Co
ditions proved to be favorable for training the women wit
men at this facility.

With the inclusion in the curriculum of 50 hours in fligh
the Bureau of Personnel immediately raised the question a
to whether WAVE officers would be able to meet this requir
ment in view of the restriction on flying by women in tl
Women's Reserve legislation. However, the Bureau of Aer
nautics solved the question to the satisfaction of that burea
by stating that the flights would be made in noncombata
aircraft. Upon the approval of this arrangement by the Burea
of Personnel, received 17 July, the first quota of 11 office
reported to Hollywood 7 August 1943.

When the first women navigation instructors were assigne
to Naval Flight Preparatory, Preflight, and Primary Trainin
centers to teach the principles of navigation to future nav
aviators, it was at once apparent that their training with tl
men was effective. They met in all respects the high standar
already established. By January 1944, the 100 WAVE office
originally requested had been trained.

Since, prior to this date, the Link celestial navigatio
trainer, a synthetic training device, had been developed, tl
Bureau of Aeronautics decided to train approximately 3
women officers who had graduated from the air navigatio
course in the use of this new aid. To do this, additional nun
bers had to be trained, so the final figure for those trained i
air navigation was 121.

Early in the spring of 1944, the Air Navigation School move
to Shawnee, Oklahoma, and the final class convened on 1
June 1944, for the 16-week course. With this class, all naviga
tion training of WAVES was terminated, the full quot
having been met.

The designation of women officers as technical observer
was approved in June 1945. Those officially designated a
naval air navigators were authorized to wear naval aviatio

observer wings. This was only just, for the WAVES had been subjected to the same rigorous training demanded by the Navy of all air navigators. They studied in the same classes as the men and flew the same cross-country check flight.

Originally, the Air Combat Information program did not include WAVES since this work was usually carried on aboard aircraft carriers or shore bases in the forward areas. Furthermore, in 1943, there were on hand an adequate number of male reserve officers.

But administration and paperwork increased as reports poured in for analysis, evaluation, and distribution. When the load reached crisis proportions, the Deputy Chief of Naval Operations for Air requested, on 8 February 1944, authorization to train 12 women officers as air combat information specialists. These women would be stationed in the United States to analyze, evaluate, and distribute intelligence data.

Once word of the proposed training was published, a hundred requests for the training came in. Five women were selected for the three months of training in a class convening 22 March 1944. Five more were selected for the class which convened the following November. In the first course, attended also by some 200 men, the five women graduated in the upper half of the class, and one of them stood second. By 1944, Air Combat Information centers had been established within the United States, and it was at these centers the women officers served.

In order that those selected for the training would be possessed of certain qualifications, the Bureau of Aeronautics had requested that the classification staff at the Midshipmen's School at Northampton be guided in its selection in terms of the following criteria: Applicants, in ages ranging from 25 to 35 years, were to be college graduates with high standings. Their practical experience should be in such fields as business, administration, library science, law, or journalism. Aeronautical experience and residence or travel in foreign countries were desirable. Their civilian experience should indicate an ability to deal with facts in such a way as to make final judgments valid. A sense of responsibility and an ability to work easily with others were essential.

Since air combat information officers continually handled classified material, discretion and appreciation of security measures were basic requirements. Each candidate had to be interviewed by a trained ACI officer before final approval for training was given. Had the war not ended in 1945, additional women would have been trained, for those already in the field had performed their duties in a highly acceptable manner.

To meet the increasing need for instructors in communication procedures in air combat, the Navy decided to train 18 women officers at the Aviation Radiomen's School at Jacksonville, Florida. In order to increase the time devoted to communications and teaching procedures, slight modifications were made to the course by eliminating such subjects as ordnance, recognition, *The Bluejackets' Manual*, etc. The Bureau of Aeronautics recommended that each candidate be approximately 25 years of age, have had two or three years of teaching experience, and possess a personality and an appearance appropriate to the teaching of young men. (The latter requirement certainly permitted scope of interpretation on the part of the classification officer.)

Early in 1944, 18 women officers were selected from a class attending the Midshipmen's School at Northampton. All candidates successfully completed the course and remained on duty at the Naval Air Station, Jacksonville, Florida, where aircrewmen were being trained. So successful were these WAVE instructors that they succeeded in dispelling, in the minds of many commanding officers, their original idea that school teachers were inflexible.

Still another field opened up to women: photographic interpretation. At first, assignments in this field were the prerogative of men since the duty was usually carried on aboard carriers, but soon it was clear there were many billets in the United States where trained interpreters were needed. Despite this fact, my recommendations concerning training women in this area met with unexpected opposition, even though I pointed to the success with which women in the Royal Navy were being used in photo interpretation. This opposition was probably rooted in the fact that screening qualified males for this training was time-consuming and, at times, a frustrating task, and the need for such persons was on a "now" basis. Introducing a search for qualified women would merely increase the pressure. The general attitude was expressed in this way: "Women haven't the background for this training, and they can't serve in the forward areas."

But women could at least serve on the teaching staff of the

school if properly trained, and, as in other fields when a shortage developed, the women were given their chance to prove the doubters wrong. Lieutenant (junior grade) Natalie Hoyt, a former architect, was permitted to enter the January 1943 class at the Naval Air Station, Anacostia, D.C. Upon graduation, she became a member of the administration staff and an instructor in the school. There was no question of her unqualified acceptance by the men of the school both as an interpreter and as an administrator.

Within a short time, the Bureau of Aeronautics requested that ten more women officers be made available for training in photo interpretation. In September 1943, the Bureau of Personnel approved the request and set up the necessary screening by which they found the desired number of ensigns with professional or business experience, between the ages of 25 and 35, who had a broad education, travel experience, were observant, and had had courses in English. The preferred professions were architecture, engineering, geology (aerial survey only), photography, photogrammetry, and archeology. Needed also was some basic knowledge of mechanical drawing.

Actually, 12 were trained as photo interpreters, Lieutenant Hoyt bringing the total to 13. All were assigned to duty within the United States in photographic interpretation billets. One needs only to recall the finding of the Russian missiles in Cuba some years ago by means of photographic evidence to comprehend the value of this type of work to combat pilots and those involved in war plans.

In the field of aircraft recognition, the Bureau of Aeronautics requested, in July 1943, that ten women officers be made available for training. Actually, only nine were sent to the regular 60-day course established at Ohio State University. Criteria for these specialists were the ability to talk well and the possession of a positive personality. Also preferred were women in their late twenties with training in a type of art which would serve to help them quickly identify the characteristic features of ships and aircraft. It was also highly desirable for the candidate to have a background in vocational training in which visual aids had been employed. Those women who had demonstrated a swift grasp of recognition material at Northampton were to be given special consideration.

Upon graduation from the course at Ohio State, eight of the women were ordered to duty as instructors at the Primary

Training Command and one was ordered to the Aviation Training Division in the Bureau of Aeronautics. Five of these officers were later absorbed in aircraft gunnery training.

As early as the latter months of 1942, a number of enlisted women trained as aviation gunnery instructors (SP-G) were eligible for officer training. Request was made at once by the Bureau of Aeronautics that upon graduation from Northampton these women be sent to the Naval Air Training Command at Pensacola, Florida, for an additional 30-day training course which would permit their later assignment to the gunnery phase of the aviation pilot training program. This was done. A total of 19 women officers was so trained; five of that number were graduates of the aircraft recognition course since it was believed that the gunnery knowledge would be valuable additional knowledge in the teaching of recognition.

In May 1943, I recommended the investigation into the possible training of women officers for some part in the radio-radar program which at that time was expanding rapidly. Only the administrative part of the program could be carried out by women, since male officers, technically trained in the subject, performed their duties as radio-radar officers at sea. Approval of this recommendation resulted in numerous conferences with the representatives of the various bureaus concerned—Bureau of Ships, Bureau of Ordnance, and Bureau of Naval Personnel. Their joint decision was that women could be used administratively and that such limited assignments would permit their preparation for the work under materially reduced training courses. A survey of the radio-radar billets of an administrative nature in the United States, made in September 1943, revealed that approximately one hundred of them could be filled by women.

The Bureau of Ships drew up a list of desired qualifications of the candidates. What was needed were intelligent college graduates who had majored in physics and, wherever practicable, women who had completed courses in electrical engineering, including electronics. Minimum requirements consisted of one year of physics and one year of college-level mathematics. A shortened course, set up originally for a three-month period, was later reduced to two months. The first group of WAVES reported to the Naval Air Technical Training Command School at Ward Island, Corpus Christi, Texas, the first of January 1944.

The curriculum was designed to familiarize the WAVES with airborne radio-radar nomenclature and give them a general knowledge of the design, structure and function of the equipment, as well as sufficient knowledge of the technical aspects of radar to enable them to handle intelligently all phases of administrative work, including the distribution of equipment and spare parts required for continuous maintenance. No attempt was made to train these officers as maintenance engineers.

In the spring of 1944, additional training was given a limited number of these airborne radio-radar graduates to prepare them for carrying out the necessary work between civilian contractors and the Navy and to familiarize them with the requirements of the shore establishments and seagoing units for radio-radar equipment. Accordingly, additional instruction was arranged at the Aviation Supply Depot in Philadelphia. Later, under a rotational system, all the earlier graduates of the Ward Island school were given the same additional training at Philadelphia. When instruction in this field was completed January 1945, a total of 121 women officers had taken the course.

Of all the types of special work undertaken by WAVES, certainly that of the air transport officer (ATO) was one of the most exacting and at the same time exciting. Whether it was dealing with carburetor trouble on an R3D or determining if an officer with a hundred pounds of excess gear had a priority high enough to get aboard a flight, the problem landed squarely on the shoulders of the ATO.

Of course, this did not mean that she had to know how to repair or replace a faulty carburetor, but she did have to know where to find another one or someone to repair it as quickly as possible in order to get the airplane on its way. In a matter of minutes, when the plane was on the ground, she had to determine where the weight in the plane should be placed. To do this, she had spent many an hour learning to use the "slipstick" to calculate weight and balance.

In short, the ATO was responsible for Naval Air Transport Service (NATS) aircraft transiting her station. She had to plan the load prior to arrival, meet the plane and supervise the fueling, cargo and mail loading, check the passengers, and oversee the loading of baggage. She completed flight papers, produced emergency assistance, arranged for passengers and plane crews to get their chow and saw to it that the flight was off on time.

The training program for the women officers got under way in September 1944 at NATS Miami base, and a bit later at Naval Air Station, Patuxent, Maryland, and lasted two months. Here the women learned to know at first hand the various types of planes used on transport service. The first group of candidates consisted of Ensigns Helen Koster, B. M. Davis, Helen Montgomery, and Margaret Randall. These young officers reported to my brother, Lieutenant Commander Ward Bright, who had done so much to get permission for this training and for later assignments of the women officers as ATOs. His confidence was not misplaced and his own commanding officer, Captain James Dyer, Commander NATS Atlantic, backed him up in the experiment.

Fifty-two women officers were eventually trained for these duties which were carried out day and night. Thoroughness and unfailing attention to detail were qualities which the administrative officers of the Naval Air Transport Service cited in commenting on the success of the WAVES as ATOs.

In the fall of 1943, WAVES were being trained to take an active part in the altitude training program for aircrewmen and men undergoing flight training. WAVES eventually assumed control of the operation of low-pressure chambers under the direction of naval medical officers, the WAVES replacing males, both corpsmen and officers.

The women officers' instruction consisted of a three-month course in low pressure environment. The academic background of those selected was in the field of physiology or psychology. Under the direction of medical officers, the women officers scheduled the "hops" in the low pressure chamber and supervised the work of WAVE corpsmen assigned to each run. These officers also delivered the indoctrination lectures in the physiology of high-altitude flights and demonstrated the use and maintenance of oxygen equipment. (Here we began to anticipate the present-day rigorous training programs for astronauts.)

Since my office was located in the training division of the Bureau of Aeronautics, I was in an advantageous position. Through conferences or just by "keeping my ear to the ground," I kept abreast of plans being made, in being, or in prospect. As a participant in training conferences I was aware of the overall planning as well as the operations and needs of the training already in action. I had been fully accepted by the other members, in fact, made welcome at all the conferences. I was free to ask questions, make recommendations, or express disagreement. No one could have had more encouragement, more cooperation, or more initial refusals than I received in the early days of the program for women. The fact that I had spent many years as a civilian working in the Bureau of Aeronautics and was personally acquainted with the men with whom I was continuing to work was certainly an advantage and one which, so far as I know, no other woman officer originally possessed.

From the time the Bureau of Aeronautics was established in 1921, one of the conflicts between the Bureau of Aeronautics and the Bureau of Personnel revolved around the fact that the Bureau of Personnel often assigned trained aviation officers (nonpilots) to general service billets. The same problem had to be faced in the women's program. Letters to the Bureau of Personnel from the Bureau of Aeronautics protesting the transfer of women officers, trained by the aeronautical organization, to other billets were unavailing. The defense of such action was conventional and repetitive: "The needs of the service."

The same problem arose in connection with enlisted women with specialized aviation training who qualified for commission. One letter of special pleading, signed by Vice Admiral John S. McCain, Deputy Chief of Naval Operations for Air, never was accorded the courtesy of a reply. This loss of specialized WAVES to general service was a costly proposition, but it continued until September 1944, when a reclassification of all reserve officers was undertaken.

The Women's Reserve section of the Bureau of Aeronautics undertook the study of approximately 2,000 billets filled by women officers and found 550 were considered eligible for the W(A) designation—Women (Aviation)—on the basis of their training in schools or on-the-job training for a period of six months or longer. These classifications were approved by the Bureau of Personnel in June 1945. This reclassification was designed to safeguard specialized aviation talent. However, I know of none who were returned to aviation, but the establishment of an "aviation desk" in the officer detail section of BuPers did serve to preclude, to a greater extent than existed before, the assignment out of aviation of both men and women officers who had had special training in aviation subjects and administration.

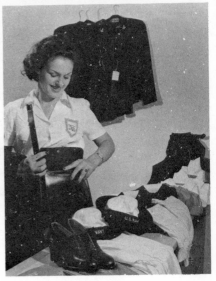

In February 1943, Hunter College, Bronx, New York, was commissioned U.S. Naval Training Center (WR). It promptly received 2,000 apprentice seamen. *At left*, inductees in the WAVES and SPARS wind their way to the commissioning ceremonies at Hunter, after just having been sworn in at City Hall. *Top, right*, swimming played a large part in a "boot's" physical fitness training at Hunter. A newly enlisted WAVE receives her issue of clothing (*above, right*).

WAVES try their marksmanship during their training program (*opposite, top*). Two platoons abreast, enlisted WAVES march down the drill field at "USS *Hunter*" (*opposite, bottom*).

"Boots" at Hunter College

To initiate any enterprise, it is next to impossible to avoid some degree of error. In the original training of enlisted WAVES, the shortcoming, fortunately not too long in being spotted, was the failure to include general naval indoctrination. In August 1942, when the Enlisted Division of the Bureau of Personnel notified its Training Division that it desired to send the first group of recruits to school by 9 October to be trained principally as radiomen, yeomen, and storekeepers, the Director of Training was definitely on the spot to undertake immediate action. On his own initiative he arranged for schools in these categories. I discovered much later that the arrangement was made by long distance telephone. The deadline was met, and, on 9 October, four training schools opened to women. Yeomen were trained at Oklahoma A & M at Stillwater and Iowa State Teachers College at Cedar Falls; storekeepers, at the University of Indiana at Bloomington; and radio operators, at the University of Wisconsin at Madison. Continued expansion of WAVE training at Stillwater, Bloomington, and Madison was accomplished by phasing out classes of men. As the men's barracks were vacated, women took their place.

Storekeepers were also trained at the Victoria Hotel, Boston, and the Georgia State College for Women, Milledgeville. At Miami University, Oxford, Ohio, there was another training school for radio operators.

In addition, by 1 February 1943, nine schools for the training of hospital corpsmen had been established at the naval hospitals at Bethesda, Maryland; Chelsea, Massachusetts; Corpus Christi, Texas; Great Lakes, Illinois; Jacksonville, Florida; New York, New York; Norfolk, Virginia; Philadelphia, Pennsylvania; and San Diego, California.

The courses were supposed to include basic naval indoctrination, but actually very little time was devoted to this training. In consequence, the enlisted women did not acquire the desired feeling of being in the Navy.

It did not take long to see that a change of course was needed. To solve this problem of indoctrination, the Secretary of the Navy on 30 December 1942, authorized a centralized recruit or "boot" school for WAVES to be established at Hunter College, the Bronx, New York. The selection was made on the basis of this school's obvious advantages: adequate space, desirable location, ease of transportation, and willingness on the part of the college to make its facilities available for training. Immediately, Captain William F. Amsden, the prospective commanding officer, Miss McAfee, and an officer of the Finance Division of the bureau passed on the suitability, adaptability, and financial feasibility of the project. That same day the Chief of Personnel wrote a letter to the Bureau of Yards and Docks recommending that $310,000 be made available to purchase necessary equipment for the school, including 1,500 double-decker bunks. On 7 January 1943, condemnation proceedings on adjacent civilian apartment buildings got under way. The Mayor's committee on property improvement of New York City cooperated with the Navy by assisting the dispossessed tenants in relocating and paying their moving expenses.

Since Hunter College had been a nonresident college, the

greatest single problem the Navy had to face in the establishment of a training school was the finding of dormitory space for its prospective on-board count of 7,000 seamen. This problem was solved by taking over thirteen apartment buildings within five minutes march of the campus; the largest accommodating 900, the smallest 300. Rooms that shortly before had steam pipes and electric switches as their only permanent fixtures were carpeted and attractively furnished. Kitchens became laundry rooms, and double-decker bunks were installed in the bedrooms, living rooms and dining rooms.

On 15 January 1943, Captain Amsden assumed his duties as commanding officer. Within three weeks Hunter was ready to receive its first consignment of enlisted women. This took some doing; shortcuts had to be taken, and it is difficult to calculate how long it would have taken if everything had been done in full accordance with regular procedures. Not only did the apartment houses have to be vacated for WAVE housing, but arrangements had to be made to furnish them and a staff assigned to direct them. Captain Amsden secured personnel from the Third Naval District (New York) to meet initial requirements. Changing a civilian day school into a U.S. naval training school with living quarters, messing, and training facilities to accommodate 2,500 recruits, with groups entering at two-week intervals, was a mammoth assignment, yet it was carried off with drive, verve, and imagination. BuPers was really rolling!

The 24-acre campus provided a spacious open area. Four main buildings served the WAVES: Gillett for administration; Davis for instruction and selection; the student hall for messing and recreation; and the gymnasium, with one large gym, six small ones, and a swimming pool, for physical training. The Walton High School auditorium with a capacity of 1,400 would be available, and for reviews and drills during bad weather, the Eighth Regimental Armory of New York was opened to the WAVES.

As for uniforming, speed was of the essence. In ten days, a combine of New York department stores equipped and set in motion a department capable of outfitting two platoons of 35 apprentice seamen in one hour. Many have been the laughs, and still bright in remembrance are the stories told and retold of the experiences of being uniformed. In fact, that phase of admission to Hunter rivals the many stories of the "daisy chain" of the physical examinations.

On 8 February 1943, in an impressive ceremony, Hunter was commissioned as the U.S. Naval Training Center (WR), which the "boots" immediately dubbed USS *Hunter*. Nine days later, the school received its initial group of 2,000 apprentice seamen. The magnitude of the job made the metropolis of New York an appropriate background.

The primary objectives of the school paralleled the regular "boot" experience for men:

1. Adequate medical examinations determined fitness for service.

2. Uniforming, drill, and personnel information requisite to the conduct of a recruit as a useful member of a military organization.

3. The selection of recruits best fitted to fill the special quotas for service training.

Each recruit went through a balanced training program. She was instructed in Navy ranks and ratings; ships and aircraft of the Fleet; naval traditions and customs; and, of course, naval history. Physical training and fitness were stressed. As the women marched in platoons to classes, medical examinations, and drills, their approach was signaled by singing, their voices providing the cadence for marching feet. The singing platoons at Hunter I shall long remember. And the singing was not confined to the marching groups. I recall particularly one evening at Hunter when I was taken to the auditorium to hear the recruit concert. Leopold Stokowski conducted the singing of 500 WAVES. Those clear, young voices rising and falling under the sensitive direction of the great conductor, combined with the rapt faces of the singers, left with me a beautiful, indelible picture and a deep emotional experience.

When the first regiment of recruits reported aboard, 173 officers (118 of them women) and 210 enlisted personnel (17 of them women) constituted the staff. The men where relieved by WAVES as rapidly as possible. Of the enlisted men retained aboard, over ninety percent either held ratings which women could not hold or performed duties which required men, such as night shore patrol.

Few changes in the basic organization were found to be necessary during the life of the school. The problem of staffing, as well as those of converting and equipping the physical plant, continued to make operations uneven at times and did cause some severe growing pains which, of course, were cured in time.

Rapidly Hunter forged ahead. In the spring of 1943, Lieutenant Eleanor Rigby, who had had experience in regimental organization at Northampton, arrived to become commandant of seamen. About the same time, the first station regulations were written, under which the position of the senior woman officer was clarified: "The Commandant of Seamen and Brigade Commander of Recruits shall be an officer of the Women's Reserve of a rank not below that of lieutenant. As Brigade Commander, she shall command the Brigade of Recruits, shall be responsible for their efficiency, discipline, and welfare, and shall be charged with the enforcement of the regulations for interior discipline of all dormitories."

As experience revealed weakness in organization, the brigade chain of command was shortened and strengthened until finally, with a minimum of administrative officers, an efficient organization was evolved. In spite of blunder and mistakes inherent in developing a new school fast, the training program was a success.

The usual indoctrination course covered a period of six weeks. The times of entrance and graduation of the enlisted WAVES were so arranged that new groups, about 2,000 strong, entered every two weeks, just at the time a fully indoctrinated group completed training.

Once the various fields of work had been approved for women and Hunter College was under way as a recruit training center, it was clear that those screening and selecting recruits should have a clear, realistic idea of what the jobs entailed. After several conferences with Lieutenant Elizabeth Reynard, who headed the training department at Hunter, we went to Captain Radford, head of the Aviation Training Division in the Bureau of Aeronautics. Miss Reynard outlined her need of visual aids, and Captain Radford immediately instructed Captain Luis de Florez, head of BuAer's Special Devices Section, to furnish equipment the aviation WAVES would come to know: a Link trainer, various airplane models, aircraft engine models, a tail gun, aerological instruments, parachute packing table and parachutes, a voice recorded and instruments to test voices for control tower aptitude, airplane dashboard equipment, and many other devices. These were collected and shipped to Hunter with gratifying results; enthusiasm for aviation billets soared.

So successful was this effort that displays were immediately set up by the Bureau of Personnel and other offices. Maps, charts, ship models, and tools found their way to Hunter where the WAVES made good use of them. Charts of naval insignia, naval organization and regulations, as well as lectures on naval history and traditions succeeded in creating high morale and a sense of pride in the service as more understanding evolved.

An effective means of instilling the habit of unquestioned obedience is military drill which the women took to as the proverbial ducks take to water. Their natural sense of rhythm combined with pride in being a part of a moving and spectacular show made reviews at the training school events never to be forgotten.

When the new second-class seaman left the center in the Bronx for her specialty school, she had been instructed in the activities of the Navy and its allied services. She knew something of its historical traditions. She had mastered the beginnings of naval lingo—bulkhead, deck, head, chow, and scuttlebutt—and in the years ahead her vocabulary would include the technical words and phrases of the activity to which she was assigned. She was physically equipped for her job and had developed a sense of responsibility for the part she would play in World War II, whatever that part might be.

On the day of graduation, the young women just reporting aboard were seated high in the stands, still in their civilian outfits. They watched with a mixture of interest and amazement as the women of the graduation group marched as one, banners held high, chins lifted proudly, eyes right as they passed the reviewing officers. Blended with the awe on their faces was something of apprehension and uncertainty. Could they emulate the perfectly synchronized team on the field? They were seeing, for the first time, a sample of what was to come as a result of their joining the Navy. In our widespread recruiting program, it frequently happened that a large delegation from a particular state would be sworn in together and started on their way to Hunter as a group. For example, when a large Texas group was sworn in, papers throughout that state carried stories on the "Texas Bluebonnets," the label given them locally. Widespread activities preceded their departure, with radio programs and much fanfare. In Arkansas, another contingent, 91 strong, were given a real brass band send-off. The celebration was arranged by the Little Rock Chamber of Commerce. The title "Arkansas Travelers" was officially conferred on the group by the governor of the state. Now all this was behind them. Already their schedules at Hunter were being set up. In the morning they would rise at dawn. Then would come the tests, the interviews, the inoculations, the classes, the drills, the marching, the lining up for mess, day in and day out—and sometimes homesickness.

Taps was a welcome sound for the exhausted, denoting another day nearer that grand review which marked their graduation.

I vividly recall such a review at Hunter when I was the reviewing officer. Flags flew from the adjacent buildings; the commanding officer, the reviewing officer, and the official party were in the reviewing stand. Approximately 4,000 women were on the field. On schedule the color guard advanced to present the colors, the flag of the United States and the blue flag of USS *Hunter*. There followed a "V" formation of officers, each accompanied by a petty officer carrying the guidon of her company. White-gloved hands executed a perfectly timed salute and the guidons dipped. Then the troops swung into the March Past while the bands and the drum and bugle corps played.

As thousands of women marched past with "eyes right," I looked into their faces and saw in them a spirit of self-reliance, pride, and dedication. As I returned the salute of each company commander, I, too, was proud that we were members of the United States Navy. At that time, I reflected: each of these young women is a volunteer in the service of her country for the duration of the war. She will go wherever she is sent, and she will be on call 24 hours a day. Her life will be very different from that which she has known. The WAVES will live in supervised quarters which they will clean. They will stand watches, eat in mess halls, wash and iron their own clothes, stand inspections, and learn new trades. Former secretaries will become machinist mates, control tower operators, instrument repairmen; in fact, learn any trade that will be needed. And they will earn their liberty passes for the weekend as do the men.

I had always held a high opinion of the capabilities of American women, and that opinion went even higher in the early days of training, assignment, and work. It was confirmed throughout the war. Largely contributing to this fine performance was the indoctrination training which was given at Hunter. In fact, Hunter, in my opinion, can be pointed to as one of the noble achievements in adult education during the war years. The teamwork that existed, the clarity of purpose, the enthusiasm for the job to be done, and the dedication of those mature and loyal women of the staff were outstanding. This same spirit was reflected in the women recruits.

From 17 February 1943, when the first regiment was graduated, until it closed on 10 October 1945, USS *Hunter* trained

80,836 WAVES, 1,844 SPARS (U.S. Coast Guard) and 3,190 Women Marines. Whatever mistakes were made during the first months of its organization were due either to lack of time under the exigencies of war or the inexperience of the officers, both men and women, of the Reserve. Offsetting every adverse criticism stands the irrefutable fact that the U.S. Naval Training Center (Women's Reserve), the Bronx, carried out the crucial task of converting civilians into members of a military organization. The fundamental naval training was not only sound but lasting. It did for the WAVE "boot" what the Bureau of Personnel and the Women's Reserve desired and what the Navy as a whole required.

After indoctrination, the WAVES were either assigned directly to a billet or, where specialized training was required, ordered to a training school. By May 1943, just ten months after the passage of legislation authorizing the Women's Reserve, a total of twenty training centers dotted the land from north to south, and from the Atlantic coast to the western bank of the Mississippi. There was also a center on the West Coast and, in later expansion, there were others between the Mississippi and the Pacific. Student bodies ranged from 4,800 at the largest school to eight at the smallest. At any one time there were places for 15,158 trainees and these places were constantly occupied except for the few hours between the graduation of one class and the convening of a new one.

All schools, with minor exceptions, were on a "flow" basis which produced graduates monthly regardless of the length of special courses, which could be as short as two weeks or as long as a year. This continuous cycle, by midnight of 31 December 1943, had put on active duty, including those in training when the year ended, over 47,000 WAVES.

In June 1945, as the end of the war seemed to be coming into view, one of the steps taken by the Navy's Bureau of Personnel was to establish a rehabilitation school at the Naval Training School, the Bronx, where the Hospital Corps WAVES would be trained in a sixteen-week course, plus practical application. One hundred and fifty WAVES, already serving at various naval hospitals, received this specialized training. This number was designed to meet the demands for skilled personnel to aid those physically handicapped during the war. Classroom instruction was supplemented by practical demonstrations at the educational schools and hospitals for the handicapped in New York City. The largest group of these WAVES was prepared to serve as occupational and physical therapists. The balance of the women trained as instructors for the blind, the deaf, or the orthopedically handicapped, providing those patients with prevocational training. They taught the blind to read and write Braille, to type, and to learn new ways of taking care of themselves. Others provided the deaf with auricular training, speech correction, and the use of hearing aids.

Ten thousand WAVES serving in the Washington, D.C., area
(*top*) celebrate their second birthday, 30 July 1944. In the
reviewing stand at the birthday review, Admiral Ernest J. King,
Chief of Naval Operations, chats with Secretary of the Navy
James V. Forrestal (*above*)·

WAVES (*opposite*), newly graduated from the U.S. Naval
Training Center, Norman, Oklahoma, prepare to board a
train en route to their new assignments.

The WAVES Come Aboard

THE estimates of the number of Women Reservists that would be needed by the naval districts, made at the time the Bureau of Naval Personnel concluded its original survey, were far too low. One district, the twelfth on the West Coast, is typical of them all.

In June 1942, the quota for that district was set at 1,200, but no sooner had the first WAVES started to report than the request escalated. The demand was a continuing one. By September 1945, 8,239 WAVES in thirty different rates were working in 130 activities in the Twelfth Naval District. Revised estimates to higher numbers were the order of the day throughout the country.

Simply to list the facilities in the Twelfth Naval District at which the WAVES served conveys the variety of tasks they performed: the shipyards at Hunter's Point and Mare Island; air stations at Livermore, Alameda, Moffett Field, and Oakland; hospitals at Mare Island, Oakland, San Leandro, and Shoemaker; the ammunition depot at Hawthorne, Nevada; supply depots at Clearfield, Utah, and Oakland, California; and the Landing Force Equipment Depot, Albany, California.

Other facilities at which WAVES served were the U.S. Naval Training and Distribution centers at Shoemaker and Treasure Island; the U.S. Naval Medical Research Unit No. 1, at Berkeley; Camp Parks Seabee Replacement Depot; the Armed Guard Center (Pacific) and the Receiving Ship, both at Treasure Island; and the WAVE Quarters in San Francisco.

The initial introduction of WAVES to the Twelfth Naval District on 21 January 1943, occurred when 42 ensigns reported to the district's communication office to be assigned to the various offices and activities. About half of them were assigned to code room duty where they quickly proved efficient. At that time, about 28,000 coded groups were handled each day with an average of fifteen women on each watch. In less than fifteen months, the traffic had tripled, but it was still handled with the addition of one or two officers per watch. It had become a complete WAVE operation; all male officers had been detached.

On 16 September 1943, the first contingent of thirty enlisted WAVES arrived from the Yeoman School, Stillwater, Oklahoma, to report for duty at the records division of the Fleet Post Office. Drafts reported every two weeks thereafter, and one year later, there were 927 aboard—seamen, mailmen, and yeomen making up the group.

Both officer and enlisted WAVES handled assignments requiring a high degree of security. One of the most responsible tasks filled by them in the Twelfth Naval District was that of watch officer, a responsibility taken over principally at night when the WAVE who held it, figuratively speaking, was the port director. It was her job to log in and out all naval service vessels. When merchant ships were proceeding independently, a woman officer made the final check on the accuracy and completeness of the routing instructions.

Not a WAVE aboard but was aware that convoy and routing operations involved the safety of Navy and merchant ships wherever they might be. Keeping track of the movements and status of each ship required detailed records which showed the entire progress of the shipment of men and material to advanced bases from the time of departure to the time of arrival.

Nearly every job in the district involved the service of WAVES in some way, whether it was routing ships, forecasting weather, making out requisitions, servicing communications, maintaining aircraft, packing parachutes, or ministering to the injured and ill. In the shipyards, their duties, routine or out of the ordinary, made the war seem very near, as ships crippled in battle at sea returned to be repaired and sent out again.

Heading the WAVES in the district was the Women's Reserve representative who acted as adviser to the commandant on all matters of policy involving the women in his command. At first, the representative labored under the disadvantage of inexperience in handling naval personnel, her knowledge being limited to the short indoctrination she had received at Northampton. Fortunately, this drawback was offset by the use of common sense and sound judgment. There being no ground rules yet established she, of necessity, set up many of her own guidelines.

And well I knew that establishing guidelines was no simple matter. In the administration of the WAVES in naval aviation, in my capacity as adviser to the Chief of the Bureau of Aeronautics, I made various decisions while on visits to the activities, and advised the Women's Reserve representatives and the commanding officer of each activity on the basis of my knowledge of what was succeeding at other activities and of existing Bureau of Naval Personnel policies. When a situation cried for a remedy, or where there was a problem in the making, I could only rely on common sense and make a policy to cover it.

One imaginative step in introducing the WAVES into naval aviation was taken when the Bureau of Aeronautics established an indoctrination course for all women officers reporting aboard at the four Naval Air Training centers at Jacksonville and Pensacola, Florida, Corpus Christi, Texas, and Glenview, Illinois. These courses, set up without the approval of the Bureau of Naval Personnel, gave the WAVES indoctrination comparable to that which male officers received. At the same time, the program opened up an opportunity to select the women best qualified to act as Women's Reserve representatives to the various activities within those air commands.

But such a program was not a complete answer to the repeated query, "What *are* the policies?" Finally, desperate for something solid in the way of interpretation, I decided to write a pamphlet. Published under the title of *WAVES in Naval Aviation*, it was sent out 16 March 1943, and included all the policies and directives regarding women which had thus far been laid down by the Bureau of Naval Personnel. I also included what information I could scrounge regarding the future assignment of women at naval air stations and seized the opportunity to record such recommendations on the matter of administration of the WAVES, opinions that I had conveyed in person to commanding officers at many naval air activities. Although these recommendations were in line with current policies, they had one fatal defect: they had not received the official blessing of the Bureau of Naval Personnel.

In all conscience, I must admit that I deliberately had not submitted the booklet to the Bureau of Personnel, for I knew full well that either it would be hopelessly delayed or it would never appear at all. Yet the definite need of some compilation of policies was apparent as the WAVES increased in numbers at all naval stations.

The pamphlet had not gone out, however, without what I considered appropriate authority. I had secured the approval of my own commanding officer, Captain Arthur W. Radford, then head of the Aviation Training Division. Rear Admiral Ralph Davison, acting chief of the Bureau of Aeronautics, had signed the letter forwarding the booklet. Although the "notes concerning the administration and employment of WAVES attached to Naval Aviation activities" were an informal compilation, they did relate to the "personnel field," an area jealously and constantly guarded by the Bureau of Naval Personnel. As was to be expected, a copy shortly fell into the hands of that bureau, and I was in trouble.

The continuing "at loggerheads" conflict which was traditional between the Bureau of Aeronautics and the Bureau of Personnel burst again into flame. The battle was joined by top-ranking officers in both bureaus, each determined to maintain his own prerogatives and defend himself against any threatened usurpation of responsibilities. I, the not-too-innocent cause of the flare-up, was apprehensive.

But the outcome was gratifying as far as I was personally concerned. There were three conclusions to the matter:

1. The Bureau of Aeronautics would send a letter to all activities on the original mailing list, making the requirement that the booklet be classified as "restricted."

2. The Bureau of Naval Personnel, in turn, would publish as quickly as possible a compilation of approved policies for

he administration of women, and this would immediately supersede the pamphlet I had compiled.

3. I was to exercise due care in the future not to overstep my prescribed tasks and missions (although these had never been prescribed).

But there was a happy ending to this bureaucratic contre-temps, for shortly there was a new and gratifying trend insofar as the Women's Reserve was concerned. Since Lieutenant Commander McAfee as director of the WAVES represented the Bureau of Naval Personnel and I, as the Women's Reserve Representative for Naval Air, was the liaison between BuAer and her office, we could cooperate on a sound working basis. We both understood the functions of our respective bureaus and, as we worked together, had far less need for recourse to our superior male officers than had characterized the first months of our association. In short, when the point was reached where the men did not have to be involved in all basic discussions and help solve all possible problems, but were called upon only for consultation and approval of final plans, smooth sailing became the order of the day.

One of the problems we encountered was that enlisted WAVES reporting to their duty stations were frequently not assigned to work for which they had been trained nor given responsibility equal to their ability. In conferences with commanding officers, I urged that women be used to the level of their capability. This needed to be done if their pride and morale in the service were to be maintained. Fortunately, as the commanding officers did assign them, more and more, to duties in various fields of work for which they had been trained, their morale and the operating efficiency of the stations increased by leaps and bounds.

WAVE officers also, in the early days of the program, faced the same problem. They too were not given, in the beginning, responsibilities commensurate with their training and experience. Perhaps the fault lay in the fact that there could be only one lieutenant commander, a few lieutenants, still more lieutenants (junior grade), and the rest ensigns, limitations that the men did not have to face. For the most part, the men were given ranks commensurate with their age and civilian experience and job responsibility in accordance with their rank. I never heard, however, until after the war was over, this question of inequality discussed by the women.

In talking it over, we recognized that the inequality was

probably helpful in "selling" the women's program to those men in the Navy who, first, frankly did not want women in the establishment and, second, certainly did not want them on a competitive basis. It was hard to convince many commanding officers that women officers were not sent to their commands merely to administer the enlisted women's program but rather to fill the billets of specialists in such fields as meteorology, electronics, public information, etc., thus releasing male officers to the Fleet. This problem of utilization was only solved gradually.

I advised the women, officers and enlisted, to the effect that we were now in what was heretofore a man's world and we had to prove ourselves step by step. This meant we must do each small assignment efficiently and cheerfully, always observing the work done by others, so that we could learn as much as possible about each task in order to be prepared to take over. And this is exactly what happened. As orders transferring the men to the Fleet came in, the women had to take over and do their job. At last the women could feel that they were needed, and that feeling was the greatest morale builder that could have been conceived.

As adviser to the Chief of the Bureau of Aeronautics on matters concerning WAVES, I relied on my years of experience as a civilian in that bureau. My long-time and wide acquaintance with naval aviators who were, when World War I came, of sufficient rank to be the commanding officers of the many naval air stations throughout the country, made it easy for me to confer with them. They welcomed my suggestions and gave in exchange their practical views, which certainly made for the better administration of WAVES in aviation.

In the matter of discipline, commanding officers were at first prone to be more lenient with the women than with the men. But this leniency did not long prevail, nor was it necessary, for the WAVES, enlisted and officer alike, had been well indoctrinated in the necessity of proving their maturity by accepting the discipline traditional in the Navy. There may have been a few tears on occasion, but this was the exception and not the rule, for the women were determined to demonstrate that they had no need for special treatment.

There remained one difference in discipline, however where confinement to the brig was prescribed, the woman was not confined, but discharged from the naval service under less than honorable conditions. In view of the overall high quality of the women serving in the Navy, there was no room for one whose conduct would reflect on the WAVES. The Navy anticipated that there would be little need of such drastic measures, and this proved to be the case. When one considers that over 100,000 women served in the Navy in World War II and that there was only one case in which a WAVE was convicted of a felony, it is clear that delinquency was really no great problem. The WAVE who was the single exception was sentenced by a general court martial to a federal prison for the crime of forgery.

On the occasion of the first anniversary of the WAVES, 30 July 1943, President Franklin D. Roosevelt lauded them as worthy descendants of "those proud pioneer daughters who first nurtured freedom's flame." In his message, he declared, "Thousands of fighting men are now at battle stations because they were released from vital shore jobs by women within and wholly part of the naval service. Other thousands will sail to meet the enemy as more women become available to take over these vital shore jobs. In their first year, the WAVES have proved that they are capable of accepting the highest responsibility in the service of their country."

Indeed, the Women's Reserve was in evidence throughout the naval establishment. WAVES, officers and enlisted, were serving in bureaus, offices and facilities of the Navy from coast to coast. Lieutenant Commander McAfee's anniversary message characterized the WAVES' "shakedown" year in these words: "Looking back on the first year of the Women's Reserve, it appears to be a year of trial and error; women were on trial as newcomers to the Navy. We made our errors, but none of them serious enough to indicate that the Navy was in error in admitting women. We are no longer curiosities, no longer assumed to be novices to Navy ways."

The WAVES had demonstrated their usefulness to such a degree that the Navy opened more and more areas of work to them. The original idea of some of the planners that WAVES' duties would be largely clerical gave way to the remarkable conclusion that, with training, WAVES could do anything, within their physical capabilities, that needed to be done. Consequently, to the fields of radiomen, yeomen, and storekeepers were added not only the aviation ratings, but various general service ratings such as cooks and bakers, telegraphers, and a line of specialist ratings.

These ratings were designated SP with an initial in paren
theses signifying the area of work: C, classification inter
viewer; G, aviation free gunnery instructor; I, accounting
machine operator; M, mail clerk; P, photographer; Q, commu
nications; R, recruiting; S, personnel supervisor; T, teacher;
W, chaplain's assistant; and Y, control tower operator. To
qualify in these specialties, seamen could train on the job or
be sent to Navy schools for the training.

Many of the women, sent as seamen to duty stations after
recruit training, found they were assigned to work which
would lead eventually to a petty officer's rating. Since the
criteria for advancement were a proved degree of intelligence
devotion to duty, and unrelenting effort, they were well qualified to meet the challenge and became bookkeepers, accoun
tants, typists, file clerks, comptometer operators, mechanical
statistical and electrical draftsmen, cartographers, commercia
artists, research assistants, laboratory technicians, reception-
ists, teletype operators, switchboard, elevator and mimeograph
operators, publication clerks, multilith operators, assistant
printers, linotype and photostat operators, photo-printers, film
projectionists, masters-at-arms, chauffeurs, and ship's service
clerks. In all these jobs, the women learned as they worked
In some cases, civilian backgrounds fitted them for the new
tasks, but for the most part, the women learned on the job

Officers who in civilian life were members of professions
found their appropriate billet in the Navy. Where additional
training was needed, they too were put through accelerated
courses. Serving as disbursing officers or dietitians, adminis
trators or physical therapists, editors or architects—the list
is too varied to put down in its entirety—they were being in-
tegrated into the naval programs and steadily releasing men
to the Fleet.

As nearly as possible, each woman's background was util
ized once the hurdle of assignment of responsibility was over
come. For example, Ensign Edwina L. Gies, who had been a
department store buyer of china and glass, became a pur
chaser of all types of mess gear. Lieutenant (junior grade
Rosalind Lifquest, a former teacher of nutrition and dietetics
carried on research into the nutritional value of Navy food.

In this area, one study, made on air stations concerning the
waste of food, revealed that in the preparation of menus suf
ficient account was not being taken of the kind of daily work
being done. Neither the men nor the women were, for the
most part, engaged in manual labor. For the women especially
the diet was too heavy, containing too much starch, and, worst

of all, unappetizingly served. Gradually, a greater variety of food, more attractively prepared, appeared. And then came the innovation of the "salad bar." On a trial basis, a large cart of salad material was placed in the cafeteria, separate from the regular chow line. Its overwhelming success marked a revolution as far as nutrition for the Navy was concerned. It became one of the most popular features of the mess for both men and women. The waistlines of the WAVES, which had been causing increasing concern, immediately started to return to their normal, attractive dimensions. The excuse of creeping obesity—"the food in the mess hall is fattening"— was eliminated.

Other examples of WAVE experience being used in the Navy come quickly to mind. In the Bureau of Ordnance, *Firepower*, a monthly magazine which went to the hundreds of thousands of workers in ordnance plants and stations throughout the country, was edited by Lieutenant (junior grade) Rebecca F. Gross, who in civilian life was the managing editor of the *Lock Haven Express*, the daily newspaper in that Pennsylvania town.

Talent after talent was utilized by the medical branch of the Navy. One small group of enlisted WAVES at the U.S. Naval Medical Center, Bethesda, Maryland, had the painstaking task of making and painting artificial eyes. Once the eye was made by the prosthetic department to fit the socket of the eye, the WAVES would do the painting, placing the almost microscopic veins on the white of the eye and coloring the iris to match exactly the patient's remaining eye. This close work with the patient, according to the WAVES, was its own reward. They were contributing directly to the rehabilitation of the men who were war casualties.

In December 1943, when a school for the training of medical corpsmen was opened at the center in Bethesda (previous training had been done at 17 naval hospitals throughout the country), Admiral Ross T. McIntire, Surgeon General of the Navy, in his address, was both congratulatory and prophetic in his comment on the WAVES: "Today we are starting something I hope will be permanent. Women have proved they can carry out the full responsibilities of their ratings. I think there is a place for them after the war." To the best of my knowledge, this was the first time a high-ranking naval officer publicly suggested that women in the Navy might well be retained on a permanent basis.

The acceptance of women in the Navy was based largely upon the superb record they had made on their first assignments. Where they were given responsibility commensurate with ability they learned to do the job quickly and carried it out efficiently. Theirs was the "can do" spirit.

The original reluctance of naval bureaus and offices (save the Office of the Chief of Naval Operations and the Bureau of Aeronautics) was overcome in less than six months after the program began. Requests for WAVES poured into the department by telephone, letter, and personal representation. In their performance, the WAVES certainly opened the minds once closed, of many a senior naval officer. A good example is gleaned from the Office of the Judge Advocate General of the Navy. In April 1943, four officers, out of the many assigned to the Washington area, reported. Ensign Lucille Pryor became the first WAVE to be admitted to practice before the U.S. Supreme Court. In the tax section, she analyzed the tax situation in the various states as it affected naval business operations and prepared opinions relating to tax questions arising in the matter of Navy contracts. Ensigns Irene Kuckinskas and Thelma Siefkus were assigned to research and editorial work in connection with a revised edition of *Law Relating to the Navy, Annotated.* Ensign Louisa Pearson edited and digested opinions of the JAG and decisions of the Secretary of the Navy which were published as *Court Martial Orders.*

Certainly the proper, efficient use of WAVES was, for the most part, the rule of every outfit. In 1943, it was the Bureau of Ships, for example, which established the "flying squad" of WAVES who were assigned for short periods of time to any section of the bureau burdened with a nearing deadline and short of clerical help. Not only did this assignment solve a problem for the Bureau of Ships, but it also gave the WAVES invaluable training and new insights into the overall work of the bureau.

Time marched on, and there was certainly good reason to mark the second anniversary of the Women's Reserve with celebrations held throughout the United States of the "WAVES Birthday." As one of the celebrants on that occasion, I shall never forget the special ceremonies in Washington, D.C.

On 30 July 1944, 10,000 WAVES on duty in the area marched in formation to the Washington Monument grounds and formed up at the Sylvan Theater. All wore grey summer uniforms with black shoes and black gloves. Except for the music of the U.S. Navy Band, not a sound was heard as each group, on signal, swung into its assigned position.

Among those on the stage were top naval officers headed by Admiral Ernest J. King, Chief of Naval Operations; Secretary of the Navy James V. Forrestal; and the Director of the WAVES.

After the opening prayer, the command was given—"Seats" —and 10,000 sank to the grass together and made the appearance of a tremendous field of grey mushrooms planted in orderly rows. In his typically short address, Admiral King reflected the praise he had earlier given the WAVES in his report to the Secretary of the Navy, in which he stated that "in addition to [the WAVES] having earned an excellent reputation as a part of the Navy, they have become an inspiration to all hands in naval uniform." On the birthday occasion, he said, in part: "All hands of the naval service have confidence that you will continue to meet every challenge, in accordance with the high standard you have set for yourselves, until the victory is won."

Secretary Forrestal said to the assembly, "I offer the Navy's traditional 'Well Done.' The tempo of the war is rising to a climax. This stepped-up push for victory will increase our responsibilities, and you will have many opportunities for varied and interesting service, certainly here, and we hope ultimately in our shore establishments abroad. Today, 72,000 women wear the Navy uniform, nearly half the pre-war strength of the Navy in 1940."

A memorable highlight of the program was a congratulatory message from Admiral Chester W. Nimitz, commander of the Pacific Fleet, broadcast from Pearl Harbor: "Although history records that women have had influence upon navies, it is only recently that women have had influence within the navies. In many naval activities maintained by the Pacific Fleet along the West Coast of the United States, the WAVES are busily doing jobs which help substantially in the prosecution of our war against Japan. To them will be owed a part of the credit for eventual victory."

All through the ceremony, an electrical storm had threatened and, just as our Director was speaking, the weather changed from sunshine to rain. In her inimitable manner of meeting every situation quickly, she remarked casually that men at sea were surrounded by water, and that the shower gave WAVES an opportunity to show that they too were not afraid of getting wet.

Luckily for the thousands seated on the ground, the rain was not continuous, but as the women marched off the field later it could be seen that their grey uniforms had become two-toned; the rear of their skirts were light grey and dry and the rest of the uniforms were dark grey and wet, but their shoulders were thrown back, their heads held high.

As we marched along Constitution Avenue, many thoughts raced through my mind. Where were those people who had doubted that America's young women could adjust to naval routine and discipline, to being dressed alike, to doing jobs never before undertaken by women? These young WAVES had proved their reliability, perseverance, and stamina. How proud I was to be one of them.

These thoughts were strangely interrupted. I felt the strap of my slip slide off one shoulden. There was nothing to do except keep right on marching and hope that the slip wouldn't show, a hope shattered when I heard Commander Jean Palmer whisper "that's mighty pretty lace on your slip."

From that day onward I have been slip conscious; my slip straps are always secured. One such occasion effected a permanent cure.

Some may ask, "What, in the first two years of their existence, had the WAVES accomplished, apart from the main purpose of expediting the World War II effort?" To answer that question, I would say that more than 70,000 American women had made new friends from every section of the country; many had traveled extensively in the course of their own training or duty assignments. War orientation lectures and movies as well as meeting representatives of foreign services had widened their horizons. Thousands had learned new skills and discovered a resourcefulness in themselves they had not known they possessed. Many of them had developed interests in music, handicraft, art, and religion as totally unexpected by-products of Navy life. These women had come to respect the Navy and to take great pride in being part of it. They marveled at its capacity to accomplish much in limited time. They watched it change long-established customs, painfully in some cases but always generously, when the needs of the service required it. They came to admire and then to demonstrate the willingness of naval personnel to subordinate themselves for the sake of the service. They became, through their training and experiences, more interesting and more interested citizens. Through the closeness of living, necessitating the need to give and take, they learned to respect the rights of others.

By 1945, women officers had learned much, and the Navy

had come to see the great contribution they made and the variety of their skills. For example, women became proficient through in-billet training as operations officers, air control officers, aviation training officers—at both station and staff level—air plot officers, and flight analysis officers. Lieutenant Katherine Hickey, who entered the Navy with several months of experience to her credit as a flight instructor for the Civil Aeronautics Authority, never received permission to fly naval aircraft, but she became assistant training officer on the staff of the Naval Air Primary Training Command where she not only did an outstanding job, but also served valuably as liaison between the Navy and the Civil Aeronautics Authority. As another example, Ensign Josephine Stauch was an adept final controller in the testing of the Navy's newly created ground control approach equipment. Lieutenant Elizabeth Ballentine at the air station at Jacksonville was influential in changing crash analysis to flight analysis, with the emphasis put on preventing crashes rather than explaining them. Her work in this field was rated as an outstanding contribution to the safety of flying.

And so, the public acknowledgments made on the occasion of anniversary celebrations really meant a great deal to the WAVES. To them it was a fine pat on the back. For them it was the knowledge that they had established in the minds of their comrades-in-arms—the officers and men of the United States Navy—a sincere feeling that they were worthy shipmates.

By the fall of 1943, the WAVE program had grown in strength to approximately 35,000. Captain McAfee was finding it necessary to spend more and more time in visiting the various activities where WAVES were stationed in order to observe the results of the training given and to strengthen the continuing progress of integrating them more fully into the Navy itself. In consequence, the billet of Assistant Director of WAVES was created so that this person could take on some of this inspection work as well as be in the Washington office when Miss McAfee was traveling. Lieutenant Tova P. Wiley of California was selected for this assignment. She was one of the first women officers enrolled in the Naval Reserve, and, like myself, went to work without benefit of indoctrination training at Northampton. Before she came to Washington she had served for one year in recruiting in San Francisco. Her new job was indeed a full-time assignment.

In connection with visits to naval activities to observe the progress of the program for women, I experienced one of my proudest duties when a trip was arranged for 30 March 1944 to 6 April 1944 to the Naval Air Training Center at Pensacola, Florida. The basic motive was to let the members of our National Educational Council for the Women's Reserve see, at first hand, an example of what had been accomplished in naval aviation. Here would be a picture of training, utilization, housing, recreation, and integration. For this trip Admiral Sidney McCain, Chief of the Bureau of Aeronautics, and therefore, my boss, provided air transportation and thus we all traveled as VIPs. The following seven members of this advisory committee had accepted the invitation: Virginia Gildersleeve, Mrs. Wallace Notenstein, Mrs. Thomas Gates, Alice M. Baldwin, Meta Glass, Alice Lloyd, and Mrs. Malbone W. Graham. In addition, Representative Margaret Chase Smith, of Maine, a member of the House Naval Affairs Committee, and, of course, Captain McAfee also made the trip.

During the five-day stay at Pensacola, the ladies were familiarized with the operation of our largest Naval Air Training Center itself and many or its outlying fields. In every activity visited the WAVES were at work. In the control towers, the hangars, the storerooms, the offices, on the flight line, in the hospitals and medical laboratories, the dental clinics, photographic laboratories, on the gunnery ranges, in the postoffice, library, communications, aerology. In all places they worked side by side with men of similar ratings. In the WAVE barracks the committee members talked with the WAVE master at arms, saw WAVE seamen on their cleaning details, saw those WAVES washing and ironing their clothes. They observed them in the chow line, at the movies, at picnics. In other words, during their visit they saw how the WAVES lived, worked, and played. They saw the grease-smeared aviation machinists at work and later saw them—spic and span— go on liberty ashore or to some recreational project on board.

A graduation of naval aviators took place while we were at Pensacola. How impressive it was to see those hundreds of young men lined up while they listened to the Commandant, Admiral George Murray, give a few words of advice about what was ahead of them in combat. I remember especially how he spoke to a group which was being retained on board as instructors. He pointed out that he knew of their disappointment because he, too, had been once held as an instructor. "But your turn will come soon to join the Fleet, and in the meantime you will help to turn out, as competent flyers,

those young men who are awaiting their turn for instruction."
And behind this fine group of combat flyers was the work of
keeping the flight logs, the daily instructors' reports, the commissioning papers, the instructions in aircraft gunnery and
instrument flying, the low pressure chamber tests—all being
done by WAVES. As Admiral Murray pointed out later to the
committee members, "Since we have had the WAVES aboard,
no graduate of naval aviation training has gone into combat
without having received some part of his training from a
WAVE. Our WAVES are making a direct contribution to the
war effort. Physically and mentally, every day, they contribute."

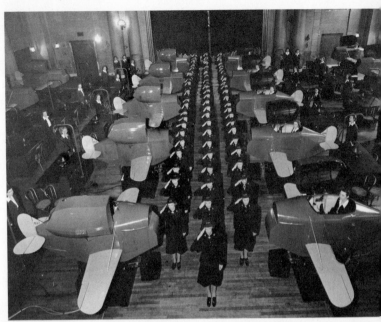

To replace men in all areas of the Navy, WAVES were sent to specialist schools. *At top*, enlisted WAVES undergo instruction as Link trainer instructors at the Naval Training School, Atlanta, Georgia, in early 1943. As control tower operator during World War II, *above, left*, this WAVE directs aircraft takeoffs and landings with radio communication and light signals.

WAVES become aviation machinist's mates the hard and practical way at the U.S. Naval Training School, Norman, Oklahoma (*above, right*).

At right, in the parachute loft at the Naval Air Training Center, Pensacola, Florida, two WAVES, qualified parachute riggers during World War II, repack a chute.

An aerographer's mate third class takes a sun sight (*far right*).

Enlisted WAVE Training

$\mathcal{T}$RAINING was a primary concern of my assignment as Women's Reserve Representative for the Bureau of Aeronautics. That bureau had urgently requested the services of women and at the same time had stated that it would train them. In keeping with this statement plans, using the coeducational concept, had been drawn up, even before the passage of the legislation, and at the same time studies were made of proper housing facilities and supervision needs. In all these activities I was given a great degree of responsibility, and concurrently, I was given the whole-hearted backing of my superior officers. No one could have been assigned a more rewarding duty.

On 24 May 1943, I prepared my first formal report concerning the aviation training for women, which revealed that they were being trained as aviation machinist mates, aviation metalsmiths, parachute riggers, aerographer's mates, Link trainer (navigation) instructors, control tower operators and 3A-2 operators (aircraft gunnery instructors). In spite of the gloomy predictions on the part of some of the older men in the Navy, the aviation schools were not disrupted when the women entered the classes. The men were all young, mostly fresh from high schools, and they were entirely accustomed to coeducation. In developing training schedules, my office kept the training section and enlisted detail section of the Bureau of Personnel fully cognizant of our need and progress. Even though the actual training was BuAer's responsibility, the scheduling and assignment of women to schools was the responsibility of BuPers. This close liaison certainly paid dividends. To Lieutenant Commander McAfee, our director, I sent periodic progress reports. Her interest in every phase of WAVE training, employment, and welfare was unfailing.

In establishing aptitude tests for the selection and screening of candidates for these courses, we looked particularly to the aviation medicine section of the Bureau of Medicine and Surgery for compilation and guidance. These tests were administered at the basic indoctrination school at Hunter.

The original numerical goals in training WAVES were passed in practically every aviation rating. One rating for which training was proposed but never authorized was that of aviation ordnanceman. Nor was regular training set up for aviation radio technicians and aviation electronic mates. However, a few women, given the opportunity of on-the-job training, did qualify and on the basis of their performance the electronics schools were opened to women. WAVES, upon being recommended by their commanding officers for training, were sent to aviation storekeepers' schools to qualify for that rating.

Of all the aviation specialities, the aviation machinist mate rating was the largest. Once the Bureau of Medicine and Surgery had its aptitude test ready for the rating, the women who passed it did well at the regular training centers in Memphis, Tennessee, and Norman, Oklahoma. In order to pass the tests, the women needed to have a desire to serve as an aviation machinist mate, the possession of a high degree of manual dexterity, a high score in arithmetical reasoning and mechanical comprehension, and more than ordinary physical stamina. Between January 1943 and October 1944, 2,730 women were graduated. Women Marines were also trained in this rating.

Recommendations to modify the training course so that women would be specialized in certain parts of maintenance —such as carburetor ignition, spark plugs, etc.—were considered, but it was finally decided that women should take the full course and develop a specialty on the job to meet the needs of the stations to which they were assigned. This method eased the problems of assignment and permitted the women to work on an equal basis with the men who had been similarly trained. The assignment of the women mechanics really worked; the efficiency curves of maintenance departments rose sharply. The women were out to show they could do the job, and the men were not going to be outdone. It was healthy competition.

As a group, the aviation machinist mates were the most versatile of the aviation ratings; their morale was consistently high. Not only did the work present a challenge but, in the minds of many of the WAVES, working with their hands on the planes which were used to prepare pilots for combat engendered a sense of nearness to the war.

The training of aviation metalsmiths (AM) was approached tentatively, somewhat with the attitude of trying it out as an experiment. Although the basic qualifications were the same as for aviation machinist mates, particular attention had to be paid to the question of physical strength. The first two weeks of training were devoted to mathematics, drawing, and basic metal work. In the advanced phases of 19 weeks, the WAVES were trained in sheet metal and shop work, welding, forging metal, finishing metals, and squadron maintenance operations. They made repairs on cowlings, fuel oil tanks, landing gear, propellers, and wings.

A great many of these women were assigned to squadron aircraft maintenance, most of which was done at night. Some worked on the engine-change crew, while others were assigned to making 30, 60, 90, and 120-hour checks on each plane. WAVES on rigging crews checked the plane for cable frays or damage to fuselage and wings.

In the assembly and repair shops, the aviation metalsmiths, together with the machinist mates and instrumentmen, adjusted, overhauled, and installed internal combustion engines or accessories such as carburetors, ignition apparatus, and starting gear. They acted as carpenters, painters, and hydraulic gear mechanics; welded parts of aircraft bodies; changed instruments and panels, and kept instrument logs and reports. Theirs was the task of replacing or repairing a part that was worn, whether it was a small strut, a wing, or a control cable.

The women who served in these mechanical ratings had the dirtiest job of all. Their normal attire was a coverall; their hair, for reasons of safety, was bound by a woolen turban, their hands and sometimes their faces were streaked with carbon lubricants. But when liberty was available and the women of the "hanger crews" went ashore, they were among the most smartly groomed of the WAVES.

Closely allied to the machinist rating in terms of qualifications was that of instrumentman (AMMI). In this field, the quality of manual dexterity was stressed. Experience in physics and electricity was desirable, as well as an appreciation of fine details combined with precision.

Because all existing training facilities in aviation instrument work were already taxed to overflowing with men training for duty with fleet squadrons, the Bureau of Aeronautics negotiated a contract with a civilian firm, the Chicago School of Aircraft Instruments. The school, designated the Naval Training School, Aircraft Instruments, was to be administered by the Naval Air Technical Training Command. Approved housing facilities for the WAVE trainees had to be set up and arrangements made for their supervision. On 2 September 1943, the first class reported aboard for the 15 weeks of instruction.

During the first three weeks, which covered the working principles of the various types of aircraft instruments and the techniques of making repairs with small tools and a jeweler's lathe, all trainees were additionally screened to determine their aptitude for the three types of specialized training during the remaining 12 weeks: mechanical, electrical, and gyro intruments. In conferring with the instructors, I learned that the WAVES were highly desirable as trainees. The smallness of a woman's hand was of great value. Not only were women more manually dexterous than men, but they were extremely conscientious and did not become bored with the details of precision work.

Two days before Christmas in 1944, after graduating 650 WAVES and 145 women Marines, the training program was terminated, the needs of the service having been met.

During October 1943, a survey revealed that approximately 300 WAVES could be utilized as aerographer's mates, and a quota of 25 per month from the recruit school was scheduled.

The 12-week training period was first conducted at the Naval Air Station at Lakehurst, but later crowded conditions forced the Navy to lease the facilities at the Newman School, a private enterprise nearby.

Since the selection staff at the recruit school did a thorough job, only a mere fraction of the women entrants failed in spite of the stringent requirements: physical endurance, 20/20 vision, emotional stability, perseverance, patience, and objectivity. To these qualifications were added the requirements of some background in scientific studies, an excellent memory, and an absolute appreciation of accuracy. Such qualifications were mandatory if the work of the aerographer was latter to be depended upon without question, since, particularly in aviation, weather information looms large in considering the safety of a flight.

The training encompassed the decoding of weather reports, hourly observations of meteorological elements, taking balloon soundings of the upper air, computing forces and direction of wind aloft, amending charts, maintaining meteorological recording instruments, working up weather data, and constantly checking teletype reports.

So successfully did the first graduates carry out their mission at their duty stations that, when another survey was made to determine the number of WAVES that could replace men as aerographers, 98 percent of the total complement throughout the aviation activities in the United States was deemed practical.

Training continued for the duration, and, when the last class was graduated in 1945, 650 WAVES, 139 women Marines, and four SPARS had succesfully completed the course. In the last class consisting of 17 enlisted men and 12 enlisted women, those in the first five places in class standing were WAVES. On the job, they did—and this is from my personal observation—everything the men did except climb the pole to fix the wind gauge. This job had been negated by area commanding officers.

Enlisted WAVES in the rating of parachute rigger were accepted with no question whatsoever. Perhaps this was due to the fact that one of the duties of the rating involved using a sewing machine. Later, when they took aptitude tests, it was discovered that only one out of every ten women knew how to operate this particular domestic equipment.

Early in November 1942, the training of women as parachute

riggers was requested at the rate of 25 per month to begin in February 1943, at the Parachute School, NAS Lakehurst. This course of training was 16 weeks. Owing to the necessity of working at standard height tables—that is, standard for men—tall women were desired, but this last qualification was not sufficiently stressed and a number of WAVES under five feet, six inches were trained.

Two months after the first WAVES were assigned to stations, I observed, while visiting NAS Corpus Christi, a hazard to safety in packing the parachutes. The shorter women, in order to secure the final closing of the pack, were holding it against their chest while another member of the team inserted the closing toggles. I immediately asked the commanding officer to bring this to the attention of the medical officer. The doctor reported that continuation of this practice might yield harmful physical results. Never was an unsatisfactory condition met with greater alacrity. Almost overnight, the Naval Aircraft Factory in Philadelphia was at work developing two small tools to give the needed leverage. Both these closing jigs were immediately sent to all schools and stations where WAVE riggers were employed. Use of these devices was made mandatory, and the men as well as the women found them useful.

Packing parachutes was only one task of the riggers. In the lofts, the chute tables were in constant use as the riggers continually inspected the chutes, watching for stains, oil spots, and mildew, as well as checking for ruptures or tears in the silk. If mending was required, the riggers in the "silk room" took over. Ripcord harnesses were regularly inspected and repaired. Every 30 days all unused parachutes were taken from their packs, aired, inspected, and again made ready for use.

In their work, the riggers also produced tarpaulins, life raft bags, plane wheel covers, blind flying hoods, and flags of all kinds. Additionally, they manufactured pack assemblies and repaired flight gear and life raft containers.

One qualification established for the parachute rigger rating was waived for the WAVES: a free jump from a plane using a parachute packed by the jumper. Though many a WAVE requested permission to make this jump, she was only permitted to make the "tower jump" while in training. Not until Kathleen Robertson, stationed at NAS Corpus Christi, was allowed to make the first free jump was the jump put in *optional* status. She received her instructions, walked to the open door, and took off into space. After a 200-foot fall, the chute blossomed. She landed feet first, fell backward in the prescribed manner and rolled back to her feet again like a veteran jumper—smiling broadly.

Before 1942, the men who were control tower operators (specialist) were trained for the most part at air stations, but in time of war the need for a formal training program was recognized as well as the need for a special rating so that trained personnel could be retained in that type of work. Specialist (T) was originally the designation, but this was later changed to specialist (Y).

Once it was decided that the use of women as air tower controlmen should be explored, I was appointed to work with the Civil Aeronautics Administration to determine the practicability of employing enlisted women in this field. The decision being favorable, the Bureau of Aeronautics on 2 February 1943, requested authorization to train approximately 1,000 women. The Bureau of Personnel speedily approved the request and agreed to furnish 25 women every six weeks to the school which the Civil Aeronautics Administration had established at Atlanta. This school was shortly taken over by the Navy and placed under the command of the Chief of Naval Air Technical Training.

The first class convened 1 April 1942. One month later the Navy took over the school. On the recommendation of the Chief of Naval Air Technical Training all future training for control tower operation would be given only to women. This recommendation was based on his opinion that women excelled men in this field of work. Lieutenant Rosanne McQuiston was named as the senior woman officer of the school. From my observations she was a powerhouse as an administrator, disciplinarian, and coordinator.

From this time on until the end of the war, WAVES continued to be trained. By October 1945, when the last class completed training, the school had graduated 863 women, of whom 632 were WAVES; 215, women Marines; and 16, SPARS.

A battery of selection tests determined the aptitude of the candidates. The exacting requirements included visual acuity of 20/20, normal color vision, normal auditory acuity, no speech defects, no pronounced area accent, no tendency to vertigo, and a clear, well-modulated voice. This last qualification was determined by voice recordings. The candidates had also to demonstrate alertness and a fast reaction time as well as an ability to concentrate under urgent and noisy conditions. The desired age range was between 20 and 30 years. The candidate must have a mature, stable personality. Those with civilian experience as telephone operators, secondary school teachers, radio announcers, salesmen, or demonstrators were considered to be desirable candidates. So did those who had studied drama or served as airplane spotters in civil defense.

After many a visit to control towers to observe the WAVES at work, I readily understood the need for high standards. The constant noise in the control rooms and the steady stream of instructions being given by the various operators constituted a tower of Babel.

Not only did the WAVES direct aircraft takeoffs and landings by means of radio communications and light, but they were also responsible for seeing that the wind T's and beacon lights were on the right course. They recorded all takeoffs and landings and notified the fields where each plane was scheduled to land, and checked landing gear before planes left the ground. In short, they checked, double-checked, and rechecked everything in sight. In an emergency, they acted instantly.

During the 1940s, low pressure chambers were in use in various Naval Aviation training centers. They were as much of an innovation as some of the apparatus used during the 1960s for the training of astronauts. In such a chamber with its hermetically sealed windows, ten or twelve student pilots and aircrewmen in full flight gear could be seated. Simulated flight in the chamber to 30,000, 35,000, and 40,000 feet demonstrated to pilots, gunners, photographers, and aviation medical officers the problems and dangers of high-altitude flight and the necessity for proficiency in using oxygen equipment.

Enlisted WAVES—hospital corpsmen—acted as observers both inside and outside the chamber. It was also their responsibility to see that the oxygen supply was turned on, that pressure was adequate, that the masks were a perfect fit for each passenger, that the equipment was in good condition, and that each person understood its use. In event of an emergency, observers took action, giving directions over the loudspeaker system. They manned the controls of the chamber, regulated the ventilation and the rate of ascent and descent. During "chill runs," the enlisted WAVES fitted the electrically heated suits on the passengers and regulated the temperature. Records and equipment maintenance were also a part of their duty.

Not until July 1944 and then only after considerable study and correspondence did the commander of the Naval Air Transport Service (NATS), Atlantic Wing, request authority to train women for the rating of air transport crewmen, specialist (V). Because of the urgent need for such personnel and the excessive time it would have taken to establish an approved school for training, the WAVES were given what was designated as an indoctrination course. In the statements of urgency and in the arrangements for the "instructions under indoctrination" the project was assisted mightily by my brother, Commander Ward Bright, who was attached to Naval Air Transport Service at Patuxent Naval Air Station.

Screening tests, administered at the Recruit Training School, were prepared in my office after several visits to operating transport squadrons and conferences at length with commanding officers and crews. The WAVES selected for training in the new rating were sent to the Atlantic Wing of NATS located at the Naval Air Station, Patuxent River, Maryland, where the eight-week indoctrination course had been set up. (Later this training was transferred to the Naval Air Station, Olathe, Kansas.) The course included practical instruction in flight control, space control, and clerical and administrative duties. Instructional watches in transport squadrons were invaluable in giving the candidates transportation experience before their assignment to actual flight duty.

Flight orderlies checked aboard all equipment, anything from aspirin to oxygen. In flight, they served meals and made out the manifest from which the next station could determine what space and weight were available. They learned the principles of weight and balance and knew how to keep the passengers comfortable. Swimming was an essential qualification. To determine the reactions and stability of the WAVES in times of emergency, they were carefully observed under simulated conditions. The specialist (V)s were to prove themselves in efficiency and stamina, in resourcefulness, courtesy and cheerfulness.

A total of 190 specialist (V)s were trained for NATS continental runs. Then, on 28 June 1945, the Bureau of Personnel permitted the use of women in Naval Air Transport Service flights to Hawaii and shortly thereafter, to Europe.

The general use of WAVE flight orderlies on cargo flights did not get under way until October 1945. In this category of service, they did not actually load cargo, but directed its proper stowage. Those who survived the rigorous training —and most of them did—liked their work. Many were the barracks tales they told after returning from flights abroad.

An example of the thoroughness of their training involved the crash of an R5D near Donaldsonville, Louisiana, in May 1948. The chief SP(V) aboard was Rubinie Pappan. The miracle was that the five crewmen and fourteen passengers escaped with their lives. The crew was commended for its excellent work, a large share of the credit for bringing the passengers out safely being attributed to Chief Pappan.

"Of course, I was scared," she told me after the crash. "We all were. But we knew our emergency procedures by heart."

Somewhat akin to the aviation machinist mate (instrument) rating was that of the specialist (P), camera repairman. I had given no thought to the employment of women in this field, nor was I, in fact, familiar with the Navy's shortage of manpower in photography. Early in November 1943, the Bureau of Aeronautics' director of photography, Commander R. S. Quackenbush, Jr., brought to my attention his need for personnel qualified in the maintenance and repair of aircraft cameras, and he suggested training WAVES in this rating. To me this was a big step forward, for it was a *request* for womanpower, rather than a suggestion on my part for the utilization of women.

Immediately, conferences were scheduled between the Bureau of Aeronautics' Training Division, the Technical Training Command, and the Fairchild Aircraft Corporation. Within three weeks, an official request was made to the Bureau of Personnel for 50 WAVES to be trained as camera repairman. In reply, the Bureau of Personnel stated it could not supply that number because of the already heavy demands on recruit classes; and furthermore, it believed camera repair work should be done by civilians.

A bit daunted but not defeated, we again made another request on 15 January 1944, pointing out that civilian personnel was not available except at the camera manufacturing plants, and those plants was so limited by personnel shortages that they could not take on the Navy's repair work. Still another consideration was that all the trained male personnel were with the Fleet. There were only three civilian representatives for camera work with the Navy and even with this limited number, it was costing the Navy up to $50,000 per year. The Bureau of Aeronautics would be willing to take the WAVES on a basis of five a month instead of a group of 50 as originally requested. This request was approved.

Candidates were selected from the enlisted women who had a high school education with emphasis on mathematics and physics rather than literature and the arts. Photographic experience was not necessary but mechanical aptitude was.

The training began in April 1944 at the Fairchild Aviation Corporation in New York City. Upon completing one month's training, the candidates were sent to the Eastman Kodak Company in Rochester for an additional six weeks. In December 1944, the course was moved to NAS Pensacola, Florida. Again, the smallness of women's hands proved an advantage in successfully repairing the intricate mechanism of aerial cameras.

One of the most unusual ratings for which women trained was that of pigeonman, and this is how it came about. While on a visit to the Naval Air Station Lakehurst, I visited the Pigeonmen's School where enlisted men were being trained in the breeding, care, and training of homing pigeons. The birds were used by airship crews for communications carried out during radio silence while on antisubmarine patrols.

On 3 September 1943, upon my return to Washington, I immediately recommended that the practicability of training women as pigeonmen be explored. While the number of persons in this rating was small, the field seemed interesting to me and would possibly constitute another area of service for the WAVES. At a conference with the officer in charge of the lighter-than-air section in the Bureau of Aeronautics, it was decided that 20 of the 26 enlisted men engaged in the work of breeding and training pigeons could be successfully replaced by women.

Accordingly, on 8 September 1943, a request was made to the Bureau of Personnel, and by 5 October, the request being approved, the WAVES were selected and ordered from recruit school to the class convening 18 November. Actually the class got under way 1 December and lasted six months.

The criterion for selection of women trainees was simple. She should be a volunteer for the training, experienced in working with birds or animals, and be able to drive a car (in order to retrieve a pigeon in training status who had lost its way). She should have indicated ability to learn the diseases of birds, their treatment as well as their care. Typing experience was desirable.

Probably because of its uniqueness, announcement of the rating aroused keen interest in the women at the recruit school. This uniqueness also caused interest among the women officers in BuPers and on my visits there I was frequently greeted with "how are your pigeoneers making out?" The selection staff was able to secure women with outstanding qualifications; several had had previous experience in the raising and breeding of birds. About one year later it was found that the 20 trained exceeded the number required—this was because of the decrease in the lighter-than-air operations occasioned by the success of our antisubmarine warfare. Thus half the women trained were permitted to strike for another rating.

The rating for the pigeonman had been established as specialist (X) (PI).

In the field of aviation instructors, enlisted WAVES proved highly competent. It is interesting to note that after women were on duty as instructors no naval aviator went into combat without having received some of his training by a WAVE.

The main instructional ratings were specialist (T), Link trainer operator (aerial navigation), and specialist (G), the designation for a gunnery instructor. The concensus was that women excelled men in these types of instruction. The reason for this was attributed to the fact that the women screened for these ratings were selected in part because of their successful teaching experience as civilians. In addition, it soon became apparent that a woman brought more imagination to her task than a man and felt more personal concern for each of her students. Still another reason may be that, knowing they were not going into battle themselves, the WAVES found in the students their nearest approach to striking the enemy. They flew and shot by proxy through the men they trained.

Utilizing enlisted instructors for training officers presented no problems; the WAVE instructors, accepted in that role, filled it effectively. This came as no surprise to the Bureau of Aeronautics which had trained 100 civilian women as instructors before the WAVE legislation passed, in order to meet pilot training needs.

In November 1942, with the WAVE program only a few months old, the Bureau of Aeronautics requested enlisted WAVES for this training. On the basis of a survey of equipment conducted by Lieutenant Colonel Carl S. Day, USMC, head of the Instrument Section of the bureau's Aviation Training Division, it was recommended that approximately 1,500 WAVES be trained in the SP(T) rating. It is interesting to note that upon aproval of this recommendation the male quotas to the schools were canceled. It was found that women could operate on a basis of 100 percent replacement of the men.

The requirements for selection of candidates as Link instructors stated that the primary desirability was teaching experience. This requirement was to be interpreted to mean that they must have good diction, good choice of words, ability to express their thoughts adequately, and ability not only to analyze a student's mistakes but to explain the proper methods of procedure. They must learn to perform the daily maintenance, lubrication, cleaning, checks, etc., of their trainers.

The first class of 75 students began training on 13 January 1943. In all, 1,970 women were graduated from the Link Trainer Instruction School. Of these, 260 were women Marines and 18 were SPARS. The general classification test score requirements for Link instructor candidates were among the three highest in the screening processes set up for aviation ratings.

On 28 January 1943, the Deputy Chief of Naval Operations for Air requested the establishment of WAVE enlisted quotas of 35 every ten weeks to be trained for the Link Celestial Navigation Trainer schools at the Naval Air Station, Seattle, Washington, and the Naval Air Station, Quonset Point, Rhode Island. Trainees for this specialized work were graduates of the Link Instructors School. A survey had indicated that 256 operators were needed as celestial navigational instructors to man the number of machines being used. All male operators (of various aviation ratings) were released to sea duty upon the reporting of their WAVE relief. A total of 235 women were trained and, the needs of the service being met in Link celestial navigation, training ended August 1945.

The training of the celestial navigation instructors covered a period of ten weeks. WAVES were given sufficient flight, navigation and radio theory to insure proper instructional techniques. This training, as well as that of the Link instructors, was subjected to far more changes and modifications than any other rating. This was due to the fact that the needs of the Fleet changed almost daily under conditions of actual combat. The problems encountered in actual combat, which could not have been anticipated, made changes necessary and modified instructional techniques.

The value of training pilots with these devices became more

and more apparent, particularly as the importance of aviation to the Fleet was increasingly acknowledged. The pilot training program was, therefore, continuously being stepped up, and there were, in consequence, changes in instructional techniques.

Another instructional rating, that of gunnery instructor specialist (G), also involved the use of synthetic devices.

The Special Devices Division of the Bureau of Aeronautics during the latter part of 1942, had delved deeply into the possibility of training pilots by these means. The devices the division had developed for gunnery were primarily the 3A-2 Gunairtrainer, the 3B-1 Gunairstructor and the Mark 3 and 4 trainers, which simulated the conditions pilots would face when they went into actual combat. But the enlisted men who had been trained as instructors became restless under the unavoidable repetitiveness of the work. The success of the WAVES as Link trainer instructors made it seem feasible to train them in the gunnery devices, so on 5 February 1943, the Bureau of Aeronautics requested authorization to train approximately 100, in increments of 20, for a period of two weeks. Based on the results obtained from the first two groups, recommendations would be made either to enlarge or cancel the quotas.

There were no facilities within the Navy available at which women could be trained because of the unusually large number of men being readied for fleet duty at the various schools. Arrangements were therefore made with the Jam-Handy Company of Detroit to train these first groups of women, and living quarters for them were set up in the YWCA. On 27 February 1943, the training was authorized.

Because of the speed with which this trial program got under way, the Bureau of Aeronautics drew up the qualifications (not the Bureau of Medicine and Surgery, as was usual) based on those in use for men in order to assist the selection staff at the Naval Training School at Hunter. In April, just before the graduation of these first groups of gunnery instructors, it was decided that upon successful completion of the course they should be rated seamen 2/c, strikers for Specialist (T) 3/c. If recommended by their commanding officers as qualified, they could, after 30 days, receive their third class rating. It was not until November 1944, when the duties had been greatly broadened, that the rating for these instructors was changed to specialist (G).

Reports received from the various aviation training stations where these first 3A-2 instructors were stationed remarked on the excellence of their performance. The experiment of using women to instruct pilots in aerial free gunnery was considered an out-and-out success.

When the Special Devices Division produced the Gunairstructor 3B-1, designed to train pilots in fixed gunnery, it was found that the size and mechanical structure required two instructors for each machine. Again it was decided to determine the practicability of using women, and, on 8 July 1943, six women selected from the basic indoctrination school were given four weeks of training at Navy headquarters in Washington, D. C., and then sent to Naval Auxiliary Air Station, Green Cove Springs, Florida, for duty.

Again, the WAVES' performance was outstanding, so the Bureau of Aeronautics established a school to train women in this field at NAS Pensacola, Florida. On 7 October 1943, the Bureau of Personnel stated it would furnish the 320 WAVES requested, and the first group of 20 arrived for the first class on 23 November 1943. During the first week of their training, the scope of the existing curriculum was expanded. In addition to being trained in handling the 3A-2 and Gunairstructor 3B-1, the WAVES were given four weeks of additional instruction in theory and practical firing at the Aviation Free Gunnery School at Pensacola. The women, originally trained at the Jam-Handy Company in Detroit as 3A-2 instructors, were brought to the school to receive this additional instruction. This broadened course allowed the original one hundred to qualify for the gunnery rating if they were also able to demonstrate their proficiency in aviation free gunnery on any firing range (exclusive of turret machine guns), on synthetic training devices, and in a classroom.

The trainee in the SP(G) rating also had to be able to fire a shotgun, service pistol, and machine gun, demonstrate her ability to assemble and disassemble arms, and operate and repair training devices. She had to know ordnance regulations, be able to recognize friendly and enemy ships and aircraft, have a general knowledge of leading and sighting in given range estimation, and comprehend standard nomenclature.

While the women met all these qualifications, there were others that had to be waived. Because of their physical limitations, women could neither set nor secure the heavy .30 and .50 caliber BAM adapters nor could they carry either of them from the armory to the firing line. There was still another limitation: they could not make emergency repairs on shotgun traps because the springs were too large and too strong for them to take off and repair. To lessen its weight, the standard Navy shotgun had to be modified for the use of the WAVES. These waivers were approved because it was felt that the physical limitations of the WAVES were more than compensated for by their superior instruction.

During the final months of 1942, a number of enlisted women who had been trained as aviation gunnery instructors SP(G) became eligible for officer training. The Bureau of Aeronautics requested that, upon graduation from the officer indoctrination training at Northampton, these women be sent to the Naval Air Training Command at Pensacola, Florida, for an additional 30-day training course to prepare them for assignment as instructors in the gunnery phase of the pilot training program. Of a total of 15 women officers who were so trained, five of the number were also graduated from the Aircraft Recognition School to determine if recognition training would augment gunnery skills. It did.

The first class of antiaircraft gunnery instructors (women) graduated in September 1944 from the Mark 3 and 4 Trainer Operators' School at the Naval Training Center, Great Lakes, Illinois. Here they were trained to instruct in the use of antiaircraft guns and .50 caliber machine guns, as well as teach the principles of aiming and firing.

The WAVES realized that as instructors theirs was one of the most responsible assignments an enlisted woman could have. They knew that on the training the men received depended their lives and the lives of those who flew with them.

The training of SP(G)s at the Aviation Free Gunnery School, Pensacola, continued until 18 November 1944. The number of women trained was 505 WAVES and two women Marines.

Officers and other instructors in the gunnery school reported, "The WAVES have been among our best students. They are proficient. They do not shirk their work."

I have discussed the aviation ratings in detail primarily because I spent the war years, 1942 to 1946, in the Navy's aeronautical organization where my particular concern was the training of the women for aviation activities. It follows, of course, that closely tied to the training programs were the matters of administration, housing, discipline, welfare, utilization, and performance. Although evaluation studies during these years were made by the Navy concerning the utilization and performance of the women, I was in the unique position of being able to observe, day by day, the breaking down of the prevalent concepts of women's ability or potential. And I watched with pride as these concepts were shattered.

The "WAVES in aviation" consisted, however, not only of those in aviation ratings, but thousands of general service and medical ratings, yeomen, storekeepers, communication specialists, hospital corpsmen and technicians, pharmacist's mates, and dental technicians. Within these thousands, at the 500 shore bases of the Navy in the United States, must always be remembered the often unheralded seamen who went to their duty stations and were assigned to do "all the jobs that needed doing." They learned special types of work on the job, and were eligible to qualify for ratings in various fields when they had gained sufficient knowledge and could pass the examinations. A large percentage of these women reported for duty immediately after recruit training because school quotas were filled. Their contributions cannot be readily evaluated. Sufficient to say they performed, and they performed exceedingly well.

Toward the end of the first year of the program for women the general service rating of recruiter, specialist (R) was available and by August 1943 over 80 women were on duty in naval districts throughout the country, proudly wearing the new rating badge of a third class petty officer. These enlisted women, chosen while in recruit training at Hunter, were the first enlisted to be given the task of helping to recruit other women for naval service. Personality was one of the chief factors considered when the selection was made, and, in addition, a number of the selectees had in civilian life done radio work and public speaking.

Also in 1942, courses for enlisted personnel in mail clerk training got under way at the Naval Training School, Sampson, New York, later moved to Hunter, to which the WAVES were sent. The course was of nine weeks duration after which the graduates received two weeks additional training at Fleet Post Offices in New York and San Francisco. Graduates were assigned the rating of specialist-mail SP(M). The last class was August 1945.

When VJ Day arrived, the Fleet Post Offices were 78 percent manned by WAVES. With the exception of tossing the huge mailbags, the WAVES ran the show.

Because of the absence of women petty officers, sorely needed at the Recruit Training School, Hunter, a school was established there in April 1944 for the training of personnel supervisors, specialist (S). The women with this rating worked directly with the recruits in all phases of their training and living. Their rating carried the same authority and responsibility as that of a petty officer. Later women trained as specialist (S) were assigned to supervisory work in barracks in all naval districts.

The Cooks and Bakers School, a Class A service school, was established at Hunter in August 1943. The training course was originally of 12 weeks' duration, but in April of 1944 it was lengthened to 16 weeks. Those women who were graduates served at the naval activities side by side with the men cooks and bakers.

Early in the program for women, a great many male officers, particularly those of high rank, had visited various installations in Canada and England where service women were stationed. Observing the large numbers of enlisted women who served as cooks, bakers and mess attendants, the men recommended not only that WAVES be assigned in large numbers to similar fields in this country but also that, if necessary to secure recruits, the educational standards might be reduced. A specialist (U) rating was therefore established to cover such work, but the project was not successful and the rate was later canceled.

Probably the reason for the failure of the SP(U) rating was basically psychological. In contrast to Canada and Great Britain, the United States had no so-called servant class; hence there was no established field of domestic workers from which to draw. Furthermore, there was no conscription of women in the United States; and those who volunteered for naval service definitely felt that "personal service" was not a direct contribution to the war effort. It was quickly acknowledged that the services of the women should not be expended in laundry operations and other similar jobs which could be performed by unskilled civilian labor. The Navy women did, of course, serve with the men on mess duties and in the galley as well as in the general household duties of their stations.

Until December 1943, the women selected for training in the Hospital Corps were, after receiving recruit training, sent in groups to seventeen different naval hospitals for further training. This practice was carried out until 6,000 were qualified. At that time a school was established at the U.S. Naval Medical Center, Bethesda, Maryland, capable of handling classes of 240 with groups entering every two weeks. Later a similar school was established at the U.S. Naval Training Center, Great Lakes. So efficiently had the WAVE corpsmen performed that the requests for them continued to multiply. This great accounting of themselves was particularly noteworthy in view of the fact that their duty hours were the longest and in most cases the most fatiguing.

Hospital apprentices, corpsmen, and pharmacist's mates released male corpsmen not only in general ward duty but in the medical storerooms, the personnel offices, the admission desks, the diet kitchens, the dental, X-ray and physical therapy departments. They were assigned also to duty in the medical and clinical research laboratories, carrying out work on autokinetic illusions.

In order to qualify them to perform the duties in the medical fields, the Bureau of Medicine and Surgery geared its training courses to cover those activities, divided into four major components:

1. Hospital. The general duty assignments in naval hospitals represented the largest group of Navy women in the Hospital Corps. In the wards they administered medicine, gave baths, served trays, distributed and checked linens and performed other professional duties. The technicians served in occupational therapy and analyzed disabilities of patients in order to determine the type of therapy most conducive to recovery. WAVES on the staff of the physiotherapy department operated whirlpool baths and gave massage. In the heart department they made reports on basal metabolism tests and administered electrocardiograms. In the X-ray department they rapidly assumed the billets in the administration of X-ray treatments, as well as performing the required photographic work.

2. At the Naval Medical School the WAVES were divided into three groups: laboratory class, orientation class, and permanent staff. Here training was intensive in the various fields of hematology, parasitology, chemistry, bacteriology, and serology.

3. In the Dental School the enlisted WAVES were trained to assume jobs in the clinics as well as working on the staff of the school. Those in training attended classes and also

performed practical assignments, such as oral hygiene, and prosthetics.

4. The WAVE pharmacist's mates assigned to the Naval Medical Research Institute had all previously attended the laboratory classes at the Medical School. Here blood plasma experiments, studies of malaria, tests of reactions to wound therapy were all part of the assignments. In the nutrition field, experiments were carried out to determine the vitamin changes that occur in food rations, and captured enemy foods were analyzed. The supervision of meals for the recording of reactions of teams of Navy men living under certain conditions of temperature were experiments of great value. In the clothing field the effectiveness of new types, in varying temperatures, was tested.

The work of the hospital corpsmen did not lessen toward the end of hostilities, for they took an increasing part in the Navy's rehabilitation program. In addition to those already associated with the program, special training was continued at the Rehabilitation School at Hunter where a 16-week course qualified the trainee to take on duties as occupational and physical therapy assistants or as instructors of the blind, the deaf, or the physically handicapped.

In attempting to present a word picture of the performance of the WAVES, it is easier to describe the activities of large groups located near or in well-known cities or at huge naval installations; but the isolated, smaller detachments often permit a more intimate study and better evaluation. The Naval Convalescent Hospital in Sun Valley, Idaho, is a typical example. I had never even heard of it until on a transcontinental inspection trip an opportunity to visit presented itself. Here, a peacetime resort had been converted with very little change into a hospital and a complete rehabilitation program had been established. One WAVE ensign was in charge of occupational therapy, another was assistant to the welfare and recreation officer (great emphasis here was being placed on athletics). Four WAVE pharmacist's mates gave physical therapy treatments; another was a dental technician; another an X-ray technician, and two were on general ward duty. Others worked in the surgery department, the laboratory, and as recorders for the survey and rehabilitation boards. They also handled pay accounts and transportation. And this group was typical of the many scattered throughout the United States.

At the opening of 1945 the enrollment of the Women's Reserve had reached 82,761; no longer was their assignment to heretofore unusual work or to responsibilities questioned, or considered on an experimental basis. Their participation in the work at naval drydocks, overseas freight terminals, submarine bases, supply depots, hospitals, navy yards, etc., and in all departments of these activities was an accomplished fact.

And what could women do at the Navy Supply Depot at San Pedro? I asked this question of the commanding officer. He looked at me with a puzzled expression and replied, "Well, after they learn about all the types of Navy supplies needed by the Fleet they just keep those supplies moving." The WAVES early learned about the types of supplies, and it was a pleasure to see with what pride they described how they "kept them moving."

One WAVE ensign had gained basic working knowledge of stevedoring operations in order to have on hand at all times adequate operating stock of stevedoring gear, such as wire rope, turnbuckles, clips, shackles, and lumber. She signed inspection reports on material for services received and certified invoices for services rendered, including those of derrick barge and crane, as well as for stevedoring, wharfage, docking, and truck tonnage. She stood duty every third Sunday and at that time was responsible for all operations of the section which involved checking ship's movements in the harbor area, coordinating the movement of equipment to the dock with the scheduled loading of the ship, and the general security of the entire area.

The radio and related materials formed a small supply depot in itself. This too was in charge of a WAVE responsible for the security of all equipment and its receipt, storage, and delivery as well as for the renewal of stock.

Duty in both the Eastern and Western Sea Frontiers was a challenge of a very high order. In order to gain the special experience and training necessary to assume the responsibilities of the many departments to which they were assigned, the WAVES became understudies of the males they would relieve. Also, in order that all at the frontiers might gain a coordinated view of the duties and objectives of all branches and an understanding of the importance of her place in the overall picture, a combined indoctrination and refresher course was established in the spring of 1944. Included was a small arms course, taught by the Marines, emphasizing the proper handling, firing, and safety precautions. They took field trips to harbor entrance control posts and coordinating naval air stations in the area where they studied the various types of aircraft and the operational control of the stations. They were taken on flights over the harbor to see the buoy system, navigation lights, and patrol craft, All this they must know for their work in a Naval District Task Unit which dealt with shipping, convoy, routing and plotting of vessels, and antisubmarine warfare, the latter including patrol readiness, rescue, defensive, and offensive readiness procedures.

The communication divisions of the frontiers were manned almost entirely by WAVES, including coding and decoding work and maintaining direct communication with surface ships. A unique duty performed in Western Sea Frontier became a part of the regular Saturday inspection program when women communication officers began inspecting the communication facilities of each ship with its commanding officer. The work of the women in the communication field of the Navy was outstanding. By June 1945, WAVES composed 75 percent of the personnel of Radio Washington, handling 50,000,000 words per month.

In November 1942, the first 15 WAVES reported to Washington headquarters of Commander in Chief, U.S. Fleet (CinCUS), now Chief of Naval Operations, Washington, D.C. By November 1944, two-thirds of its enlisted personnel were women. They were engaged in writing technical summaries of operational bulletins and reports and preparing Navy bulletins for publication. They plotted and charted the routes of vessels. They did a large amount of the courier work. They logged in correspondence and microfilmed reports from the fleets.

In his annual report to the Secretary of the Navy, released 23 April 1944, Admiral Ernest J. King, Chief of Naval Operations, included this statement concerning the program for women in the Navy:

"The organization has been a success from the beginning, partly because of the high standards WAVES had to meet to be accepted, partly because no effort has been spared to see that they are properly looked out for, and partly because of their overpowering desire to make good. As a result of their competence, their hard work, and their enthusiasm, the release of men for sea duty has been accomplished. The natural consequence is an esprit de corps which enhances their value to the Navy, and it is a pleasure to report that in addition to their having earned an excellent reputation as a part of the Navy, they have become an inspiration to all hands in naval uniform."

The "new look" in uniforms for the women of the naval service (*top*), was designed by Mainbocher of New York shortly after World War II, and proved to be so classic it has changed but little over the years. Left to right: blue dress uniform, gray summer working uniform, evening dress uniform, white dress uniform, and raincoat with havelock.

The handsome navy blue bridge coat (*above*), worn by women officers in winter during World War II.

A "working smock" was the attire for enlisted WAVES when the job required it (*right*), while slickers, sou'westers, and boots became the "uniform" if one was assigned to guard duty on a rainy night (*far right*).

The Proper Thing to Wear

ABOUT the time of the first anniversary of the WAVES, an informal survey at the Naval Air Station, Jacksonville, Florida, yielded an interesting statistical picture of the enlisted women serving there. They represented fifty-four civilian occupations, with office workers predominating at about 57 percent. Professional women, including teachers, students, and technicians, accounted for 27 percent; telephone operators and manual workers constituted the remaining 16 percent.

In terms of education, 37 percent of the enlisted WAVES had had from one to six years in college; of these, 15 percent held bachelor's or master's degrees. Sixty percent had finished high school, and of these, 19 percent had had additional business school training. The remaining 25 percent had a minimum of two years of high school plus business experience.

In height, the enlisted WAVES stood between five and six feet. Seventy percent were between five feet three and five feet seven, and the height tallied most frequently was five feet four and a half inches.

Seventy-three percent of them had brown hair in varying hues; blonde ranked next with 22 percent; four percent were red-headed; and only one percent black-haired.

But in Navy blue, they all stood tall and became truly composite, and their similarity was marked as one saw them in review. Their heads were held a little higher because they believed themselves to be the best-dressed women in America. They owed this distinction in large measure to the efforts of Mrs. James V. Forrestal, wife of the Assistant Secretary of the Navy, in procuring the services, without cost, of the noted American fashion designer, Mr. Main Bocher, who headed the house of Mainbocher in New York. His design has withstood the test of time and fashion; with but few changes, it is worn by the women of our Navy today.

Not as dark as the standard Navy blue of the men's uniforms, the original WAVE outfit was still dark enough to serve as a background for the light blue stripes of the officers and the appropriate insignia of the ratings.

The officer's hat, which owed its characteristic style to the hat worn by John Paul Jones, was almost universally becoming, so much so that at the present time it is still worn by all WAVES.

The original hat for the enlisted women was of the snap brim variety, turned up in back. This very youthful-appearing fashion was finally considered somewhat inappropriate for the more mature women, mature in both age and experience, who were pouring into the enlisted ranks. Actually, this snap brim hat was really nudged out with the coming in of the overseas cap, authorized primarily for use on air stations where high winds frequently made the wearing of the regulation hat impracticable. Soon permission to wear the cap was extended to all activities, and both officers and enlisted wore it except on formal or prescribed occasions. Later, when the hat designed for the women officers was adopted for all women in the Navy, the snap brim model of the early war days was retired with honor.

Variations in the uniform continued during the first years of the war, and one scarcely knew from day to day what the next change would bring forth. At one conference with the officials of the Naval Clothing Depot, one distracted male officer vehemently remarked, "May the Lord be thanked that underwear for the WAVES is not prescribed!" To this, an officer from the distaff side of the conference table retorted, "I agree one hundred percent. The only regulation on that matter is that 'it will be worn and it will not show.'" And that is the basis for the uniform regulation which later appeared, "Slips shall not show."

Oxfords, primarily for daily use during indoctrination and recruit training, were originally "things to behold." All women were instructed to report with well-fitting oxfords and plain pumps with a one and a half inch heel. In reality, they wore what could at that time be found in the retail market, for it was not until much later that the Naval Clothing Depot was able to let contracts for women's shoes under the heading of war priorities. Because the production facilities of the country were being geared to meet war needs, these new contracts had to be officially declared war necessities.

Many retail stores in the vicinity of the basic training schools did yeoman service during the early months. Members of the early classes recall ruefully the exciting days when the tailors and fitters arrived, and then the day when the finished uniforms were delivered, all several sizes too large. This "plenty of room" uniform may have been the reason it soon became necessary to start a crash watch-your-weight program.

Navy blue bridge coats were worn in the winter. This handsome coat followed the lines of those worn by the male officers except that, in the interest of femininity, the shoulder boards worn by the men to denote rank were not prescribed for the women. Raincoats with havelocks gave WAVES weather protection as well as a distinctive appearance, the havelock somehow reflecting the look of the Foreign Legion. Worn with the uniform was a black handbag, the leather strap slung over the right shoulder, crossing aslant so that the bag hung at the left side, somewhat reminiscent of the Sam Browne belt. Black gloves were regularly worn, and white gloves were donned with the white uniform in summer, the materials being leather or cotton, according to the season. Later, white gloves were worn for dress with the blues as well.

When the summer of 1943 struck with heat wave after heat wave in Washington and throughout the South, the WAVES donned the newly prescribed blue cotton gabardine suits, which were duplicates in design of the blue winter uniforms.

This uniform was an unqualified failure, and the WAVE quite properly called them "gremlins." I myself never owne one of these suits, for, after viewing those in the fir procurement lot, I decided I'd rather die of the heat than t found alive in one of them.

Unfortunately, there had not been sufficient time for pro erly testing the cotton material. At the same time, the wa had cut off the nation's dye sources. Furthermore, blue prove to be a most difficult color, for each dye lot differed marked from the previous one. When the sun rapidly faded th uniforms, the WAVES called them sun-kissed gremlins. Som endured the gremlins bravely; others found themselve slinking around corners to avoid observation, and still other reverted to the winter blues and endured discomfort for season.

In the early spring of 1944, the WAVES were heartened b a welcome announcement: "Grey and white striped seersucke dresses with separate jackets will replace the present Nav blue cotton suit as the summer uniform for officers an enlisted personnel. White will continue to be the summer dres uniform."

Actually, the change in summer uniform was not so muc an act of mercy as an attempt to provide more convenien washable, hot-weather attire. The seersucker was a cotton dres with a set-in belt, a round collar, short sleeves, and a fittec collarless jacket with long sleeves. It could be worn on an occasion short of one which called for dress whites. The gre seersucker was an appropriate parallel to the summer uniforr of male officers.

The summer uniforms for men were also in a state of flux Gabardines—grey, green, and khaki—were being "wear-tested. The green gabardines were fashioned after the already existin winter work uniform of the naval aviators. The color of th greenish cotton uniform quickly faded, and the grey gabardin was finally approved, largely because it didn't fade as rapidl as the green. Furthermore, it permitted the Navy not t embrace the khaki which the Army was already wearing.

Interest in the adoption of the new service uniform for th men extended to the very top. I frequently met the Commande in Chief of the Navy, Admiral King, my former boss in the Bureau of Aeronautics, in the corridors of the old Nav building, wearing either one of the grey or green test suits. O one occasion, he told me he personally favored the greens (he secured his naval aviation wings very late in his naval career but was fearful that the greys, because of the dye situation, would win out, which they did.

The original approval of the grey gabardine for men was behind the choice of the grey and white seersucker for the women. When the grey for men was discarded in favor of the khaki, the seersuckers were already in production. With this reversal in the decision of the color of the men's uniform, the grey lost its significance in Navy tradition. However, this reversal did help the women in one way. We no longer, while attending uniform conferences, heard the remark "Can't you women make up your minds?"

At the time the seersuckers were introduced, other changes were made: Several types and colors of shirts were eliminated; the button-on ties were adopted to avoid bulkiness under the collar of the shirts and the grey dresses; a lightweight, shower-proof raincoat and havelock were procured.

Hosiery was a problem. Nylons were not yet available, and the wearing of rayon and cotton lisle stockings presented anything but a chic appearance. Wrinkles were unavoidable; not even the most conscientious WAVE could be sure that she fulfilled at all times the regulation which read, "Seams shall be straight." There was no answer to the problem until nylon stockings appeared on the market. The WAVES had them from that moment onward. Representatives of the Naval Clothing Depot, recognizing the great improvement in appearance and hence heightened morale, immediately registered a priority on nylon production for the WAVES. The first consignment received was of the conventional "seam up the back" variety.

Later, the first seamless nylon stockings appeared on the retail market, causing a furor. They became a vital issue! Inspecting officers were at a loss as to what to do. In some instances, the WAVES were put on report as being out of uniform. But were they? The question quickly reached the office of the Director of the WAVES. During a regular conference, the subject was seriously discussed and there actually were some who thought seamless stockings should not be permitted because they gave the appearance of bare legs. But the "ayes" won that day and the permissive change was written into uniform regulations. With the passing of time, local commanding officers in very hot climates permitted the elimination of stockings altogether when the WAVES were in working uniform and within the station confines.

Inspections of the WAVES in the Bureau of Aeronautics

were regularly held between the wings of the Main Navy Building on Constitution Avenue in Washington, D.C. I called these inspections in order to keep the WAVE program a part of the regular Navy schedule and not have it seem that the women were only part of some special wartime program. If the men stood inspection, so should the women. Then, in order to keep the male side of the Navy alert to the fact that the women were an integral part of the service, I would ask various officers, such as the Chief or Assistant Chief of the Bureau of Aeronautics or some high civilian official, such as the Assistant Secretary of the Navy for Air, to be the reviewing officer. In spite of the great workload these men carried, they all graciously responded though not—I found out later— without some fear and trepidation. Still, it was an experience worthy of later discussion and some boasting. Occasionally the reviewing officer exhibited some timidity while making the inspection.

Before making his first WAVE inspection, Admiral DeWitt Ramsey, an officer I had known most of my working life called me to his office and asked, "Joy, just what do I look for?"

"It's very simple, Admiral," I replied. "Today we will concentrate on three of the uniform regulations which state 'Hair may touch but not fall below the collar,' 'Slips shall not show,' and 'Stocking seams shall be straight.' "

With this agreed upon, we headed for the inspection area where hundreds of WAVES awaited our arrival.

Every part of the inspection was carried out with precision every command was given clearly and responded to smoothly Every woman stood sharply at attention, eyes straight ahead.

The admiral passed in front of each line and then the rear After completing inspection of the first company, he relaxed and several times paused to ask questions of the women in ranks.

"Where do you have your laundry done?"

The WAVE, bless her, kept eyes straight ahead and replied "Sir, I do it myself." Then she added with a touch of pride "We have laundry facilities in our barracks."

Admiral Ramsey then remarked that everyone's shirt was so white and starched that great care must have been taken to get them that way.

As I passed the young woman, still rigidly at attention but with a startled expression on her flushed face, I could not refrain from whispering, "Nice going." I saw the muscles of her face relax a trifle.

One part of that inspection will never be forgotten by those of us who were there. The admiral stopped at the end of the front line of the fourth company and stood looking along the rear of the line of women before proceeding. He suddenly turned to me and, out of a clear sky and in a voice which could be heard by a large number of women, said, "You know, this is the first time in my life it has been part of my official duties to look at women's legs."

The following day when I had occasion to go across the river to the Bureau of Personnel, I was greeted in the office of the Director of the WAVES with the query, "Is it true that Admiral Ramsey said he was having a fine time inspecting women's legs?"

Scuttlebutt worked as well for the women of the Navy as it always had for the men.

Soon after the war ended additional modifications to the uniform were undertaken. The Navy Nurse Corps during those years had gained, through legislation, recognized commissioned status. Captain Nellie Jane DeWitt, director of that corps, and I had many discussions regarding our uniforms, endeavoring to find a meeting of minds on what features of our two different uniforms would be welcomed by both. In the interest of economy of procurement and as officers of the regular Navy we felt that the only sensible thing to do was to combine our ideas. A survey was conducted of both the nurses and the WAVES. The nurses were entirely in favor of their gold stripes, while the WAVES favored the light blue stripes which they had become accustomed to. The nurses preferred the dark navy blue color which was that of the male officers; the WAVES preferred the lighten navy blue. There seemed to be unaminous agreement, finally, on the Mainbocher-designed uniform, hat and overcoat. Neither the WAVES nor the nurses felt that the grey seersucker dress and jacket was alluring. After the results of the surveys were in, and throught the efforts of Mrs. John Nicholas Brown, wife of the Assistant Secretary of the Navy for Air, the matter was taken to Mainbocher for his advice and recommendations.

The result of all these prolonged efforts was that Mainbocher designed a grey seersucker work uniform and a formal evening uniform. He used the dark navy blue favored by the nurses and put gold stripes on the uniform which he had originally designed for the WAVES. He added the gold embroidery (scrambled eggs) to the hat for senior officers which followed the procedure for senior male officers.

When all these changes and compromises had been made, a showing was arranged for the General Board of the Navy. It was quite an affair! Mainbocher came to Washington from New York, bringing his chic and beautiful models who showed off each item of uniform—the greys, the new color of blue with its gold stripes, and the entirely new evening uniform. I can still recall every detail of that afternoon; the row of high-ranking naval officers of the General Board of the Navy, Secretary and Mrs. Brown, and various chiefs of bureaus of the Navy Department. I'm sure that nothing like it had ever happened before in the history of the Navy. Approval was secured.

At an official inspection of the USS *Winston* (*left, above*), Captain Hancock asked to see the garbage grinder and meet the lone seaman in charge of that detail.

Captain Hancock (center) participates in the recommissioning ceremony for the *Earle B. Hall* (APD-109) and the *Bassett* (APD-73), about to see service again in the Korean conflict (*above, right*).

The *Lewis Hancock* (DD-675) *opposite,* named in honor of Lieutenant Commander Lewis Hancock, who lost his life in the crash of the rigid airship *Shenandoah* in 1925. Joy Bright Hancock acted as sponsor for the ship bearing her husband's name.

Of Ships and Men

 DURING the summer of 1943, I participated in two ceremonies of great personal significance to me. On
2 July, the Goodyear Tire and Rubber Company staged a special day of events at its huge plant in Akron, Ohio, in connection with the christening of the airship K-X. The K designated
her type and the X was used instead of the usual numeral, in
the interest of national security, to conceal the total number
of this type of airship on hand.

Also, on this day, in a simple, moving manner, a memorial
plaque was dedicated to the eight Navy men who had been
trained as lighter-than-air pilots in the first class at Wingfoot
Lake, Ohio, during World War I, and who had later lost their

lives. One of the names on the plaque was that of my first husband, Lieutenant Charles Gray Little, who had been killed in the crash of the ZR-2 (British R-38) on 24 August 1921.

Later, fifty thousand people, almost all of them workers at Goodyear, gathered on the landing field for the K-X christening. The president of the company, Mr. P. W. Litchfield, and Rear Admiral Charles E. Rosendahl, senior surviving officer of the rigid airship, the USS *Shenandoah*, made the principal addresses. "Not one of the thousands of transports and supply vessels that have been escorted by non-rigid airships has been lost through submarine attack," Admiral Rosendahl pointed out. Heartening words indeed at a time when the United States was working unremittingly to replace the ships lost at Pearl Harbor.

And then came the moment for which I had been asked to come to Akron, the christening of the K-X. In my hand I held the bottle of liquid air so appropriate to the christening since it was used in the repurification of helium with which the ship was inflated. Speaking the traditional words, "I christen the K-X," I smashed the container on the nose of the control car and the vapor rose in the air. The airship, released from her moorings, soared to join two of her sister ships circling overhead.

Such a ceremony, so inherently dramatic and symbolic of the work and will of the nation at war, could not but evoke in the thousands of workers present a joy of accomplishment, for each airship, upon completion, immediately joined the patrol in the fight against enemy submarines. Too frequently the tasks of civilian workers in the war effort went unmentioned, but on this day the officials paid high tribute and gave them high praise for their achievement which was on parade in the sky.

Less than a month later, I was the sponsor of another ship. Admiral Marc Mitscher, then Assistant Chief of Naval Operations (Air), told me that one of the new destroyers, DD-675, was to be named in honor of my husband, Lieutenant Commander Lewis Hancock, who had lost his life in the crash of the rigid airship, USS *Shenandoah*, in 1925. Admiral Mitscher and my husband were members of the Naval Academy class of 1910. This notification was followed by a formal letter from the Secretary of the Navy which stated that "a destroyer, now building, will be named in honor of your husband, the late Lieutenant Commander Lewis Hancock, Jr., U.S. Navy.... Will you please advise the department at your earliest convenience if you will be able to act as sponsor for this vessel when she is launched."

Would I act as sponsor? From some recess in my mind, a hope, almost buried that day in 1925 when the *Shenandoah* had crashed and Lewis Hancock had been killed, had come to fulfillment that some day the Navy would pay tribute in just this manner to his devotion and sacrifice. Now I, who had shared his life and his death, was to have the opportunity and the honor of participating in the Navy's recognition of his service.

The first of August finally arrived and with it the unfolding of the orderly planned ceremonies, including my arrival at the yard of the Federal Shipbuilding and Dry Dock Company, Kearny, New Jersey. On all sides, the work of keel laying, building and launching was being carried on. Such activity made me wonder if those men and women at work on the hulls on the ways were conscious of the fact that they were building more than ships? Did they know that every section plate riveted into place, every bulkhead erected, every bracing inserted would enter somehow into the lives of the men who would fight her?

Near the foot of the ladder leading to the launching stand, a sign announced the date the keel of the USS *Lewis Hancock* had been laid and the date of its launching. In an incredibly short time those men and women had readied another ship. I mounted the ladder and peered over the railing of the platform to see the two steel plates on either side of the bow which held the ship on the ways. Men stood ready to cut away, simultaneously, the two restrainers.

Because we were at war, only a few members of my own family and those of Commander Hancock were present. An official of the shipbuilding company handed me two telegrams, one from the prospective commanding officer of the ship, Commander C. H. Lyman, and one from the secretary of the Naval Academy class of 1910. These telegrams reflected what I have always found true of the Navy, that it is never so big as to forget courtesies of a kind and personal nature. War duties were so pressing that not one member of Lewis' class could be present, but they had not forgotten, they were there in spirit. Their greetings included the knowledge that the vessel would live up to the splendid record of bravery and devotion to duty exemplified in their classmate's career. The prospective commanding officer, a thousand miles away, wired, "Give her a good send-off and may her colors always be proud to fly from her." I was no longer alone in this ceremony. Around me hovered the earnest thoughts of Navy men.

"Lieutenant Hancock," someone said to me, "when I give the word, break the bottle about here." A hand was laid on the bow of the ship to indicate the place. When the hand was lifted I noticed a faint, smudged fingerprint which at once became my point of aim. I wondered who had made that imprint, little knowing that his mark would go to sea under successive coats of paint. My thoughts led far away. Then the photographer's flashes were exploding. I raised the ribbon-wrapped bottle each time I was requested to do so—just one more—but I kept my eyes on that smudged fingerprint. Silently and smoothly, the fingerprint began to draw away.

"Now!" came the voice of my instructor. I swung hard, and the fingerprint was covered with foam. "I christen thee *Lewis Hancock*," I said as the ship drew farther away. I could no longer put out my hand to touch the ship; she was slipping rapidly and easily toward the water. "Down to the sea in ships," ran through my mind. I turned to face the moving ship and saluted. As she gathered speed I sensed the spirit of Lewis Hancock, but it was more than that. He would live more than ever in the hearts of those who remembered him. He was going to sea. The name of Lewis Hancock was once more on the active rolls of the Navy, back to the first line.

I heard, as if from a distance, the shrill whistle of the tugs as the ship slid out on even keel into the water. I saw dimly the debris of the shorings floating about her as her bow swung gracefully toward the pier, where she would receive the last items of fighting equipment.

Someone spoke to me. "Look," the voice said, "they are swinging another keel into place before the ways have cooled. Isn't that marvelous?" And indeed it was.

It was all over and I left the christening stand. Already the *Lewis Hancock* sign had been removed and another sign put in its place. The keel-laying date was painted on it; a new name was up. In a few months another sponsor would mount the same steps.

On all sides, the clang of metal against metal went on. Instructions were shouted. I shook hands with the shipyard officials and saluted the naval officers superintending construction. I made the usual remarks and finally departed.

When people later asked about the ceremony I answered, "Well, it was really a grand affair. Yes, I broke the bottle successfully. I was terribly proud." But my deepest feeling was not the pride of sponsorship but the sheer joy of knowing that Lewis Hancock had again gone to sea.

Time passed and the *Lewis Hancock* chalked up a fine record. Commissioned on 29 September 1943, at the Brooklyn Navy Yard, she completed her shakedown and departed on 5 December 1943, via the Panama Canal, to join the Pacific Fleet. On the bulkhead in her wardroom were mounted Lieutenant Commander Hancock's sword, a photograph of him, and one of me as the ship's sponsor. So often I thought of that small display and wondered how she was faring.

The *Lewis Hancock* remained in the Pacific until 14 September 1945. In this period she steamed 200,000 miles, and her path from Pearl Harbor led to the Carolines, Hollandia, New Guinea, the Marcus-Wake area, the defense of the Marianas, and the Philippine Sea. In all, she participated in nine "star" operations, plus the Philippine liberation campaign, for which the crewmen of the ship were authorized to wear that campaign ribbon with two stars.

In the Battle of Leyte Gulf, the *Lewis Hancock* was part of the task force which trapped and destroyed an enemy cruiser or large destroyer off San Bernadino Straits in the darkness of 26 October 1944. Stationed twelve miles in advance of the fast striking force, the picket ship which discovered and reported the enemy was the *Lewis Hancock*. Then, on 19 November 1944, with USS *Collett*, she was credited with shooting down six enemy aircraft, four of which were bombers, disposing of them in the space of five minutes. In addition, the *Lewis Hancock* recovered sixteen U.S. pilots and crewmen from crashed aircraft at sea.

Following World War II, the *Lewis Hancock* was placed in the Reserve Fleet January 1947, where she remained until 19 March 1951, when she was recommissioned at Long Beach, California. On that day—Armed Forces Day—it was my privilege to deliver the address at the recommissioning ceremonies of the *Lewis Hancock*, the USS *Miller*, and the USS *Erben*, and to meet the officers and men of these ships which were going into service in the Korean conflict.

After Korean service, the *Lewis Hancock* was again returned to mothballs, this time at the Naval Base, Philadelphia. There she remained until 2 August 1967, when she was given to the government of Brazil. She was renamed CT *Piaui*.

Another unique and interesting experience was mine when I was invited to make an official inspection of the USS

Winston, at Norfolk, by her commanding officer, Captain Nicholson. My brother, Commander Cooper Bright, was the executive officer, and it was at his suggestion, I'm sure, that the invitation was extended. It constituted another first for me.

An official request from the commanding officer was approved by the Navy Department and the inspection was placed on my schedule for my next visit to the Norfolk area. In the interim I asked many questions of male officers in Washington regarding the proper procedures and the proper remarks. I knew that I would be briefed when I reported on board, but I wanted to have an intelligent background for listening so that the briefing would be most meaningful.

In June 1949, I was in the Norfolk area and the inspection of the USS *Winston* was scheduled. I have often wondered since just what were the reactions of the members of the crew to the fact that the inspecting officer was a woman. Outwardly, of course, all the formalities were carried out in a most precise and military manner. For my part, I was truly interested in all departments of the ship, and I did have enough background to ask the leading chiefs some intelligent questions regarding the functions under their cognizance. I climbed and descended the ladders to the engine room, the store rooms, the sick bay, the crew's quarters, the mess hall, the galley, the wardroom, the bridge. It was a lengthy but fascinating procedure for me. Finally, the captain asked me if I had covered all activities desired. I replied that the one place I had not seen was the garbage grinder. He looked at me with a rather astonished expression until I said, "I really have a reason for wanting to see it. My brother, your executive officer, served for thirty months in USS *Yorktown* in the Pacific, and when he returned to the United States he told me that there was a particular 'word' passed several times each day: 'Now hear this, now hear this, will the man with the key to the garbage grinder lay below and grind same.' My brother was detached from *Yorktown* without finding out if the man with the key had ever received the word. I'd like to see the garbage grinder on this ship."

The captain was most amused and said, "We'll go to the garbage grinder," and away we went, aft, the entire length of the ship and below to the waterline. We entered a compartment approximately 12 × 15 feet which was immaculately clean, smelling of disinfectant, and there, at attention, stood a lone seaman in spotless uniform. To me, this was a very lonely sight—this very young man standing and ready for the inspection party which, I'm sure, rarely arrived. I talked to the lad and told him that it was my first visit to the grinder of a ship, and that I had not expected to find a compartment so immaculately clean. I asked him to explain to me how the equipment worked. A look of astonishment came over his face and he glanced rather imploringly at his commanding officer, who nodded in the affirmative. The lad knew his job and was enthusiastic in his recital. I learned something and I felt sure that the young man in charge received some satisfaction in telling someone about his duties.

Later, at a reception, I told the Secretary of the Navy about this experience. He was thoroughly interested and remarked that he, too, had never seen a garbage grinder, and that next time he was on board a ship he would make it a point to visit it, and meet that "lone seaman." Later, I heard that he had actually done so.

After coffee in the captain's quarters I departed, being piped ashore. A sense of great fulfillment always came to me in boarding or departing a ship. Carrying out the ceremonies of the Navy made me feel so definitely a part of it, for I realized that I was expected to do these things correctly. Although some of the so-called little things, like saluting at the proper time under unfamiliar circumstances, brought worries to me, I later learned that the men, even though their knowledge of ceremonies was more detailed, were at times also faced with some uncertainties.

Here I am reminded of the time I was the reviewing officer at the U.S. Maritime Academy at King's Point. New York. The occasion was a graduation. It was a beautiful setting and the cadets were of the smartest. I stood on the reviewing stand and returned the salutes of the marching companies, at the proper time. And then the drill team performed ending the performance by the company officers dropping to one knee with swords pointed to the ground. I stood transfixed. I instinctively knew that I was supposed to do something. But what? The moment was saved for me when the aide to the admiral, standing behind me, whispered, "Salute." It was truly a sincere salute. I had never before seen a Queen Anne salute. As long as I live I shall retain the shock of those seconds of utter uncertainty on my part.

While on an inspection trip to naval air activities in the south, I was given an important role in a most impressive ceremony for which I was again little prepared. It was another first for a woman officer. In looking back I realize that some of the duties which devolved upon me were assigned on the premise that I was a captain, and as such I was expected to know the how and why of any occasion that might arise. This certainly exemplified the acceptance by the men of the Navy that the program for women was designed to promote. The fact that I did not know so many of the "little things" of the Navy I hope I was able to keep hidden. But on many occasions my internal uncertainty was often disquieting, to say the least. On this specific occasion I was informed that I was to take part in a planned event at Green Cove Springs Naval Station, headquarters of the Florida group of the Atlantic Reserve Fleet. There, combined, were the observance of its fifth anniversary and the ninth anniversary of Pearl Harbor Day. The great number of ships moored at this base had been in mothballs for several years, and now the Korean conflict saw many of them being rapidly prepared for recommissioning. On this date, 7 December 1950, two APD, fast attack transports, were ready: the USS *Earle B. Hall* and the USS *Bassett*.

Captain Chauncey Moore, U. S. Navy, the commander of the Florida group, explained to me briefly that I was to place these two ships in commission, and he handed me the orders from the Navy Department that I was to read. He also gave me a brief rundown of the history of each ship and said that I was to make a very short speech to the assembled crews aboard each ship. With that we proceeded to dockside where the ships were tied up, their crews waiting. I accompanied Captain Moore first to the USS *Earle B. Hall*, APD 109, where, after the usual formalities of going on board, I was greeted by the prospective commanding officer, Lieutenant Commander William Mack, and taken to the stern of the ship where the microphones were set up and where we could all face the crew standing in precise formation on the deck forward. And what a sight that was. Captain Moore, Lieutenant Commander Mack, the chaplain, and I formed the official commissioning party. I remember so well a feeling of inadequacy as I heard my own voice over the loud speakers when reading the orders of commissioning. Inadequate because I knew that these men were to sail to the Pacific and fight their ship if necessary, while I remained in the safety of the continental United States. The reading of his orders by the commanding officer, the presentation of the Bible to him by the chaplain and his following prayer, and then the hoisting of the flag while the band played the national anthem—all hands standing at salute—combined to make another indelible picture in my mind. Immediately, we crossed the deck and proceeded to the USS *Bassett*, APD 73, where like ceremonies were carried out.

The event, because of a certain uniqueness, made headlines in various news media. The Florida papers especially made much of the occasion, with headlines "WAVE Captain Commissions Ships, Makes Navy History." "A 'first' in the annals of the U.S. Navy." I was, of course, honored to have had this part in the ceremonies, at the same time realizing that favorable publicity would also aid our recruiting people to secure the women we wanted on a career basis.

My rank of captain, in one instance, produced some complications. It was in August of 1949 when the opportunity arose for me to observe, at first hand, the possibilities of using the services of WAVES on board naval transports. I was anxious to survey this possibility, particularly in the interest of more diversified assignments for hospital corps WAVES. I felt that if transports, which carried dependents, and which already included Navy nurses in their complement, could provide living accommodations and supervision, certainly the services of corpsmen could be most helpful. If this proved a helpful and practical assignment in might lead the way to their future assignments in hospital ships.

With this in mind I secured permission to travel in a naval transport between Norfolk and San Juan, Puerto Rico. The official transportation request was forwarded so that accommodations would be available and assigned, I flew to Norfolk and went aboard the ship just prior to its sailing, and when I checked in for my room space there was considerable consternation. It developed that no one knew that one of the four captains assigned to one cabin was a woman. The ship's sleeping spaces were all filled, and as we steamed through Hampton Roads the burning question was what to do with Captain Hancock. Within the hour all was settled. I was placed in a cabin with a Navy wife and her three children. There were three berths in the cabin, mounted on one bulkhead, from ceiling to floor. The mother and baby slept in the lowest, the other two children couldn't possibly be put in that top berth about 14 inches from the ceiling, so I inherited it. Unfortunately, we had a rough voyage and my cabin mates were all seasick. The children were up at dawn and turned in at

6:00 P.M. With the evening meal on board served at 5:00 P.M., I soon changed my sleeping habits to conform.

However, I didn't always come out on the short end of the stick in the matter of transportation.

I remember my first trip to the lighter-than-air station at Glynco, Georgia. I was a lieutenant, having but very recently received my commission. I was to accompany a captain, the lighter-than-air representative in the Bureau of Aeronautics, on this inspection trip where I was to check on facilities which could be converted to accommodate WAVES. The Navy transportation office had taken care of the train reservations. When we boarded the train in Washington for the overnight trip to Glynco, we found that the accommodations consisted of a bedroom. Immediately the captain searched out the conductor and explained that he wanted a berth other than in the bedroom with the lieutenant. As was usual during wartime, the accommodations were entirely sold out. And then the conductor asked if there were any objections to a captain and a lieutenant sharing the same room. "In this case, yes," replied the captain. "The lieutenant happens to be a woman." The result was that I had the room to myself and I've always had a hunch that the captain slept in the smoking car.

The old saw that "no man is without honor except in his own home," was disproved for me on several occasions. The first such came about when I received an illuminated resolution passed and signed by the commissioners of the city of Wildwood. This resolution set forth, in glowing terms, that my services in two wars, my promotions and my appointment as Director of the WAVES, had brought honor and distinction to my home town and, therefore, I was offered the congratulations of all its citizens. Naturally, this brought about a great sense of warmth, particularly in view of the many occasions, which still must certainly be remembered by those citizens, when my high spirits had had to be curbed; when my tomboy behavior and pranks were certainly sources of annoyances for them.

In addition, I was invited to be the principal speaker at the annual beach-front services on the following Memorial Day (1947). My father had been the speaker, as Mayor of Wildwood, just prior to his death. I had first taken part in these exercises in 1918 when I was in the naval uniform of World War I, but then I certainly was not the speaker of the day.

Nor were New Jersey honors limited to my home town. On 20 March 1950, very impressive ceremonies were held in the New Jersey State House in Trenton, presided over by Governor Alfred E. Driscoll. Members of the Senate and House of Assembly and representatives of the various veterans' organizations and officials of Wildwood gathered to "publicly honor, for distinguished service in two wars, Vice Admiral Dorsey Foster, SC USN, and Captain Joy Bright Hancock, USN."

After Governor Driscoll presented us with scrolls, we were taken to the Senate chamber where a resolution honoring the admiral and me was adopted. Accepting and acknowledging these honors did, of course, occasion deep emotion, but even greater was my reaction as I stood facing the hundreds of kindly people who had gathered there from all sections of the state; many I had known as a child, many I had not seen in years; and then I glanced up to the visitors' gallery, and there was mother, a smile on her face. She gave me a small affirmative nod as I started to speak. She knew, as I did, that as I stood on the rostrum of the President of the Senate, so long occupied by my father, that again, as at the hearings in the Congress two years earlier, he was there, and through her smile and nod she was expressing his pleasure.

Northrup and Gillett, the twin dormitories at Smith College, Northampton, Massachusetts (*top*), "home" to WAVE officers undergoing indoctrination during World War II. At naval stations, the shortage of housing for WAVES often proved critical. Hotels and apartment houses were taken over, or barracks were modified. Whatever the housing, one of the first tasks was to make up the double-deckers, as these WAVES, newly arrived for duty in Hawaii, are doing (*above, right*).

Duty during World War II was not all work for the WAVES. This couple (*left, above*) seems to be enjoying the "Big Apple." The occasion, a dance given by enlisted personnel at NAS Honolulu for their sisters in the service. In the photo *opposite*, WAVES at Stillwater, Oklahoma, raise their voices in song.

Housing and Recreation

ONCE the program for women in the Navy had been approved and recruiting and training were under way, the scramble was on to provide housing at the activities scheduled to be assigned to the WAVES. On the assumption that legislation would be passed, air stations had earmarked buildings for the WAVES and had commenced modifications.

In establishing the standards for WAVES' housing, officials had dug out of their files approved barracks plans for men. The Bureau of Medicine and Surgery had recommended that the usual open-dormitory spaces be divided into cubicles in the interest of privacy for the occupants, as well as the prevention and spread of communicable, particularly respiratory, diseases. These changes which had never been implemented for men were put into effect for the women.

Doors were hung on toilet stalls and partitions erected in the showers. Wherever practicable, limited cooking facilities were furnished, as well as a refrigerator, a washing machine, and irons. A lounge was provided for receiving guests. WAVES were permitted to "dress up" the cubicles to a limited extent with curtains and bedspreads in the hope that they would spend more time in their barracks than the men did in theirs. So desirable and acceptable were these modifications in the basic requirements that later these became the rule for all new construction for men.

In New York, San Francisco, and other large cities, WAVES were generally housed in leased hotels. Arrangements for these women, usually included in the "general service rating," were made by the Bureau of Naval Personnel. As for housing in Washington, where adequate housing for men in the Navy had never existed, the situation was tight to very nearly the end of the war. Hotels and apartment houses were taken over and a series of barracks was built, each one designated by a letter of the alphabet. WAVES poured into the Capital until more than 22,000 were there, and housing designators reached the halfway mark in the alphabet. This situation was true in most of the metropolitan areas where WAVES were assigned.

Quarters I, located near the Lincoln Memorial in Potomac Park, sprawled on and on, section after section, but the amenities were preserved and Sunday morning on the quarterdeck was a prized affair for guests. In this area, the girls were permitted to come in housecoats to serve coffee, doughnuts, cereal, etc., and sit around and talk Navy. Afterwards, they would conduct a tour of their barracks, pointing out their own cubicles and showing the touches they had given them to make them a personal retreat.

Naval stations found a way to handle their housing situation. A barracks could be readied or built for the first group of women to arrive. Generally, the space was secured by taking one of the men's barracks and crowding the men into others. As the WAVES took over the jobs, the men went off to join the Fleet, and crowding lessened.

I was on hand to see the WAVES received at the Naval Air Station, Anacostia. The station officers seemed to think that the WAVES should have their own mess facilities, an idea which, with the approval of my superior officers, I opposed. At Anacostia, the third floor of the Administration Building had been converted into a WAVES barracks. Housing was scarce at Anacostia, and the majority of the men lived ashore.

The Chief Master at Arms felt that if the men and women used the same mess there would be rowdyism and show-off tactics on the part of the men. So emphatically did he stress the problem of keeping the men in good order that he sowed doubts in my mind. But I resolutely ignored them and told him that the plan for the joint use of the mess halls was approved, and we must go through with it, assigning certain tables in the cafeteria to the WAVES if he wished, until we found out what the problems if any, might be.

Late that night, forty WAVES came aboard: control tower operators, yeomen, storekeepers and seamen. The WAVE officers had reported a few weeks earlier. I have never seen a finer group of girls, all eager to see and do everything. They made up their bunks, took their showers, and turned in.

The Chief Master at Arms' account of the breakfast next morning was a classic.

"I never was so surprised in my life," he said. "The WAVES filed into the mess hall, picked up their trays, went through the line and then to the tables assigned to them. There wasn't a loud word of any kind by the men. What is more, all of the men had their hair combed and had on clean dungarees. You can send me more WAVES any time, and I'll start hunting for more barracks space for them."

What happened at Anacostia was typical of bases throughout the country. Recreation facilities were enlarged, group participation in sports was organized, dances in the hangars were scheduled, and drill teams on a competitive basis got under way. More and more the men found it unnecessary to go ashore every free evening for entertainment, and the number of cases at mast went to a new low. The men watched their language; ladies were present.

The commanding officers' reaction to inspections of WAVE barracks always amused me. I do not know where it originated, but very early in the war, some WAVE Master at Arms, upon the approach of the inspection party, shouted, "Man aboard!" It became the accepted warning everywhere. Communications watch-standers, who were sleeping in, merely remained in their bunks and out of the heads until after the inspection, thus saving themselves and the inspection party embarrassment.

The WAVES took pride in their barracks, made it their home, and accepted the rules and regulations. Talking with a group of them at a barracks meeting, I asked if they had found it difficult to adjust to barracks living with its strict rules and supervision.

One girl looked me squarely in the eyes and said, "At first, yes. But then I realized that it was the first time in my life that anyone cared whether I was home and in bed at a certain hour."

Such barracks meetings were arranged at my request so that I could meet firsthand as many enlisted WAVES as possible and discuss with them the plans under way in Washington. Sometimes they had in mind a matter not already resolved with their WAVE representative aboard. After a short period of informal conversation, we generally came to the heart of the matter. Usually it was something trivial, but still something that needed to be talked out. I found it a great advantage that I had been a Mustang, for many times, a WAVE would say, "We know you understand because you once were an enlisted woman also."

These meetings not only meant much to me, but I learned a great deal. Certain helpful suggestions I could pass on to other stations as I visited them. For example, at one station the interior of the barracks was gloomy and painting was needed. In talking with the commanding officer, I learned that paint could be made available by the Public Works Department. Upon learning this, the women volunteered to do the painting. Permission being granted, WAVE working parties on their liberty time did the job. The next station I visited, where similar painting was needed, I suggested how it coud be done.

The WAVES' willingness to do the work generally produced the paint and the men often helped out. At one station, the WAVES agreed to do four sailors' laundry for a week if they would, in turn, help with the painting. This worked out well until an inspection party noted the men's clothing on the lines in the WAVES' drying area. The final solution was that the station installed washing machines in the men's barracks also.

The problem of providing toilet facilities often proved to be a stumbling block when plans for receiving a contingent of WAVES were under way. For example, a commanding officer of an air station would say, "We want to have the WAVES but hangars, storerooms and other facilities are not equipped with toilets for women." Fortunately, early in the WAVE program, I found an answer at one naval air station where WAVE mechanics were happily working in the hangar. With the aid of an old-time male chief petty officer, they had solved the problem by installing a peg on the outside of the toilet facility and posting a sign, "Before entering here, hang up your hat." It worked. When a sailor's hat was on the peg, only a man entered; when a WAVE hat hung there, the women entered.

I quickly passed the word to other stations. The solving of this small problem meant that the immediate assignment of women to those stations not having additional toilet facilities need not be halted until they could be made available. Sometimes, because of the shortages caused by the war, such additional installations would require months.

In the matter of housing, particularly during the first year of the program for women, in-service non-agreement on policies between the Bureau of Aeronautics and the Bureau of Personnel caused frustration and unfortunate stalemate. An example of the stalemate was the matter of the assignment of personnel. In order for an activity to receive WAVES it was first necessary to have approved housing available. This policy was logical and acceptable to the Bureau of Aeronautics, but in attempting to carry it out is where the frustration arose. BuPers's stand was, "when you have housing ready, we will start sending personnel." The stand of the Bureau of Aeronautics was, "Tell us how many, and when you plan to send WAVES, and we will build accordingly. We must have that information in order to justify our requests for necessary funds to the Secretary of the Navy." Finally, in desperation, BuAer started building at several aviation activities to which BuPers admitted that they would send, but not how many, women. After approximately six months of discussion, sometimes heated and always frustrating, which I, as liaison officer, also experienced, every logical argument was exhausted. The Bureau of Personnel agreed to break the deadlock by providing estimates of the number of WAVES which would be supplied and the approximate date of their arrival. From that point on, the Bureau of Aeronautics was able to justify its building requests and a huge construction program got under way.

But trouble was not yet over. On the strength of proposed assignment figures, BuAer had its house in order to receive 1,300 enlisted women on 15 January 1943. On 1 January, this entire number was diverted to Naval Communications at the request of the Cominch (later Chief of Naval Operations). Fortunately, 525 enlisted WAVES had been screened for special aviation training and they, on 15 February, were supplied to meet the quotas of the first schools to train WAVES: aviation machinists mates, aviation metalsmiths, aerographer's mates, Link trainer instructors, and parachute riggers.

A carefully prepared list of activities where WAVES housing was available and the dates when additional facilities would be completed, was furnished. Unfortunately, this list was not used to any great extent. Assignment of enlisted WAVES, without due regard for ratings and housing, brought strong protests in writing from the field activities. Each of these air activities practically demanded that they do the assignment of WAVES to the air activities which were prepared to house them and utilize their services immediately. This procedure did follow the procedure already in existence for male enlisted personnel ordered to aviation activities. Finally, toward the end of 1943, BuPers delegated the authority of detailed assignment to the commandants of districts and chiefs of the functional air training commands, which method most satisfactorily met the needs of the service. Actually, the mechanics of screening and asignment were not completely correlated until the last days of the war program.

Part of the confusion was, of course, unavoidable on account of the pressure of the times and the overall shortage of personnel. A case in point is the priority given to Communications, which I have mentioned—a priority which the Bureau of Personnel could neither anticipate nor reject.

Always, when I visited a station, I would meet with the chaplains. They almost always had the "in" on what might become a problem, and always they worked closely with me to prevent them. Actually the chaplains welcomed the women aboard as an aid in their work with the enlisted men.

At one time, to a great number of men, liberty meant leaving their stations for a night or weekend on the nearest town. Movies were provided on the station and generally there were facilities for bowling, billards, swimming, shopping, etc. but as one young man told me, they saw "the faces of the same guys that you worked with all day, and no chance to see any gals except when a USO show comes." The arrival of the WAVES created the need for expanded recreational facilities. The WAVES didn't all go out on the town and more and more men started to stay on board. Dances, organized picnics, athletics, and chapel attendance increased greatly. One chaplain told me that the WAVES had brought an air of refinement to the service. "I know that many men are attending chapel now because the girl he is wanting to date sings in the choir. What the reason is for his attendance really doesn't matter, what does matter is the fact that he is renewing or forming a church habit. The mere presence of WAVES in the chow line brought more orderliness and courtesy than was ever achieved by the stoutest chief boatswain. And we do know that with more and more men staying on board instead of going out on the town, the discipline cases have decreased tremendously."

I remember, while on my visit to Hawaii in connection with inspecting housing facilities which might be converted for the use of WAVES, I pointed out to the public works officer on the commandant's staff who accompanied me, that the Quonset huts currently being used as chapels would probably prove to be entirely inadequate. He looked at me in amazement and remarked that they were never more than half occupied and that the number of WAVES planned would constitute a relatively small group. I was interested to note on subsequent inspection trips to Hawaii that all naval stations had found it necessary to almost triple chapel facilities.

One of the many outlets for WAVES was the writing and production of shows, usually in some form of musical comedy. One such effort was USS *Petticoat*, produced at Corpus Christi air station. For this venture, the WAVES not only constituted the *dramatis personae*, except for two men, and composed the entire score, but also wrote the dialogue and made the costumes, all on their own time, for this was recreation.

The show, which celebrated the WAVES' second anniversary, was such a huge success during its three performances that, on request, it was repeated for the public in the city of Corpus Christi.

Captain Radford, hearing of the signal success of the musical comedy, invited a group of leaders from the theatrical world to see the show in Corpus Christi and evaluate the possibility of putting it on in various cities to benefit recruiting. I was designated to accompany these representatives of five major motion picture companies along with three New York producers: Gilbert Miller, Oscar Hammerstein II, Howard Reinheimer, John Byron (Paramount), Sidney Phillips (MGM), Hal Horden (Columbia), Paul Peters (20th Century Fox) and Jake Wilk (Warner Brothers).

The trip to Corpus Christi was in itself dramatic. After a one-day visit at Pensacola, where the guests were introduced to aviation training, saw WAVES at work, and witnessed flight operations, we departed for Corpus Christi early in the afternoon in order to be on time for an official dinner given by Rear Admiral C.P. Mason, preceding the presentation of USS *Petticoat*. Unfortunately, just after goodbyes were waved, the plane ran off the runway and only finally stopped when its tail was high in the air and its nose buried deep in the mud. The pilot appeared forward and announced "Keep your seats, gentlemen, until we get a door open." Simultaneously I heard sirens as ambulance and fire-fighting equipment tore down the runway toward us. One by one we crawled toward the door, with those nearest to it going first to clear the aisle for others. My turn was not long in coming.

Captain Lester Hundt, the station CO, was by this time standing below the plane's door, and said, "Jump, Joy, and I'll catch you."

I jumped into his outstretched arms, and we both went sprawling in the mud. By the time all passengers were on the ground and the baggage removed, another plane stood by and we all went on board.

What a sorry sight we were when we deplaned at Corpus Christi to be met by the official party, headed by Admiral Mason, all in gleaming whites.

However, no one had been injured and there had been no fire. In the light of these blessings, our appearance was a minor inconvenience quickly rectified by a bath and change of clothing.

The banquet and show went off without a hitch, and my traveling companions were very much impressed, so much so that upon returning to New York, the group formed a committee with Oscar Hammerstein II as chairman. The consensus was, in their recommendations to Admiral Radford, that the nucleus of excellent entertainment in proper directional hands could be put on Broadway, provided that it was performed by naval personnel and not by professional actors, since it was a satire on the WAVES, and might be considered bad taste. Because of this and by reason of the fact that WAVES could not be spared from their jobs, the Navy decided against any attempt to put the play into general production.

But the tours to see the activities and work of the WAVES on the part of these men did have its effect. They spoke of these experiences as unforgettable and illuminating. Several members of the group requested any and all material regarding the WAVES; later several Hollywood pictures indicated the interest generated by this trip.

It is almost impossible to set up a program for WAVES at a school or activity without some contretemps. Such an occasion occurred in connection with the introduction of eleven WAVE officers into the navigation course at the Naval Aviation Training School at the Hollywood Beach Hotel in Hollywood, Florida, in August 1943.

The commanding officer, who in the spring had welcomed the idea of training the women, had departed, and his successor, who had just returned from sea duty, found the arrival of WAVES upsetting. When this word came, Captain Radford at once told me to head for Florida: "You'd better get down to Hollywood and see what you can do to calm down the commanding officer. He's scared to death because the women officers have just reported aboard for training."

I knew that all the proper arrangements had been made for the WAVES' housing, feeding, recreation, etc. Furthermore, as adults the women were entirely capable of looking after themselves. Nonetheless, I lost no time in catching a plane to Florida the next morning.

Lieutenant Florence Judge, one of the students as well as the senior woman officer in the group, met me. On the way to the school she described the arrangements for the women. Everything was satisfactory. Only one question had yet to be settled, probably because we had never visualized its being raised. This was a matter of wearing slacks, a necessity during instructional periods, as the WAVES climbed in and out of planes. Of course, the reasonable and proper thing to do was to declare slacks the uniform of the day for women officers. We did this at once, without consulting anyone, and it became policy. (This may seem like making a mountain out of a molehill, but these were the 1940s, not the 1970s.)

For the housing of women, Lieutenant Judge had recommended that the women be quartered in one wing of the hotel, the men in another; the public rooms would be used jointly as they are in any hotel. Later, in going over these plans with the new commanding officer, I congratulated him on making such satisfactory arrangements. A smile reflected his pleasure.

I always found it desirable to maneuver the commanding officers into a position of suggesting or recommending a plan which had already proved itself elsewhere and soliciting his opinion as to whether he thought it sound or workable at his installation. Almost without exception, we were in full agreement by the time our conferences ended. If there was no definite policy covering a specific situation—and this happened again and again in the early days—I had no qualms about establishing one, never giving away the fact that the rule had just that moment come into existence. Occasionally I slept uneasily after such a session, but I comforted myself with the thought that, by trusting to common sense, I had at least avoided making a grievous error.

The matter of housing for women officers did not present any great problems. At naval stations when bachelor officers' quarters were in existence the women were quartered there either in a wing or part of a wing, depending on the number of women originally reporting. As their numbers increased and as they relieved more and more men, they simply continued to take over more space. In the event no quarters were available as occurred in areas such as Washington, D.C., and San Francisco, hotel accommodations were commandeered. This take over was necessary because of the otherwise unavailability on a regular rental accommodation basis. The commandeering of entire hotels was also carried out in urban areas in order to house the enlisted women until barracks could be constructed for them.

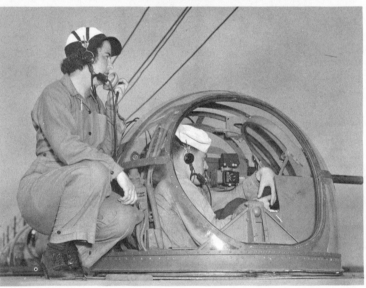

Garbed in coveralls, enlisted members of the Women's Reserve help attach the basket to a free balloon at the U.S. Naval Air Station, Moffett Field, California (*top*).

Girls behind the men behind the guns—members of the Women's Reserve instruct on electrically-operated .50 caliber machine gun turrets. They pass along their knowledge to male marksmen at the Naval Air Gunners School, Hollywood, Florida, training the aerial gunners of World War II (*above*).

A WAVE aviation machinist's mate (*opposite*) spins the prop of an SNJ training plane at the Naval Air Station, Jacksonville, Florida. She spent four months in training, learning how to repair and overhaul Navy fighting planes.

On the Job in Naval Aviation

FROM the beginning, when the legislation for the WAVES was being considered, the Bureau of Aeronautics addressed itself to the problem of determining the number to be trained. As a preliminary step in planning, the bureau made an analysis of the number of women that would be required by the aeronautical organization. Taking into account the physical limitations of women, the planners proceeded on the basic assumption that women could, nevertheless, be trained successfully to replace men. Based on the requirements of 50 air stations within the continental United States, the preliminary estimate was that 20,326 women could be utilized as follows:

Yeomen	1,801	Parachute riggers	257
Storekeepers	1,473	Link Trainer instructors	535
Line assistants	841	Aviation machinist mates	6,993
Messengers	333	Aviation radiomen	1,041
Chauffeurs	361	Pharmacist's mates	748
Tower watch	225	Aviation metalsmiths	1,253
Telephone operators	316	Cooks	1,406
Mail room clerks	169	Bakers	483
Chaplain assistants	139	Officers' stewards	232
Information assistants	122	Officers' bakers	340
Aerographer's mates	161	Waitresses	891
Photographer's mates	206		

It was this estimate of strength which Rear Admiral John H. Towers, Chief of the Bureau of Aeronautics, sent to the Chief of Naval Personnel on 14 September 1942, confirming the many conversations which had been carried on during the two months since the passage of legislation establishing the Women's Reserve. In his letter, Admiral Towers made certain suggestions which strongly reflected the recommendations of Captain Arthur W. Radford, then head of the Aviation Training Division:

"It is proposed that the training of enlisted personnel in specialized aviation ratings be carried out at existing establishments and in the same schools now in operation for the training of men in the same ratings. Recruit training would be given at the same time as is now done with general service ratings. This same plan, in general, is recommended in the case of officers of the Women's Reserve (administrative), in that those applying for aviation duty upon completion of the present naval indoctrination course at Smith College could be selected whose qualifications seem best designed for aviation activities. A short naval aviation indoctrination course can be arranged for this group at the existing school for AV(S) officers at the U.S. Naval Air Station, Quonset Point, Rhode Island." *

This insistence that the technical aviation program for WAVES be coeducational wherever practical was a principle which the Bureau of Aeronautics advocated and adhered to. This method, and the additional recommendations of Captain

* When the Bureau of Personnel did not agree to this plan, BuAer set up facilities at various naval air stations for aviation indoctrination of women coming on duty during the first six months of the program. Thereafter, when these officers were performing their jobs satisfactorily, officers subsequently arriving were given on-the-job indoctrination in naval aviation.

Radford, carried the program for women in aviation far beyond the initial goals.

As has been previously pointed out, the Bureau of Personnel leased college facilities for the training of women, separate from the training of men, and their indoctrination and training in general service ratings was conducted on this basis. But for aviation specialist training, the plans of the Bureau of Aeronautics were carried out. Actually, the Bureau of Personnel had its hands full to deal with the training of recruits already reporting for duty in other fields and was, I believe, relieved that BuAer would give the specialized aviation training needed by the women assigned to its stations and facilities.

The coeducational method proved to have definite advantages. First, it was far more economical since the naval facilities already in being could be utilized with fairly minor changes. Only one teaching staff was needed and any additional administrative staff was held to a minimum; such economy was particularly evident when only a small group of women at one time was to be trained. And since men and women would be working together as a team, being trained together insured easy adjustment.

Another advantage stemmed from the identical training—healthy competition. The women would go on duty knowing where they stood as compared with the men, and the men were bound to recognize that the women had been trained in exactly the same way and had competed for class standing. Such integration in the Navy also served to break down the idea of a separate corps and gave the women a sense of belonging to the Navy on the same footing as men.

For example, an early report on the training of metalsmiths at the Naval Air Technical Training Command at Norman, Oklahoma, read in part: "The WAVES proved early in the training that they could hold their own. In a class of 120, graduating in January of 1943, there were ten WAVES. Only 50 percent of the graduates could be rated. Seven of the WAVES or 70 percent of their number received their crows. In the class graduating in July of 1943, the two highest standing students were WAVES; in fact, five out of the top eight were WAVES."

This proficiency was honored. One instance I recall with pride and amusement. I was attending the graduation of a class at Norman. The assembly hall was filled with trainees—Navy men, WAVES, and women Marines. It was the custom of the commanding officer to present a heavy gold signet ring to the top-ranking graduate. When the Number One graduate was called, a five-foot-two WAVE came up on the stage. The commanding officer, with an appropriate remark, hung a red, white, and blue ribbon around her neck, from which was suspended the ring. In her case, it might more nearly have served as a bracelet. The trainees, as if they were one, rose and gave a lusty cheer.

The qualifications for women officers were very high, and advanced degrees were commonplace. The age span was set at from 20 to 50 years, and the majority of women represented in the service, in the beginning, were those in academic fields; that is, they were teachers, deans of women, school staff members, and administrators. This was fortunate, for there was a great demand for women on the staffs of the many schools the Navy was conducting. Later, when these needs were met, it was natural to shift the emphasis in recruitment to those with administrative, technical, and business experience, particularly in expanding industries.

While some male officers strongly expressed their desire for WAVES with experience other than in teaching, they discovered that women officers of diverse talents could, given proper training, assume the responsibilities of their assigned jobs. Whatever their academic or professional background, WAVE officers made a remarkable adjustment to the Navy and its way of doing things.

On-the-job training became an exceedingly useful system in preparing and adapting those enlisted WAVES who had not attended specialist schools to new tasks. As rapid technical advances, gained by constant and intensive experimentation, opened up many hitherto unexplored fields, both men and women had to be trained on the job. So rapidly did these fields expand many specialized jobs were, for the most part, not covered by specific ratings when the war ended.

Women proved invaluable as laboratory technicians and were particularly gifted in the assembly and repair of testing equipment. As the number of men ashore dwindled, more and more the women were, of necessity, placed in new projects. For example, they became the operators of secret aviation ground control devices (ground control approach in its experimental stage) and, in similar capacities, participated as specialists and operators in a highly secret night fighter training project.

In these and other experimental programs undertaken during and immediately after the war, the women were, of necessity, carrying out the jobs at hand. Before World War II ended, the Navy had reached the bottom of the manpower barrel. The Fleet needed all the competent and trained men it could get and supplying this need depleted the staffs of the shore establishment. The WAVES stepped in as replacements and, to the surprise of many seniors in the service, the stations continued to repair and fly planes. The voices coming from the control towers were those of women. As new experimental projects developed, the Navy depended on women. The early assumption of officers like Admiral Towers, Captain Radford, and many other forward-looking naval aviators, that women, given the proper training, could satisfactorily fill the aviation billets ashore, was entirely substantiated.

The typical enlisted WAVE was a woman of better than average ability, well motivated and eager to do a job in the Navy. On her primarily rested the burden and largely the success of the WAVE program. The qualifications for enlistment were high and attracted one of the finest groups of young women in the United States. As enlisted WAVES they could see at once the direct results of their efforts and in consequence, their morale was high.

For the thousands of young men who were being trained as pilots, the presence of WAVES presented no problems of adjustment. They had no preconceived notions about the Navy, for the Navy was new to them also. From the day a man checked into his air station for training until the day he was designated a naval aviator, he found the WAVES part of every phase of station operations: administrative, clerical, mechanical, or instructional. In the primary and secondary schools, the young men had had women teachers; they had attended classes with women in their high schools and colleges and now the Navy was "coeducational".

At the training centers, WAVES scheduled each pilot's flights, logged his flight hours and directed his takeoffs and landings. They packed, checked, and issued his parachute; checked and recorded his grades; inspected and refueled his plane, and also repaired it; sorted and delivered his mail, gave him his pay and made out his allotments; and instructed him in instrument flying and free gunnery.

I remember one WAVE "mech" (AMM), a plane captain. Grease-streaked, wind-blown, her hands raw and red, she watched intently, almost reverently, as her plane soared into the skies in a squadron formation. You could see her pride in its beauty and precision. Impulsively she spoke to me, "Funny thing; when civilians talk of my being in the WAVES, they usually mention the word *glamor*. I'm not sure quite what they mean, but when I see my plane flying safely in the sky and know it will come home safely, I feel sure that it is due partly to my taking the best care of it I can. Well, there is a feeling inside me that is so completely satisfying and so sort of uplifting that perhaps that is glamor. If it is, we have plenty of it."

Just like this WAVE, many others became plane captains. As aviation machinist mates they were on duty 12 hours a day, seven days a week with every eighth day free. The pride and devotion of the captain of a ship could not be greater than that of each WAVE plane captain as she worked steadily and meticulously to make sure her plane was ready for flight. In preparation for the flight of a squadron she warmed up the engines, turned the oil strainers and propellers, set the controls and started on signal. It was she who checked and initialed a daily inspection form listing 66 items that constituted her maintenance checkoff list before she certified that the plane was ready. After the pilot had signed the check sheet accepting the plane, she removed the chocks and guided the plane out from the apron by signalling it or by pushing it, with the aid of one or two WAVES on a wing.

Nor was her task complete at that point. When the plane returned the plane captain guided it to chock, signalled the pilot, chocked the wheels, and checked the pilot's report on the condition of the plane. After the pilot left, she refueled the plane, checked the switches, then wiped down the struts, cowling and air scoop, the windshield and the sides of the plane. In case of trouble she notified the schedule board and stood by the plane to aid with repair. She repeated this procedure for six flights a day.

While visiting one of the naval training centers one day, I talked with the chief in charge of the line. He was a typical old-timer: clean dungarees faded to a light blue, his cap perched at a jaunty angle, his voice pitched almost to a growl, and the small, almost undetectable, wad of tobacco in his mouth. I seized the opportunity to ask how the WAVES were doing.

He answered me bluntly that he hadn't wanted WAVES but he'd had to take them or nothing. "But now I have hundreds of them. They're all over the place."

I followed his glance. I could see the WAVES in their overalls, their hair in turbans, climbing in and out of the planes, cleaning, inspecting, and repairing them.

One WAVE approached the chief with a report on a certain plane and departed. The chief then said to me with a twinkle in his eye. "She was the first to be made a plane captain. She's good. I'll have to admit that I've never had cleaner planes on the line, and I've never had more careful inspections. I'll keep the WAVES even though they have one big fault I can't seem to correct."

"What it that, chief?" I asked.

"Well, they don't take to shortcuts. When I tell them how a certain gadget is to be repaired, they say, 'But, chief, on page so-and-so of the manual it says....' They've had good training and, given time, they'll work out their own shortcuts."

"How do the pilots react to the WAVES servicing their planes?" I asked.

"They're satisfied. Why shouldn't they be? The WAVES teach them aircraft gunnery and instrument flying; they man the control towers and pack their parachutes."

He lifted his hat by the visor, scratched his head with his three free fingers, looked me straight in the eye and said, "To think I have lived so long!"

One Navy custom the student pilots were quick to adopt was that of personally thanking the packer who had packed the parachute that had saved him in an emergency. One day at a primary training command station, a cadet, having completed a safe parachute landing, checked the tag on his chute and found it had been packed by "Weiderman." At the packing loft, he asked for Weiderman. In response, WAVE Weiderman appeared. The pilot could only gasp, "Are you Weiderman?"

The answer was affirmative. Without waiting to greet her further, he fled, but half an hour later he was back, this time with a box of candy which he delivered with the fitting expressions of gratitude.

A simple visit to a control tower at a naval air station makes it clear why the standards for air controllmen were high. I shall never forget one occasion when, with members of the Educational Advisory Council, I visited a control tower with its ear-splitting din. The voices on the receivers were deafening and certainly confusing, yet there sat the WAVES, each at her own microphone, directing the many training planes in the air and keeping the traffic pattern organized.

Suddenly, it became obvious that something unusual was happening. A plane had developed landing gear trouble and the pilot's radio was not functioning. The controllers stepped up the action. Though there was tension, there was no confusion. Each controller instructed the planes in her landing pattern to form a new pattern in order to clear the runways for the aircraft in trouble. The WAVE operator directing this complicated maneuver continued to give directions in a clear, steady voice.

We all watched the plane while a pilot/instructor went aloft waving a wheel to alert the other pilot that only one wheel on his landing gear was in the *down* position. All fire-fighting equipment and an ambulance took their places on the field, and all hands held their breath, and, I believe, prayed. The lad made it down safely with no great damage to his plane. But what I remember chiefly is the calmness of the WAVES in the control tower and the clarity of the voices that gave instructions to all other planes to resume their former, prescribed landing procedures.

The young men training to become pilots accepted the WAVE tower operators and their instructions without question. However, combat pilots, trained in an earlier day and rotated from the Fleet, found it something of a shock to hear a woman's voice coming from the tower.

One pilot described his experience. He had arrived in San Diego, fresh from the Pacific theater, and was ferrying a plane to the east coast. All went according to standard procedures until he neared the naval air station at Jacksonville. After identifying himself, he requested instructions for landing. They came to him precisely and clearly. In relating the incident to me he said, "I was so confused on hearing the beautiful voice of a woman that I sat in stunned silence until the voice said, 'Navy 51700, do you read me?' and then I was still so confused I said 'Yes, Ma'am'."

Upon landing, this pilot did what many another returning pilot did. He climbed to the tower to make sure that he had really been brought down by a woman.

"We'd been hearing from the new pilots all this talk about WAVES and what they were doing, but we just didn't believe them," he said.

When the war ended and the prospect of mustering out all WAVES was imminent, the word from many pilots ran like this: "Don't take our gals away. Their voices are better and they have more patience. They have cheered us many a time when that was just what we needed."

Like all other WAVES, the tower operators had mastered their task. They had been trained to be alert to any factor outside the normal pattern of a plane or pilot in the air. If the flight was in any difficulty or if a pilot's voice was uncertain or indicated stress or confusion, the controller was prepared to assist.

But the WAVES in special aviation ratings were certainly outnumbered by the WAVES in the so-called general service ratings who were assigned to aviation activities, large and small, from coast to coast. They were the yeomen, storekeepers, communication specialists, hospital corpsmen and technicians, pharmacist's mates, dental technicians, and other specialists. In this last group there were recruiters, mailmen, masters-at-arms. A very large group of women designated as seamen when they completed training at the recruit school, went to their duty assignments and received "on the job" training.

The many assigned to air stations as seamen carried out the multitude of tasks of a general nature crying to be done. They learned specialities on the job and were eligible to qualify for ratings in the field of their service once they had gained sufficient knowledge to pass the examinations, or they were recommended for training at one of the prescribed schools.

In addition to the seamen, the largest number of enlisted women serving in the general service ratings at air stations were yeomen, storekeepers, radiomen, and hospital corpsmen. The very fact of being assigned to naval air stations meant that their duties made them a part of the naval aviation establishment. At air stations, they received additional and specialized training, particularly storekeepers who became thoroughly at ease in the air nomenclature and were as deeply committed to naval aviation as the aviation ratings.

Storekeepers functioned in supply and disbursing offices, clothing and small stores, and, of course, the commissary, devoting themselves to tasks not far removed from civilian pursuits. Other WAVE storekeepers were in the shop stores where they requisitioned, checked and stored aircraft parts and accessories, from diverse and multiple types of nuts, bolts, washers, gaskets, etc., to complete wing assemblies, center sections, flaps, and ailerons. Like the WAVE machinists and metalsmiths, they found their tasks vastly different from their civilian occupations.

The yeomen were the clerks of naval aviation, the clerical force that kept the innumerable records of which there seemed

to be no end; operational and statistical reports, flight
schedules, flight hours, engine checks, crash and accident
reports, training records, and a multitude of others. Their
paperwork was never done—at least, not for the duration.

Admiral John H. Towers, Lieutenant Commander Joy Hancock, Lieutenant Commander Jean Palmer, and Admiral R. L. Ghormley (*top*) discuss necessary preparations prior to the arrival of members of the Women's Reserve for duty in Hawaii.

WAVES board a Navy transport en route to Hawaii—the first time in history members of the Women's Reserve were transported overseas for duty (*left, above*). They arrived on 6 January 1945.

These two WAVES (*right, above*) were assigned to the control tower at the U.S. Naval Air Station, Honolulu.

Greeted with a traditional welcoming kiss and a colorful flower lei, Captain Hancock (*opposite*) arrives in Hawaii to visit WAVES stationed there.

The WAVES Overseas

Now that the WAVES had proved their worth in the minds of skeptics, the Navy, needing to rotate men to the continental United States and from the Fleet, largely as a morale factor, requested the Congress to enact legislation to permit WAVES to serve at certain overseas bases in the Pacific area and in England. Requests from those bases for their services were accumulating and BuPers moved strongly for this permissive legislation. Two bills to permit this overseas service were introduced but both were defeated.

While the matter hung fire, the Bureau of Aeronautics made a survey of its aviation overseas needs. This survey indicated that men could be replaced by WAVES according to these percentages: yeomen, 85 percent; storekeepers, 60 percent; radiomen, 35 percent; telegraphers, 50 percent; aviation machinist mates, 15 percent; aviation metalsmiths, 20 percent; aviation machinist mates (instruments), 35 percent; seamen, 30 percent; control tower operators, 90 percent; Link trainer instructors, 65 percent; gunnery specialists, 50 percent; hospital corpsmen, 50 percent; aerographer's mates, 50 percent; parachute riggers, 70 percent.

On 23 June 1944, the Deputy Chief of Naval Operations (Air) forwarded a letter to the Chief of Naval Personnel, requesting 3,759 enlisted WAVES for naval air stations in the Tenth and Fifteenth Naval Districts and Hawaii. As we looked toward the eventual passage of permissive legislation, many a conference was held with Captain McAfee and the women officers assigned as assistants on the staffs of the commandants and air command directors. We studied and tentatively agreed on criteria on which to base the selection of the WAVES for overseas service, centers for staging and distribution, uniform requirements, and housing facilities. Even the form for application for overseas duty was drawn up. All of these findings were presented as recommendations for approval, which was granted.

We were, therefore, prepared to go into action when the third attempt to obtain legislation permitting overseas duty succeeded, as an amendment to Public Law 441, and passed by the Seventy-eighth Congress, becoming law on 27 September 1944. Although this measure restricted the overseas assignments to the American theater (Alaska, West Indies, and Panama) and Hawaii, it was felt that real progress had been made. Two days later, a letter containing the results of the studies which we had made became the bible for overseas assignment of WAVES. This letter was entitled "all naval activities in continental limits of the United States for members of the Women's Reserve—policies and procedures covering selection for an assignment to." The restrictive clauses in the original legislation regarding the assignment of women to duty on board naval vessels or in aircraft were modified, so that orders to duty involving flying for personnel of the Women's Reserve were not limited to certain types of aircraft. Only aircraft engaged in combat missions were excluded, and duty aboard noncombatant ships of the Navy (transports) could be had.

For members of the Women's Reserve making application for duty outside the continental limits of the United States, these were the ground rules:

1. Only those who had served six months on continuous active duty, exclusive of time spent in training, were eligible. If two individuals were equally qualified, preference was to be given to the one with longer service.

2. Satisfactory conduct, health, and work records were required.

3. Only those who had demonstrated maturity, a sense of responsibility, adaptability, and emotional stability were to be considered.

4. Only those free from any form of dependency which would require their presence in the United States were considered. Dependency arising after the assignment overseas would not normally be considered as a reason for returning to the United States. Any individual who had at any time submitted a request for transfer or discharge, based on dependency, was ineligible for overseas duty.

5. Applicants had to volunteer additionally for duty outside the continental limits of the United States. Preference of area could be stated, but definite assignment to the area was, of course, not guaranteed. (Due to war's ending, women were sent only to Hawaii).

6. While overseas assignments were normally made for a minimum of 18 months, no commitment was made to return personnel to the United States at the end of that period.

7. No leave to return to the United States would be granted to one on an overseas assignment.

8. Individuals who submitted applications would be considered available for selection unless cancellation of the application was submitted through official channels before orders were received.

Women officers were also required to meet strict, high qualifications. Whether an officer or enlisted women, the candidates had to be certified by their commanding officers as approved in work, conduct and health after their records had been carefully reviewed by a board appointed by the commanding officers. Such screening boards were also established for each bureau in the Navy Department.

Early in October 1944, Lieutenant Commander Jean Palmer (assistant to Captain McAfee), and I, then a lieutenant commander, were sent overseas to survey proposed WAVE assignments and to report on housing in the Hawaiian Islands. I had no question in the matter of job assignments since I knew firsthand the quality of the work which the WAVES had done in the United States. The big question in my mind was whether the housing facilities would be adequate. I need not have worried. I had not taken into account the presence and the proficiency of the Seabees in the Pacific area. No combat group, in my opinion, had a more spontaneous "can do" attitude. Furthermore, since the WAVES had been requested, much of the preliminary planning for their well-being had been done before we arrived.

Others making the trip to Hawaii were Colonel Ruth Streeter, director of Women Marines, and Major Marian Dryden, the Women's Representative for women in Marine aviation. The day after our arrival in Hawaii, Captain Dorothy Stratton, director of the Coast Guard's SPARS, arrived.

Our flight from San Francisco to Hawaii had differed from the flying I had done on my constant inspection trips and for Jean Palmer, who was ordinarily all but fastened to her desk job in BuPers, it was a real experience. The cross-country trip to San Francisco in a nonpressurized cabin was made uncomfortable for Jean by a flareup of sinusitis, but, nonetheless, in the middle of the night, she disembarked at a twenty-minute stop to greet some relatives.

The clearance routine in San Francisco, as well as the fact that we were not told the time of our plane's departure west, or from which field, made me feel that finally I was getting nearer the actual combat area. Just before dawn, I received a telephone call which entirely satisfied my "who-dun-it" type of thinking. The caller merely stated: "An official car will pick you up in twenty minutes. Be on hand." We were.

At once we were whisked to a field twenty miles away where we were put through the final check-out procedures. Final they may have been, but brief they were not.

Much, much later, as we flew over the Golden Gate Bridge, the sun, a huge red ball, was just slipping down over the edge of the horizon, so utterly beautiful that even now in memory I can see it. The old jingle, "Red sun at night, sailor's delight," kept running through my mind.

We traveled on a chartered Pan American flying boat with a lounge and several bunks, one of which was assigned to me. During a visit to the control cabin to watch the pilot, navigator and engineer at work, a silent gesture on the part of the navigator made us look down to see, on the dark waters below, a ship burning. I never learned the outcome or if any measures were taken to get aid to the flaming vessel. I do know that we were maintaining radio silence.

While I was in the control cabin, the navigator said that we had just reached "the point of no return," a phrase I heard for the first time, and one that can still cause a shiver, so poignantly does it suggest hazard.

I turned in shortly and lay listening to the roar of the motors. On the metal deck adjacent to my bunk, and near the piled-up baggage, six male ensigns wrapped in blankets were sleeping. Other passengers were distributed in the remaining bunks and in the lounge. I awakened near dawn and went into the washroom. When I returned, on my bunk were three of the ensigns, dead to the world but warm. In the dim light I managed to find my shoes and jacket and I proceeded to sit on the deck with the other three ensigns until daylight. I just didn't have the heart to disturb the lads in my bunk.

Toward noon, Diamond Head loomed ahead, surrounded by beautiful colored tropical waters. Down we went to the water runway cut into the coral at the Naval Air Station, Honolulu.

What a reception awaited us! On the dock were Admiral Chester W. Nimitz, Commander in Chief, Pacific; Admiral John H. Towers, Chief of Staff; General Beresford Waller, USMC, as well as the commanding officers of the naval air stations, and the Commandant of the 14th Naval District, Admiral Robert L. Ghormley. Picture after picture was taken to record the arrival of the first WAVES in Hawaii.

From that point on, an unbelievably heavy schedule got under way. Every minute was planned for that week, but we managed to survive. We went from one activity to another for a succession of conferences and inspections at which we made some on-the-spot recommendations.

Our headquarters were in the bachelor officer quarters at the Naval Air Station, Honolulu, commanded by Captain David S. Ingalls, USNR. These accommodations turned out to be only a place to rush to, bathe, change and secure fresh uniforms, and catch some sleep. Every activity on Oahu and the other islands had proposed barracks accommodations, ready with alterations and with personnel requirements drawn up. For the women in the general service ratings who would serve under the direction of the general shore establishment, a huge section of Quonset huts was set aside on Oahu.

This hut city, originally constructed for Navy men, was being converted for the women; many of the huts had never been occupied. When converted for the women, each hut, arranged in cubicles with double-decker bunks, accommodated thirty-two. One of every eight huts was a recreation facility. The occupants of every three huts shared a Quonset hut equipped with laundry, head and shower facilities. A dispensary and a chapel would be available.

A large recreation area, which included an open air movie theater, playing field, tennis courts, ship service store and a dance floor, was provided. Such extensive recreation facilities had been provided at all stations primarily because of the

6:00 P.M. curfew for all enlisted personnel and 10:00 P.M. curfew for all officers and civilians. Since all personnel were required to be on board at these hours, each activity provided the recreational activities which would ordinarily be found off station.

Jean Palmer and I were invited to speak to many civilian groups, to answer all questions regarding the WAVES. An influx of several thousand young women was bound to have impact on the civilian population since dependents of servicemen stationed there were not permitted to come to Hawaii.

One young man at the Junior Chamber of Commerce luncheon, during a period of questions, asked, "What are the WAVES really like?" This was my answer: "They are the same as your sister or the sister of your best friend. They come from families on many levels of American society. They have met and maintained the high standards set for them for their initial entry into the Navy. They are all volunteers and, to serve in Hawaii they are obliged to volunter again, and be carefully screened. They have passed rigorous tests in terms of efficiency, conduct, stability, and devotion to duty. I doubt if anywhere in the world you will find a group of women so catalogued."

The first women to arrive in Hawaii on permanent duty orders were Lieutenant Commander Eleanor Grant Rigby and Lieutenant Winifred R. Quick, the first to be the District Director of the Women's Reserve and the latter to be assistant to the District Personnel Officer.

On the day before I flew back to the United States, I was, as usual, moving at a quick pace toward the exit of an administration building on Ford Island (Pearl Harbor), headed for another conference. As I passed through the door I encountered a group of male naval officers. I glanced at them, then gasped with astonishment, for I looked squarely into the eyes of my brother, Lieutenant Commander Cooper B. Bright, whom I had not seen in nearly two years. He had been serving aboard the aircraft carrier, USS *Yorktown*, which had just come into Pearl Harbor for repairs. Our instantaneous bear hug brought looks of astonishment to the faces of the officers. The explanation was classic and true. Cooper turned to his companions and said, "Believe it or not, fellows, she's my sister."

My evening schedule was immediately changed, and I went aboard the *Yorktown* as the guest of my brother for dinner. I was told that I was the first WAVE aboard a combatant ship outside the continental limits of the United States.

On leaving the ship it was necessary for us to cross the hangar deck where a movie was being shown. Even in the semi-darkness, my uniform was spotted. A young sailor suddenly shouted, "WAVE aboard!" and a lusty cheer rose from a thousand throats.

With the same enthusiasm, the WAVES were welcomed when a little later they arrived in Hawaii. Even en route they proved to be those same "eager beavers." Yeoman second class June I. Read reported their activities aboard ship:

"We didn't swab the decks or navigate the ship, but our unit of WAVES did give those aboard one ship an idea of how landlubbers can correct manuals, type reports, and do many other jobs while en route to Hawaii. It all started a day or so after we got underway. After exploring the ship and getting our sea legs, we were actually looking for something to do— even work. Our ship had been in dry dock for several months, getting repairs and new equipment, which involved many extra reports and changes in records. So when the officers heard we were anxious to go to work, they asked for yeoman, store-keeper, and pharmacist mate volunteers.

"The storekeepers told me storekeepers made all the manual changes. It was a great help because the manual hadn't been changed during the past six months while in dry dock. I guess the boys had been kept too busy preparing to again go out and fight rather than take care of those minor details. One of the officers told me our ship had been in seven major engagements. The manual was so thick and the hinges so rusty, it took two of the men to take it apart.

"With my usual Navy luck, which has been all good, I was assigned to the first lieutenant's office. It gave me an idea of shipboard procedures, for all the activity seemed to center around this office. The first lieutenant planned the battle station watch bills, and the chief bos'n was on hand bellowing orders to be piped to the crew.

"We all found typing aboard ship quite a feat. We had to type furiously when the ship rolled to port, and only shift the carriage when she'd roll to starboard; otherwise there was so much force the carriage wouldn't move at all and the letter keys would pile up. So we soon learned to throw the carriage with the roll of the ship; it was like typing to music. We had to learn also to balance our weight in our chairs to keep them from sliding from one side of the office to the other....

"We accepted our mid-morning and mid-afternoon 'joe' as a Navy tradition, but we learned that the coffee was a treat from the men. One of the male yeomen told me that they had heard scuttlebutt that the WAVES were to be on board, but no one believed it until we came up the gangplank. The men were a little unhappy about it at first, for they felt that drastic changes would be made in their way of life, but they didn't know they would be pleasant ones.

"We like to think the crew really appreciated our help as much as we enjoyed working. We feel we are real 'salts' now that we have worked aboard ship. And the sea stories we will tell our grandchildren!"

The WAVES selected for overseas reported to the Naval Training and Distribution Center, Camp Shoemaker, California, in December 1944 to make their final preparations before sailing for Hawaii. Here they received special instructions dealing with war orientation; the Hawaiian area, military courtesy, censorship, shipboard procedure, abandon ship drill, and deportment aboard ship. In addition, all were given additional physical examinations. All uniforms were inspected for serviciability and additional items were purchased. All excess clothing was shipped home before embarkation. The WAVES were organized into platoon groups and these platoons were maintained all during the wait for space aboard the transports and continued while on board ship. Two officers were assigned to each platoon.

On 6 January 1945, the first contingent of WAVES reporting for duty in Hawaii marched down the gangplank to the music of a Navy band playing "Aloha." Shouts of aloha and the waving of white caps accompanied the marching tread of the women as platoon followed platoon ashore. The first WAVE ashore was Mary Babine, seaman first class, of Gloucester, Massachusetts. A brilliant lei was placed around her neck by a photographer's mate, and with the flowers went the traditional kiss of welcome to Hawaii.

The WAVES were wearing their summer grey and white seersucker uniforms and the newly authorized garrison cap. Each carried her musette bag and raincoat; the heavy gear of more than 200 duffel bags was handled by a working party of sailors. The officer in charge of the contingent was Lieutenant Winifred Love of Moorefield, West Virginia. Lieutenant Commander Rigby was on hand to greet the women. At the pier, grinding a motion picture camera to record the occasion was Lief Erickson, photographer's mate first class, a former motion picture and stage star. So intent were the WAVES in this overall, unusual experience of landing in

Hawaii, that he went unnoticed as he crouched behind his camera, at least for the time being.

The WAVES were mustered on the pier and then loaded in busses for the journey to the receiving station at the Naval Air Station, Honolulu, where they were housed while awaiting further assignment to the facilities throughout the islands where they would be serving. Although everything was carried out in military fashion, in between salutes the WAVES craned their necks to get their first view of Hawaii.

Among these first arrivals was one WAVE who was particularly eager to see the islands with which her name was associated. She was Aloha M. Cassity, yeoman second class, of Modesto, California.

The arrival of the WAVES in Hawaii was in sharp contrast to their departure from the West Coast, where their embarkation had been surrounded with the secrecy common to all troop movement for overseas in wartime. Only the port director officers were on the docks to bid the women farewell. The first unit was followed by monthly quotas of several hundred until VJ Day.

A letter written at the time by one of the WAVES in Hawaii describes the reaction of the women who served there: "It can be truthfully said that not one WAVE here would want to turn around and go back; each girl wanted to be here, and the fact that they wanted us here is also important.... There's a big job to be done and the WAVES are helping to do it. When the war is over and someone says, 'Remember Pearl Harbor?' we can answer, 'Yes, I was there.'"

Another WAVE, writing after six months in the islands, described something of life overseas: "In all our minds, there was the same question, 'What was it going to be like?' We were to find the answer gradually. Our jobs were much the same. We worked in warehouses and offices, in control towers, gunnery schools and dispensaries. We typed, kept pay accounts and service records, checked supplies, drove jeeps, directed air traffic, worked in laboratories and wards, taught combat air crewmen. We lived in a barracks and ate in a chow hall. We wore grey seersucker uniforms and hit the sack at lights-out. We learned, in short, that be it Maryland or Maui, the Navy is the Navy.

"But in our leisure hours, our liberty days, there was a difference. This was Hawaii, and we began to find our way around. True, it was wartime Hawaii and there were many restrictions, but the old 'Paradise of the Pacific' was still there. On our liberty days, we went sightseeing. We rode the

10,000 feet up Haleakala to take a look at her fifteen-mile-long crater. We went to luaus and ate poi and lomi-lomi salmon, and pig roasted in a pit.... We rode through miles and miles of growing sugar cane and vast fields of pineapple. We sunned ourselves on coral beaches and swan in the blue Pacific....

"We began to pick up a few of the more common Hawaiian words. Newcomers like ourselves, we learned, were *malihinis*. Things that were bad were *pilou*. When a thing was finished, it was *pau*. We no longer say, 'hello,' 'goodbye,' 'good luck,' but 'Aloha'....

"It has been more than six months now since the first WAVES came to Maui. We're still *malihinis*, but we've begun to feel at home, and we're beginning to know the island. We can play a few songs and mix Hawaiian words with our own. We've begun to recognize the flowers—the scarlet showers of blossoms on the royal poinciana trees, the blue-purple of the jacaranda, the many colors of the hibiscus, the unforgettable odor of the ginger.... When the day comes for us to go back to the mainland, it will not be easy to say 'Aloha'. "

In all, 350 officers and 3,659 WAVES served in Hawaii. In the naval aviation establishment were 127 officers and 1,526 enlisted women. Their duty stations included Headquarters, Commander Naval Air Bases; 14th Naval District; Naval Supply Depot at Pearl Harbor; Naval Air Stations at Barber's Point, Honolulu, Kahalui, Kaneohe, Pearl Harbor, Puuene, the Navy Weather Central, and communication stations.

While Hawaii was the first of the approved wartime overseas activities to be opened to WAVE assignments, it also turned out to be the last during World War II, for a little over seven months after the arrival of the first WAVES, the victory was won and demobilization was under way.

Captain Hancock confers with Fleet Admiral Chester W. Nimitz, Chief of Naval Operations (*top*). Admiral Nimitz, one of the doubters in the early days, changed his mind and became a firm backer of integration of women into the regular Navy.

Advanced to captain and sworn in as director of the Women's Reserve on 26 July 1946, Joy Bright Hancock (*above*) receives her "eagles" from Vice Admiral Louis E. Denfeld, Chief of Naval Personnel. Proudly looking on are her brothers, Commanders Cooper B. Bright and Ward H. Bright, USN.

By the end of World War II, the WAVES could proudly look back on their accomplishments. Thousands were demobilized, but many, like these trainees at Hunter (*opposite*) stayed on to serve in the peacetime Navy.

Victory and Demobilization

W<small>HEN</small> victory came in 1945, first in Europe and then in the Pacific, there came the summing up—and demobilization. No sooner had we enjoyed the excitement and exhilaration of victory than every effort was directed toward a fast return to peacetime ways.

At the end of the war, the Women's Reserve of the Navy had on duty approximately 8,000 officers and 78,000 enlisted personnel, with 8,000 in training. The WAVES could, with good reason, take pride in their record. In terms of percentage, the women comprised 18 percent of the total naval personnel assigned to the shore establishment in the United States. They had not only released 50,500 men for duty afloat or overseas but had also taken over some 27,000 other jobs in the greatly expanded naval shore establishment. Approximately 20,000 WAVES, twice the number originally proposed for the entire Women's Reserve, were serving in the Navy Department, Washington, D.C., and the Potomac River Naval Command. They comprised 55 percent of the uniformed personnel in the Navy Department.

In their first three years, the responsibilities assumed by the WAVES had steadily increased. They were handling about 80 percent of the work involved in the administration and supervision of the Navy mail service for the entire Fleet and the Navy's extra-continental activities. In Radio Washington, the nerve center of the Navy's entire communications system, WAVES filled 75 percent of the total allowances. In the Bureau of Personnel, 70 percent of its workers were WAVES.

Thirty-eight ratings were opened to enlisted women, with approximately 14,000 serving as yeomen. In the Hospital Corps ratings there were 13,000, and 1,000 additional recruits per month were being selected for training in this service because of the expanding rehabilitation program. More than 23,000 were serving in naval aviation, and, of this number, 1,000 were teaching instrument flying to 4,000 men each day. Others taught aircraft gunnery and celestial navigation. In the Naval Air Transport Service, flight orderlies were serving on almost all domestic routes, as well as on the runs to Hawaii and Europe.

Over 100 women had qualified as chief petty officers and more than 1,000 former enlisted WAVES had been commissioned.

The WAVES were privileged to be a part of the forces preparing for peace. Dean Virginia Gildersleeve, chairman of the Advisory Council for Women in the Navy, was the only woman in the U.S. delegation to the United Nations Conference for International Organization held in San Francisco in the summer of 1945. Her request for WAVES to be assigned to assist the U.S. delegation was readily granted by the Navy. The Navy temporarily relieved Commander Elizabeth Reynard of her duties as Commandant of Seamen at the Recruit Training School at Hunter College in order for her to assist Dean Gildersleeve, whose office was entirely staffed by WAVES, the only military women to be assigned to this great historical conference.

Also on loan was Lieutenant (junior grade) Mary Ely McDonald, who was attached to the joint post-war committee of the Joint Chiefs of Staff in Washington. Hers was the difficult task of setting up the secretariat for the U.S. Military-Naval Delegation of the conference. Lieutenant Mary Bowman, Ensign Catherine Harty, and Yeoman first class Mary Bradburn were loaned by the Fleet Post Office. They handled the tremendous volume of mail that poured in.

That the hours were long and the tasks occasionally tedious seemed not to matter to the WAVES for they knew it was an honor to be part of the history-making process of creating the United Nations.

With the arrival of VJ Day, the problems of demobilization seemed suddenly to descend upon the Navy. Although much work had been done by the demobilization section of the Bureau of Personnel, its recommendations had not been confirmed. Thus machinery for the separation centers had not passed the experimental stage and no definite plans had been made for implementation overnight. As one officer observed, "The Japanese have betrayed us again with a sneak surrender."

Uncertainty and reverses in planning were not new, and with this the Women's Reserve had some experience when a slow-up in recruiting and training was ordered a year earlier. When, during the first part of 1944, large numbers of men were released from naval hospitals as limited-duty personnel, it was evident that the Bureau of Medicine and Surgery was doing a better salvage job than the Navy had dared to hope and was returning to active duty ashore an unexpectedly large proportion of casualties. The increase of limited-duty men obviously diminished the need for additional WAVES at shore bases. Accordingly, the figure of 87,000 was to be considered the full quota for women and their procurement was reduced to a "replacement only" basis. The task of closing schools began when the last class of officers left Northampton in December 1944. Drastic reductions were ordered in the number of enlisted women at Recruit School, Hunter.

But these steps proved premature. The Bureau of Personnel had agreed to provide replacements for WAVES transferred out of a command or discharged, and these demands were unexpectedly high. Furthermore, the Bureau of Medicine and Surgery obtained permission to procure and train 10,000 WAVE corpsmen, over and above the manpower ceiling, for service in convalescent hospitals. Accordingly, the "replacement" input for indoctrination training at Hunter, once cut to 500 monthly, was raised again to 2,000 and continued that high until VJ Day.

The indoctrination school operated until October 1945, and the activity was not decommissioned until February 1946. The last class of Hospital Corps WAVES graduated from Corps School at the Naval Training Center, Great Lakes, Illinois, in October 1945. Also, during that month training was completed for Link trainer instructors and control tower operators at Atlanta, Georgia, and for mailmen at San Francisco. In November, the last group of aerographer's mates finished at the Naval Air Station, Lakehurst, New Jersey.

In April 1945, arrangements were made to train fifteen women officer candidates per month in Washington, D.C. This was established because of the need for additional officers in certain specialities. Enlisted women composed the majority of each class with approximately six to be commissioned in the Supply Corps and the others to become medical specialists, primarily occupational and physical therapists, selected from either civilian life or enlisted ranks. The course was of four weeks duration and the curriculum covered basic indoctrination, supplemented by lectures and by field trips to naval stations in the Washington area. The unit was administered by Naval Barracks whose commanding officer, Captain H. W. Underwood, had formerly commanded the Naval Reserve Midshipmen's School at Northampton, Massachusetts. Lieutenant (junior grade) Jeanette McPherrin, Assistant for the Women's Reserve to the Director of Training of BuPers, was officer-in-charge of the indoctrination unit.

The indoctrination school operated until October 1945 and the activity was not decommissioned until February 1946.

The complexities and reversals of the demobilization policy which ensued offer a lesson of some importance. In the future, the armed forces in the national interest must not only prepare, during the years of combat, their officers and men to face the problems of demobilization with some patience, but also the wives and parents. The United States faced, after World War I and World War II, demands of the civilians through their congressmen, for almost instantaneous demobilization upon the cessation of hostilities.

Failure on the part of all the services to formulate and to make known an acceptable plan of demobilization gravely damages national prestige and foreign relations, involves our effectiveness in areas of occupation, and undermines public support of the armed services. Furthermore, it does not forward domestic reconversion, care of veteran's needs and interests, and actually stands in the way of the preservation or disposal of tremendously valuable equipment.

Now as to the WAVES, the first big question concerned the rate of their demobilization. The Women's Reserve section of the Bureau of Personnel was inclined to undertake a separate demobilization of women to be completed within six months of VJ Day. This plan, which might have worked were the WAVES a separate unit, proved unfeasible because they were not a separate unit, but a part of the overall naval personnel. Since the majority of the yeomen and storekeepers at stations within the continental United States were women, the entire naval organization would have been disrupted if they had been demobilized within six months.

Furthermore, yeomen and storekeepers were obliged to carry a major part of the workload at the separation centers. In the face of these considerations, it was therefore determined that the WAVES would be demobilized at the same rate as men for the year ending the first of September 1946. This date was based on the assumption that the president or the Congress would declare the end of the national emergency 1 March 1946, so the reserve enlistment "for the duration and six months thereafter" would expire on 30 August 1946.

Separation-point scores for WAVES were set to provide their separation monthly in proportion to the men. The score for enlisted women ran about 15 points lower than for men because few WAVES could claim points in terms of dependents, and their entry into service had not been possible until 1942. But before a final decision was reached, some official words—and many more unofficial words—indicated the WAVES would be out in six months, a scuttlebutt that did much to damage planning and lower morale. For example, all contracts for items of WAVE uniforms were canceled at once, and this brought about such critical shortages by 1 January 1946, that remedial steps had to be taken in the way of new contracts.

Training reserve personnel, except in the case of hospital corps schools, was discontinued. This step, which appeared reasonable at the moment, created a critical shortage in ratings for which the early training quotas had been heavy. The large percentage of high-point personnel in these ratings stripped the Navy of trained people to carry on during the spring and summer of 1946. Continuation of training for a class or two would have eased the strain. Such training, while undeniably expensive in the light of service expected, would have justified itself in terms of general efficiency during the period in which demobilization was being carried out and property was being disposed of or stored.

The same criticism applies to the immediate discontinuance of recruiting. As shortages became apparent, efforts were made to retain personnel, but these efforts were hampered by the premature action already taken. On 15 August 1945, AlNav 196—45, which set up the point scores for separation, was published. Certain ratings were exempt from immediate demobilization, but the yeoman rating was not one of them. Personnel who wished to remain on duty after becoming eligible for separation were required to address a request for retention to the Bureau of Personnel, but this possibility was stated rather grudgingly, and unfortunately was interpreted by reserve personnel as an unceremonious invitation to be gone—at once.

But this impression was directly contrary to the hopes and plans of the Navy as expressed at that time by Secretary of the Navy James Forrestal. AlNav 202, which followed hard on the heels of the earlier AlNav, invited reserve officers to consider transfer to the regular Navy. It was, however, not sufficiently cordial to offset the earlier impression that the reservists had interpreted as an invitation to get out, so the oldest and most experienced reserves left and gaping holes began to appear in the naval organization. Since it takes months to decommission a naval activity, those men separated left unfinished tasks behind them.

On 9 September 1945, AlNav 252 canceled former AlNav's on demobilization and restated the procedure for separation. In this document, two paragraphs were devoted to explaining that personnel "might" request retention after they became point eligible. On 29 November 1945, under AlNav 395—45, yeomen were frozen at the point score of 45 for males and 25 for females. These scores were not lowered until 2 February 1946. By that time, the score on unrestricted rating for WAVES had dropped to 22.

But separation continued to outrun the process of consolidation; critical shortages of personnel continued. Admiral Ezra Kendall, who was in charge of *Magic Carpet* (transportation to the United States of military personnel in the Pacific), warned that the service could not continue without replacement. Officers charged with disposition of materials cried havoc, with good reason, when clerical personnel were ordered to staff separation centers. This situation was further complicated by the fact that Civil Service could not provide enough persons to fill the gap. Yet all the while the public and the Congress screamed for more rapid demobilization. In view of world conditions the situation in the Navy was disquieting, and that in the Army alarming.

In October 1945, AlNav 325 authorized commanding officers to request spot promotion for officers up to the rank of lieutenant commander, provided that additional rank was required for the duties they were performing, and that the officers so promoted would remain on active duty 180 days past their normal separation date. Ordinarily such a promotion, that of a lieutenant becoming a lieutenant commander, was infrequent but, under the pressure of a personnel shortage, the interpretation became more and more liberal. Almost any officer recommended by his commanding officer was promoted in exchange for an extra six months of duty. A considerable number of officers remained.

Similar inducements for enlisted personnel were difficult to arrange. The law required that a man shipping over from the reserve to the regular Navy must be enrolled in the highest rating held. The rating structure was already top-heavy and this, combined with the expectation that reservists would prove the best field for U.S. Navy recruiting, meant that wholesale promotion of enlisted men would wreck the rating structure of the post-war Navy.

But this difficulty did not apply, or was presumed not to apply, to women. Accordingly, AlStaCon 52346 of January 1946 provided a "free" advancement in rating up to pay grade A for all enlisted WAVES who signed an agreement to remain on duty until 1 December 1946. This provision was a godsend to many activities, especially smaller stations where a single individual became highly important in its operation. This was manifestly undesirable on the ground that it created special privileges for a chosen class of personnel, but its promulgation was eloquent testimony to the acute shortage of workers. Now having said all this, I must add that once under way, demobilization functioned smoothly, and even kept a bit ahead of schedule, passing the midmark in January 1946. By the first of September 1946, three million reservists had gone home, and the Navy was still an effective organization. Almost all separation centers did an excellent job, giving each veteran full information about his opportunities and bidding him a pleasant goodbye.

Perhaps this announcement of success should be followed by a general observation of all things naval, including the WAVES' program. In the Navy, the normal situation is frequently described as "snafu" (situation normal—all fouled up). Everyone has the idea that he struggles with unnecessary difficulties. Any report of his work is an account of the stumbling blocks encountered; the reader would expect no outcome but complete failure and disaster. Then when all complaints have been voiced, the summary of results comes with a contrast that is either incredible or comic: "The results were excellent," or again, "Progress was satisfactory." Or yet again, "The schedule was met." And all the cries and groans acted as incentives and the gripes were but laments that herald final success.

At the time that many WAVES were volunteering to remain on active duty to aid in demobilization, Vice Admiral Louis Denfeld, then chief of Bureau of Personnel, announced: "Our plan is to keep a WAVE component in the Naval Reserve. Further, if Congress approves, we will seek to retain on active duty reasonable numbers of WAVES who wish to do so and who may be needed in certain specialties. The Navy is proud of the job done by its women during the war. We know from experience that they can be extremely useful after the war in such specialities as communications, the medical corps, and certain types of naval aviation duties."

The Advisory Council for Women in the Navy (*top*), takes a trip to Pensacola, April 1944, to see WAVES at work. At left is Representative Margaret Chase Smith, who had long furthered the cause of women in the Navy; center, Director of WAVES Mildred McAfee; Dean Virginia Gildersleeve converses with a WAVE at far right.

Secretary of Defense James V. Forrestal congratulates the directors of the four women's services following the president's signing of the Women's Armed Services Integration Act of 1948. *Above*: Colonel Geraldine P. May, Director of Women, Air Force; Colonel Mary A. Hallaren, Director Women's Army Corps; Mr. Forrestal; Captain Joy B. Hancock, Director of the WAVES; and Major Julia E. Hamblet, Director of Women, Marine Corps.

Vice Admiral Thomas L. Sprague, Chief of Naval Personnel, (*opposite*) together with other naval officers, presented the Navy's request for the continuing services of women to the congressional committees in 1946.

Post–War Legislation

$\mathcal{E}$ARLY in 1946, Captain McAfee, the WAVES' first director, returned to her position as the president of Wellesley College. Actually, from the beginning of demobilization,
she had been permitted to spend increasing amounts of time
at the college, the day-by-day administrative tasks of her office
being carried out by her assistant, Commander Jean Palmer,
who, when Captain McAfee resigned in February 1946, was
named director. While plans had been discussed that I suc-
ceed Captain McAfee, the appointment of Jean, who served
until July 1946, was most appropriate, even though she did not
plan to remain in the Navy in the event permissive legislation
was enacted. Her familiarity with the work of the director's

office plus her previous experience in personnel detailing were of great value during the rapid demobilization which was taking place.

My release from the Bureau of Aeronautics and the duty which I had so thoroughly enjoyed with its many challenges and its many rewards engendered, after so many years as a civilian and as a naval officer, a great feeling of nostalgia. One of those rewards I could carry with me—the Secretary of the Navy's commendation:

"For exceptionally meritorious conduct in the performance of outstanding service as Assistant for the Women's Reserve to the Deputy Chief of Naval Operations (Air) and for her assistance to the Director of the Women's Reserve in the formulation of policies for the administration of the Women's Reserve, United States Naval Reserve. Since her entry into the naval service on October 24, 1942, her leadership, judgment and superior abilities have played a vital part in the development, expansion, and administration of the comprehensive program of integration and utilization of the skills of women in the naval service. The success of this program is reflected in the splendid performance of women in Naval Air activities throughout the Continental United States and the Fourteenth Naval District. Her outstanding service and performance of duty were at all times in keeping with the highest traditions of the naval service."

I reported to the Bureau of Personnel 24 February 1946 as Assistant Director (Plans) of the Women's Reserve.

Nothing could have suited me better, for I firmly believed that women should be an integral part of the Navy and in such a position I could make that my goal in my planning. In naval aviation particularly, the Women's Reserve had demonstrated that integration was not only the practical approach to the best methods in training and utilizing the services of women efficiently, but it was also economically the soundest approach. Experience after World War I, in which 10,000 women had at once been demobilized, with no opportunity to serve in the peacetime Reserve, resulted in the fact that some 20 years later practically no naval officer of junior rank knew, and few older officers remembered, that women had successfully served in the enlisted ranks of the Navy; hence, in World War II the very idea of women in service had had to be sold and planning undertaken from the ground up.

There was good reason to continue to make womanpower available to the Navy. The public demand for the rapid demobilization of the World War II armed forces personnel, both enlisted and officers, meant that volunteers for this tremendous job were to remain on active duty beyond the date of eligibility for release, not only to carry on the demobilization functions, but also to continue some of the peacetime programs of the Navy.

On 13 March 1946, women officers were asked to remain on active duty until 1 July 1946, and on 29 March enlisted women were made eligible for voluntary retention until that same date. This voluntary extension of service permitted the women to remain until their place in the peacetime Navy could be determined, while at the same time making available their urgently needed skills. An example of this need was clearly demonstrated by the GCA (Ground Controlled Approach) program which was, in the spring of 1946, in its earliest experimental stage. I vividly remember visiting the Naval Air Station at Banana River, Florida. The commanding officer explained very carefully that because of the loss of many men owing to demobilization, he had decided to use women in the experiment—the only available "manpower." When I asked how they were performing, he replied that they had absorbed the training readily; that they were efficient in the operation of the equipment, and their instructions to the pilots were clear and accurate. This commanding officer had spent most of the war years abroad or in the Fleet and was not too familiar with the work done by the WAVES as navigation instructors, and in manning the control towers where they had directed air traffic for several years. These WAVES at Banana River had been trained to perform duties as operators of the ground radar system and thus directed the movements of aircraft, manned by pilots simulating blindness, so that a safe approach to a runway could be made under conditions approaching zero visibility. Today such procedures are not unusual, but at that time, as I stood behind these young women seated in the darkened room of the mobile trailer, watching the approaching aircraft appearing as tiny blips on their radar screens, carefully instructing the pilots by voice, to correct up or down, left or right, and coaching them into a landing, a feeling of great satisfaction and pride came to me. It was another example of the women successfully meeting the challenge of a job that needed to be done.

Another field which was particularly hard-pressed because of the loss of personnel was the rehabilitation program in the hospitals. Here the retention of the services of trained women hospital corpsmen proved to be a godsend.

It was my task to draw up a logical presentation of a permanent complement of women for study by the various offices and bureaus of the Navy Department. I started my work by basing it on the major premise that women in the service should, insofar as practical, fit into the structure already in existence for men. I visualized women as serving not only in the regular Navy on a career basis, but also in the Naval Reserve, active and inactive. The wisdom of this latter feature, which was later approved by the Congress, was demonstrated during the Korean War when women in the Naval Reserve were recalled to active duty, along with the men, bringing with them their .Navy skills plus the experience they had gained in civilian life.

Looking back on those months of work and the many conferences in which I was involved, I recall frustrations of mind because of the apathy on the part of a large number of persons with whom I must deal. At times this apathy appeared to me to be lack of cooperation and it finally brought me to the point where I began conferences by saying, "I have been instructed by the Chief of Naval Personnel to prepare these plans concerning the possible use of the services of women in the Navy on a permanent basis. If you care to work from an absolutely negative recommendation, I will be glad to append your views to my report to the Chief." Such an approach was a measure of my desperation.

I must confess that a great deal of my material was obtained, out of necessity, through this "if" approach. For example, I would ask the officer, with whom I was conferring, this question: "Based on the fact that permissive legislation has been requested by the Navy and assuming that it is passed by the Congress, to permit women to be an integral part of the Navy, Regular and Reserve, as a permanent nucleus, in which ratings of the peacetime structure do you think they could most effectively serve?" Or I might ask, "In which field do you think women officers, during the war, have been of greatest assistance?" Perhaps I would get, offered with reluctance on the man's part, one or two possible fields of service; additional conversations with other representatives would elicit a few more, and these responses combined to furnish a small basis on which to proceed. I even went so far at times as to say, "Of course, I don't think the legislation will pass, but we have to make this study." This approach usually inspired cooperation.

One month after I reported to the Bureau of Personnel, H.R. 5919, "To amend the Naval Reserve Act of 1938, as amended, so as to establish the Women's Reserve on a permanent basis and for other purposes" (79th Congress, 2nd session), was introduced by the Honorable Carl Vinson and referred to the House Committee on Naval Affairs. The burden of presentation before that committee was carried largely by the members of the Women's Reserve who were not in a position of sufficient authority to speak with the necessary assurance of Navy plans and policies.

During and after the hearings, 9 May 1946, the proposed legislation underwent major revision, and on 21 May, the bill was reported by committee with certain amendments. The Navy Department records reveal a letter, dated 22 May 1946, to Representative Margaret Chase Smith, signed by Vice Admiral Louis Denfeld, then Chief of Naval Personnel, outlining his views as to what the legislation should embody. Subsequently, a draft of a bill was prepared and sent to the committee in which Section IV read as follows: "All laws or parts of laws which authorize the appointment of persons to commissioned grades or ranks in the Regular Navy and Regular Marine Corps and which authorize the enlistment of persons in the Regular Navy and Regular Marine Corps should be construed to include authority to appoint and enlist women in the Regular Navy and Regular Marine Corps in the same manner and under the same circumstances and conditions as such laws or parts of laws apply to the appointment and enlistment of men." This simplified language was good. Another point in its favor was that the Marines were included in the legislation.

The seeds which had been planted several times now appeared to be sprouting. Great credit for this is due Margaret Chase Smith. Unfortunately, time ran out and no further action was taken before the 79th Congress adjourned. Thus legislation died in committee and new legislation would have to be introduced in the next session.

On 26 July 1946, I became the director of the WAVES, and as such I was in a position to devote great effort to legislative activity. Recognizing that a tremendous amount of work had to be done to prepare properly for future hearings, I took steps to secure training in approach methods from Captain Ira Nunn, who was a member of the staff in the office of the Judge Advocate General. His tutelage insured that the errors of the first hearings would not be repeated.

The next step was to convince the Chief of Naval Personnel, Vice Admiral Thomas L. Sprague, that he and other men of the Navy, not the women, must present the Navy's request for the continuing services of women to the congressional committees, just as was done in the case of all other naval legislation. It was at this time also that I secured Admiral Sprague's approval to request information and help from all heads of divisions in the Bureau of Personnel and other offices of the Navy Department, of an affirmative nature, regarding the practicability of and need for the services of women in naval service. My last request of the admiral was that a senior male officer of the Plans Division of the bureau be assigned to assist in preparing the material needed for congressional hearings.

In response to this last request, Captain Fred R. Stickney, USN, was designated to "run with the ball." He frankly admitted at the onset that he, personally, was not in full accord with the provisions of the proposed legislation, nor was he convinced that the Navy needed women in peacetime. Nevertheless, his objectivity left nothing to be desired. On many an occasion, he worked in my office with me and my assistants until midnight. He was positive in his approach and, without his assistance, I am sure the Navy would not have been in a position to answer clearly, logically, and convincingly all the questions asked by the congressional committee members. Captain Stickney also appeared before the Naval Affairs Committee, as one of the Navy representatives, to present a comprehensive analysis, section by section, of the proposed legislation.

Captain Nunn, who represented JAG's legislative division, worked diligently to redraft the terms of the proposed bill to bring it into line with what he knew would be needed for favorable action, but at the same time worded in such a way as to assure that the Navy's requested terms were practical and justifiable. I remember so vividly one of the hearing sessions, filled with rapid-fire questions, during which I inadvertently addressed Mr. Vinson as admiral. I was beginning to wonder if I was really following the many instructions Captain Nunn had given me, or if I were floundering. He passed this note to me: "You are doing all right." That was just the booster I needed!

Mr. Franklin J. Schuyler, a civilian legislative aide of long standing in the legal division of the Bureau of Personnel, proved to be a marvelous kibitzer as well as an understanding and patient co-worker. He had a talent for studying what looked to be a perfectly logical statement in the proposed draft of a bill and finding a weak spot. Also, he subjected much of the material being prepared for the hearings to the same rigorous scrutiny.

The expenditure of effort during the ensuing year was great, and many were the delays and disappointments in spite of the fact that as early as 24 September 1946 the priorities listed by the Navy in its legislative program for the 80th Congress placed in the fifth and sixth places the legislation:

a. To authorize female officers and enlisted personnel in the regular Navy, and
b. To provide permanent authority for female officers and enlisted personnel in the Naval Reserve.

During this time, we worked closely with the Army in order that the proposed bills would be as nearly alike as the similarities in service made logical. Now that the military services had combined to become the Department of Defense, and the House and Senate committees became known as the Armed Services committees, it became mandatory, in July 1947, that a single bill be introduced which included women in the Army, Navy, and Marine Corps. It was not until 21 November 1947 that Title III was attached to the bill to cover the women in the newly formed Air Force.

I find it interesting to remember that I experienced the creation of the Bureau of Aeronautics in 1921, which had necessitated the relinquishing, by existing naval bureaus, of their aviation functions, and the intraservice contentions this occasioned. I also saw the growing pains occasioned by the unification of the several services into the Department of Defense when the service rivalries, which had always been in existence, became a real battle and James Forrestal, the first Secretary of Defense, was faced with the almost insurmountable task of calming the new organization and making it work. To be able to observe his untiring efforts and note the increasing good results was indeed an educational experience.

Fortunately, the service rivalries were not carried into the formative period of the programs for women. The first women who were chosen to head these programs had not been previously subjected to service rivalries and each worked entirely with a view to having their program established as to best fit into the structure of the department they represented.

Cooperation and interchange of ideas, when I became director of the WAVES, were even more desirable, for at that time we of the services were facing up to the legislative battles ahead. The directors of the various women's programs during these unsettled years were Colonel Mary Hallaren, WAAC, Colonel Geraldine May, WAF, Colonel Katherine Towle, USMC, and Commander Beatrice Ball, USCG. Discussions of procedures for the solving of problems under peacetime conditions, recruiting standards, uniform regulations, disciplinary procedures—in fact, all phases of our various programs were discussed, each from the viewpoint of the varied differences within each service, but with the view of reconciling such differences satisfactorily and practically. And this we did.

When the preparations for the congressional hearings got under way, every different requirement of each service was reviewed, and worked out so that it could be readily stated that such differences in the legislation that existed were necessary because of the existing differences within each service. We rehearsed what we contemplated would be questions from members of the congressional committees, and reached agreement on how our explanations were to be presented. There was never a semblence of seeking prestige.

At the close of one such session, one of the participants smilingly remarked, "Why is it that our meetings never end in a big fight? Why do we never pound the table?" To which another member of the group replied, "Because we let the men fight the battle of unification. We need all the time we can find to polish up our programs."

Subcommittee hearings in the Senate got under way 2 July 1947 and continued through 15 July on S.1527 (Navy) and S.1103 (Army), which were now combined to form S.1641. These hearings, compared with those of the House committee, were a pleasure to attend. Each member present had apparently familiarized himself with the subject matter and past correspondence and was prepared to make his final analysis based on these materials and the current hearings. The committee room had something of the atmosphere and dignity of a court; one sensed the opportunity to voice honest opinions as well as to present the facts.

One of the questions, which had been raised in the early part of the hearings, concerned the possible incapacitation of women during menopause. In reply, Admiral Sprague had pointed out that during the five years of service, none of the 18 disability retirements of the WAVES was related to menopause or any female disease. The Army presented a letter from the Surgeon General's office which stated the there were now adequate treatments and medicines for any of the discomforts of menopause. I sensed that these answers did not entirely satisfy the questioners and that they were perhaps visualizing a large number of women who might eventually need to be retired for this physical reason. Feeling that we needed a firmer statement for the record, I went to Admiral Swanson, the Surgeon General of the Navy, that evening and asked him if he could and would prepare a strong statement on the subject that I might have for the hearings the next day. He did exactly that:

"In reply to your question concerning the probable incidence of retirement for physical disability in prospective WAVE officers as compared with male officers, it is my opinion that there will be very little difference. The commonly held idea that women are invalided in their middle years by the onset of the menopause is largely a popular fallacy. It is well known that men pass through the same physiological change with symptomatology closely resembling that of women.

"Experience with our Navy nurses has shown that the question of the climacteric or menopause has never been a problem. The average professional woman is well balanced mentally and physically, and this normal physiological change occurring in late middle life is usually passed with little or no serious disability or residual effects. As I recall, since 1931, 440 nurses have been physically retired from the naval service and of these only one was retired with the diagnosis of 'menopause.' The proposed retirement age as contained in the bill, i.e., lieutenant commanders at age 50 and commanders at age 55, is earlier than the age at which a considerable proportion of active women reach this physiological period.

"In conclusion, I consider the menopause a normal physiological change which, in the vast majority of women, is passed through with little or no real difficulty. Also, we now have certain medical preparations which have proved most useful in preventing or in allaying the untoward symptoms which occur at this time. Finally, in comparing the possible extra hazard in the female officer due to this condition, I repeat, a similar involutional period occurs in the male."

The Navy Surgeon General's statement not only laid to rest all doubts in the matter, but was also something of a bombshell to many members of the Congress, particularly the statements which included the male of the species. In fact, for several weeks after the statement was read into the record, I was told that any congressman who showed signs of abruptness, irritation or irascibility was accused by his colleagues of going through the menopause.

At the conclusion of the hearings, Senator Raymond E. Baldwin asked the directors of the women's services, past and present, if they desired to make a final statement. All those present did so and those absent had sent written statements, favoring the legislation. When I was called upon I stated:

"I should like to make a very brief statement, if I may, on my feelings regarding this legislation.

"I simply believe that the legislation requested for the inclusion of women in the Regular Navy and in the Naval Reserve is realistic and wise. To me it is a wise acknowledgment that in any future emergency the services of women will be needed, and in overwhelmingly larger numbers that we even visualized during this war.

"The peacetime Navy has always been the nucleus on which expansion could be carried out economically, effectively, and rapidly. I think, therefore, that the nucleus must contain all the necessary basic components. In evaluating the lessons of this war, their services constituted one of the studies.

"The Navy was offered a valuable experiment on how women could best help in the national defense by the services of the WAVES. This legislation being requested is based on the results of those studies.

"It would appear to me that any national defense weapon known to be of value should be developed and kept in good working order and not allowed to rust or to be abolished.

"We all know, I think, that women, of necessity, long since emerged from the days when the males of the family were supposed to support all the unmarried females. I think we also must remember that, fortunately or unfortunately, females now dominate in the numbers constituting the population of this country. I believe that the future functioning and survival of our country depends to a great extent on the amount of responsibility that each citizen assumes.

"Another important reason for retaining a nucleus of women volunteers in the armed services is that it would emphasize to women generally that their country needed and expected contributions from them. It is my opinion that the women will be proud and eager for an opportunity to contribute directly and vitally to the welfare and security of their country through continuing services in the armed forces.

"In this respect I speak particularly for services in the Regular Navy, because it is only there that we can offer the permanency, the advancement, and the security of a career. Knowing as I do what women have contributed and what they can continue to contribute, I sincerely and honestly believe that the Navy has need of their services."

Many years later, my mother sent me a letter which she had received from my brother, (Commander Ward H. Bright, USN) who, without my knowledge, had been present in the committee room during the final days of the hearings. It is a letter I treasure:

"Dearest Mother,

"Today the voice of William H. Bright was heard in the Armed Forces committee room of the United States Senate. You can take my word for it, Mother, Dad was there, for I was on hand and heard him. To this same committee room General Eisenhower and Admiral Nimitz came to admit publicly that their early strong belief that the use of women in the armed services would not work out had been reversed by experience. They now strongly asserted the critical need for women to insure our country having the best possible fighting machine. They loudly told of the great accomplishments of the American Girl in the present war and how she had proven herself in the combat area and on foreign duty.

And then Senator Baldwin asked our Captain Joy if she cared to make a statement.... As her words came forth clearly and sincerely it was obvious that something real was being said and everyone listened. You may wonder if she said something entirely different. The answer is no, but she spoke from experience as a leader of a movement of which she was a vital part even as long as two wars ago. Here was the embodiment of the mustang who had greatly succeeded and, as is so rare, had achieved greatness....

"Yes, Mother, you should rightly feel proud, as should all the clan, for through Joy, Dad and you spoke to the Nation on Capitol Hill today and as usual it was in the furtherance of another 'cause.'

...your son, Ward"

The Senate committee approved the subcommittee's recommendations providing a permanent status for women in the Armed Services, and, on 16 July 1947, the bill was reported by Senator Baldwin and placed on the Senate calender. It was passed by the Senate on 23 July 1947 and referred to the House committee, where it assumed and retained an inert character until the adjournment of the first session. Fortunately, this did not involve starting all over again, although necessary redrafting of various sections had to be done. It was not until 18 February 1948 that hearings before the House subcommittee were scheduled, and a month later, 23 March, hearings before the full House committee were begun.

For me, those hearings were packed with high tension. In spite of all the tremendous preparations we had made, many questions, which had neither been visualized nor contemplated, had to be answered on the spot. For example, we were queried on the number of pregnancies with, in my opinion, the innuendo that the women were not married. The majority of the questions, however, related to overall policy and the implementation planned for the proposed program. As had previously been decided, these questions were answered by Admiral Sprague, Captain Thomas Darden, and Captain Stickney. Having the men of the Navy carry the weight of the presentation was certainly wise. It was only proper that this be the procedure since the Navy women were to be an integral part of the service and not a corps. Furthermore, the Navy, and not the Women's Reserve, was requesting their services.

From the beginning of the House committee hearings, sleep was hardly on our schedule as we prepared for the next day's hearings. However, all went well and, on what was scheduled to be the "wind-up" day, we all relaxed, optimistic about the outcome. We were assembled in the committee room to await the committee's favorable report when Mr. Vinson announced that the members of the House committee had reached agreement. The majority had approved only the permanency of the women in the Reserve components of the services. The blow left us speechless. I had been seated alongside my boss, Admiral Sprague. We looked at one another in absolute astonishment, so convinced had we been that our presentations had met with approval.

On 29 March 1948, the bill was reported to the House with amendments, and on 21 April it was passed; but on that same day, the House asked for a conference with the Senate committee to reconcile the differences in the two versions. Representative Margaret Chase Smith had voted against the committee's version of the bill.

The time that elapsed between 29 March and 21 April was a period of mad and determined activity. Telegrams and letters to the House Armed Services committee from business and professional women throughout the country urged that the legislation, as passed by the Senate, be approved by the House. Civic and patriotic organizations as well as individuals wrote or telephoned their representatives, even those who were not on the committee, in support of the Senate's version. I learned later that communications numbered in the thousands.

It was heartwarming to realize that when the chips were down the strong declarations that the services of women were needed and wanted in the armed services came from all the necessary high places in the Army and Navy, and included Secretary of Defense James Forrestal; General of the Army Dwight D. Eisenhower; Fleet Admiral Chester W. Nimitz, Chief of Naval Operations; the Commandant of the Marine Corps, General A. A. Vandergrift; and Vice Admiral Donald B.

Duncan, Deputy Chief of Naval Operations (Air). Mrs. Oswald B. Lord, chairman of the Civilian Advisory Committee for the WAAC, spoke for that committee and also for such women's organizations as the Business and Professional Women's Club, the General Federation of Women's Clubs, the Women's Patriotic League, Women's Overseas League, the Daughters of the American Revolution, the American Association of University Women, and several others.

These speakers established a convincing pattern of endorsement, and in the Navy, Vice Admiral Thomas L. Sprague and the chiefs of other bureaus and offices, such as Supplies and Accounts, Medicine and Surgery, and Communications recalled vividly the splendid work of the WAVES.

General Eisenhower, in his testimony, stated in part:

"Not only do I heartily support the bill to integrate women into the Regular Army and Organized Reserve Corps, but I personally directed that such legislation be drawn up and submitted to this Congress.

"My experience in the utilization of WAAC is long and covers both war and peacetime conditions. The first WAAC to serve in an active theatre of operations were assigned to my headquarters in North Africa. That initial wartime experiment in utilizing trained WAAC, my later experience in the European theatre where 10,000 were on duty, and my knowledge of their contribution to the peacetime military establishment have convinced me that a modern Army must have WAAC....

"I was the first officer in the field, I am sure, who had women sent to them as regularly enlisted people in the services; and like all others, I am sure that we had our regular number of opponents. Older officers were horrified and it was a terrific thing to get it started [the program]."

Fleet Admiral Chester W. Nimitz, Chief of Naval Operations, in backing the legislation, said:

"I was one of the doubters in the early days, and I was definitely reluctant to see this program started. However, after it started and after I saw it work, I became a convert.

"This legislation has been requested after careful study of the overall requirements of the Navy, now and in the future. It is the considered opinion of the Navy Department and my own personal belief that the services of women are needed. Their skills are as important to the efficient operation of the naval establishment during peacetime as they were during the war years.

"During the war, women were actively employed in all the duties for which they were found qualified, making available large numbers of men for combat.

"Not only were they equally efficient in many of the duties previously performed by men, but in certain types of work they proved to be more efficient and psychologically better fitted. This was particularly true within the Hospital Corps, the Supply Corps, aviation specialities, and communications....

"These conclusions are based on observation and study of their services during nearly five years at approximately 950 shore establishments in the United States and Hawaii. They served in practically all ratings except those from which they were excluded because of physical limitations, combat nature, or seagoing requirements. I was able to observe their work closely in the Hawaiian Islands where nearly 5,000 served and in the United States when I returned after VJ-day....

"The Navy's request for the retention of women is not made as a tribute to their past performance. We have learned that women can contribute to a more efficient Navy. Therefore, we would be remiss if we did not make every effort to utilize their abilities."

General A. A. Vandergrift, Commandant of the Marine Corps, stated:

"There can be no question of the importance of the role played by the Marine Corps Women's Reserve in the recent war.... They filled 87 percent of the enlisted billets at Headquarters, Marine Corps, and comprised one-third of the troops at the major continental posts and stations....

"Experience during World War II has demonstrated that there are certain military-type duties for which women are inherently fitted—in some cases to a greater extent than men. It is strongly urged that this legislation be enacted."

And so it came about, when the bill emerged from the joint conference of 2 June 1948, that the House committee was in accord with the Senate report. Ten days later, 12 June 1948, Public Law 625, the Women's Armed Services Integration Act, was approved and was signed by the President 30 July 1948.

The victory was sweet.

Captain Hancock (right) and Secretary of the Navy John L.
Sullivan (left) look on as the first group of enlisted WAVES
(*top*) are sworn into the Regular Navy by Rear Admiral George
L. Russell, Judge Advocate General of the Navy, 7 July 1948.

Above, the first women officers to be sworn into the Regular
Navy under the Women's Armed Services Integration Act of 1948
receive their commissions from Secretary of the Navy Sullivan
(second left), while Admiral Russell administers the oath of
office. Left to right: Captain Joy Bright Hancock, Lieutenant
Commander Winifred R. Quick, and Lieutenant (jg) Betty
R. Tennant.

Young women in training at the U.S. Naval Training Center,
Great Lakes, Illinois (*opposite*).

Reserve to Regular

THE entry of the WAVES into the regular Navy in accordance with Public Law 625—Women's Armed Services Integration Act—was an event of such significance that
a special ceremony took place 7 July 1948 in the old Main Navy
Building on Constitution Avenue, Washington, D.C. Six WAVES
were duly sworn in by the Judge Advocate General, Rear Admiral George Russell.

Each of these enlisted women represented various activities
and areas of service: Kay L. Langdon, Naval Air Transport
Service; Wilma J. Marchal and Edna E. Young, Bureau of
Naval Personnel; Frances R. Devaney, Bureau of Supplies and
Accounts; Doris R. Robertson, Naval Communications; and
Ruth Flora, Naval Medical Center, Bethesda.

As I watched the ceremony, it seemed almost unreal, for the path to this accomplishment had been long and, at times, discouraging and frustrating. But this feeling was immediately offset by a sense of accomplishment as I looked at these WAVES, meticulously attired in uniform, their right hands raised and their eyes fixed on the Judge Advocate General as they repeated after him the solemn oath of allegiance. I knew each of them well. I knew, too, their true and lasting desire to continue to serve their country in the Navy.

Immediately after the swearing in, the Honorable John Sullivan, Secretary of the Navy, hailed their new status in these words:

"On behalf of the entire United States Navy from Admiral Denfeld, Chief of Naval Operations, on down, I want to welcome you into the regular Navy. This is a milestone in the history of this department. You are the first enlisted women to become part of the regular Navy. Captain Hancock, during the war years, your WAVES, 86,000 of them, not only made it possible to assign to combat duty 86,000 men who would be otherwise employed, but your girls, in their own way, developed talents and techniques that were superior to those of the men whom they released. Like the women of the Women's Reserve of the Marine Corps, the WAAC of the Army, the SPARS of the Coast Guard, and the WAF of the Air Force, your girls served with distinction and honor. Although you have now been reduced to 2,000, it is my understanding that within the next two years you hope to induct 6,000 enlisted women into the WAVES, and I assure you the Navy will welcome them. In such highly specialized fields as communications, aerology, aviation training and many other fascinating and interesting fields, they are better than any men we have ever had, and we are proud to have them."

Thus began the program, which was to be completed by 31 August 1948, to transfer those WAVES on active duty to the regular Navy if they applied and were between the ages of 20 and 31. Since the Women's Reserve was established for the duration of the war and six months, the WAVES who did not apply for enlistment in the regular Navy could be retained until 30 June 1949 and beyond that date, if the necessary funds were appropriated.

In accordance with the legislation, the Navy, during the first two years, was permitted to achieve the strength of 500 officers, 20 warrants, and 6,000 enlisted women. The swearing in of the first six enlisted women was, therefore, a very small beginning, but these women represented the type of women who would be attracted to the naval service on a career basis.

The terms of enlistment set up for the regular Navy were for two, three, four and six years in the rating held at the time of discharge from the Reserve. On 15 September 1948, plans were put into effect to enlist civilians and those WAVES with former enlisted service, their training to be carried out at the Naval Recruit Training Center at Great Lakes, Illinois.

Lieutenant Commander Kathryn Dougherty was selected to head this Recruit Training (W) school. Because of the relatively few officers remaining on active duty, letters were sent to several officers who had been demobilized, asking them if they would volunteer to return to active duty to serve on the staff of the new school. The response was enthusiastic and a sufficient number was recalled for administration and teaching purposes.

Most of these officers had been lost to the women's program under the terms of the demobilization point system. Miss Dougherty was serving on the staff of the Commandant, Sixth Naval District, Charleston, when she was questioned as to her willingness to head up the new enlisted recruit training at Great Lakes. Her response was a strong affirmative, even though it meant that she would lose her "spot" and revert to the grade of lieutenant.

The Recruit Training (W) convened on 5 October 1948. The length of the training period was eleven weeks with planned input of a company every six weeks. During the Korean War, the size of the classes was doubled.

The first class of 134 graduated in December 1948. The recruit training continued at Great Lakes until the U.S. Naval Training Center was opened at Bainbridge, Maryland, in October 1951, at which time the enlisted training was moved to that place.

Not until 15 October 1948, was the first group of women officers sworn into the regular Navy. This delay was caused by the terms of the legislation which established the numbers of officers on a percentage basis. Therefore, the augmentation program (for both men and women) had to be in effect long enough to permit the enrollment of junior officers on active duty, for on the basis of these totals were determined the higher rank percentages. Finally, this was accomplished.

The swearing in of the women officers constituted another ceremony, again in the old Main Navy building, with the Judge Advocate General and Secretary of the Navy Sullivan on hand.

These eight officers represented the various branches of activities of the Navy.

Sworn in with me were Lieutenant Commanders Winifred R. Quick, Ann King, and Frances L. Willoughby, (MC); Lieutenant Ellen Ford, Supply Corps; Lieutenant Doris Cranmore, Naval Medical Service; Lieutenants (junior grade) Doris A. Defenderfer and Betty Rae Tennant. We represented the initial group of 288 women officers selected for commissions in the regular Navy.

Again the ceremony seemed unreal to me, but it really happened. Strangely enough, the month of October 1948 was exactly six years from the month in 1942 when I had been sworn into the Women's Reserve of the Naval Reserve.

The establishment of facilities for the training of women officers of the regular Navy was a new and interesting enterprise. The commanding officers of various training schools were requested to submit full information and recommendations concerning facilities which could be utilized with the maximum economy and the minimum disruption of existing operations. In addition, I was sent off on a tour of inspection to various naval activities in order to secure a firsthand view and to make a firsthand evaluation and report my findings to the Chief of Naval Personnel via the Training Division.

One of the first activities I visited was the U.S. Naval Academy at Annapolis where the revelation of my mission had about the same effect as would have had the announcement of the placing of a time bomb. Vice Admiral James L. Holloway, superintendent of the Academy, however, seemed to be entirely unshaken by the nature of my visit. In fact, he sent me on a tour of all the academy facilities. I do believe that it had taken all of five minutes for the word to pass that "WAVES were going to attend the Naval Academy." I conferred with various heads of departments and all were most interested as well as concerned. Was the last stronghold of the male Navy about to fall?

That afternoon I stood beside Admiral Halloway as he took the review of the Plebes. The "eyes right" seemed to me to be more intent than usual, and I later learned that the "word" had also penetrated the body of midshipmen.

On Sunday morning, before leaving the Academy, I attended Chapel. I had always been impressed with the religious ceremonies there and also seeing the Chapel filled with such fine and clean-appearing young men. On this particular morning, as I glanced up at those seated on the balcony, I thought I detected almost a smile on several faces as we sang that line of the Navy hymn, "Whose arm hath bound the restless wave."

The facility finally agreed upon was the Naval Base, Newport, Rhode Island. This selection had much to recommend it for already established there was officer training for general line. An officers' quarters building was available, as were also necessary classrooms. Recreation and messing facilities would be shared with the men, and a fine drill field immediately adjacent to the women's quarters was also available. And so, Newport was selected for Officer Indoctrination Unit (W), and became a part of the U.S. Naval School (General Line).

The choice of a woman officer to head up the new school was of primary importance and the Bureau of Personnel made an excellent choice when it ordered Lieutenant Commander Sybil A. Grant, USN, to this duty. She had been attached to the Training Division of the Bureau where her duties involved administration of policies for Naval Academy preparatory schools and selection of candidates; liaison officer on Naval Academy matters and coordinator of development of the curriculum of officer indoctrination training.

The first group of trainees, twenty-nine in number, reported to Newport on New Year's Eve, 1948, and operations started on the five-month course on 1 January 1949. The training of women officers for the regular Navy was under way.

In the summer of 1950, the ROC (Reserve Officer Candidate) program was inaugurated for women at the Great Lakes Training Center. The program, designed for undergraduate women, was similar to the Navy's program for college men.

The living facilities available at Great Lakes for the use of the first class were a wing of a Junior Bachelor Officers' Quarters. In these buildings, of wartime construction, toilet facilities were generally without much privacy. Gang showers, toilet stalls without doors, and rows of open latrines were the order of the day. Upon taking over the wing assigned, the senior woman officer recommended that a temporary plywood casing be erected around the row of latrines. The WAVES had long since learned that patience was more than a virtue, and apparently in this case patience did not produce the enclosures. I had known of this request but deemed it one that would be solved at station level and that if it weren't solved the heavens wouldn't fall in. Following my call upon the commanding officer, the inspection tour started. All went extremely well, everything apparently shipshape, until we reached the "head" area. I walked into the area at the side of the commanding officer, with the staff officers, men and women, bringing up the rear. There, in each urinal, a flower-pot sprouted a lovely red geranium plant. The captain and I burst out laughing at the same moment. The following day a working party arrived and threw up a temporary enclosure around the fixtures.

The first ROC class was graduated 18 August 1951 at Great Lakes, the women having completed two summer training sessions of six weeks each. Those graduates who were not yet 21 years of age or had not yet earned their degree were not commissioned until these requirements were met. The others were commissioned as ensigns and placed on active duty.

The school was moved in 1952 to the U.S. Naval Training Center, Bainbridge, Maryland, and then was superseded by the College Junior program in December 1953. This latter program was established at the U.S. Naval School, Officer Indoctrination, (Women) at Newport, Rhode Island.

There was something a bit different about the ROC program when compared to various other training programs of the Navy. Doubtless this was caused by the collegiate note which the coeds added to the existing military medley. Both the training centers and the coeds profited by it. However, the ROC made the sudden change from casual campus living to the swiftly paced military schedule with apparent and surprising ease. They spent six hours a day absorbing a "listening knowledge" of naval history and traditions, of gunnery and navigation, of logistics and communications. By their own reports they found the indoctrinational tours as informative and much more fun than classroom instruction. Of the 1952 tours, which included the David Taylor Model Basin in Washington, a destroyer escort and a submarine, and the Philadelphia Navy Yard, the ROC rated as "best of all" the visit to the Naval Academy at Annapolis.

Despite these tours, the ROC school was no summer camp. Trainees rose at 6:00 A.M., policed their barracks, stood watches around the clock, and kept the log. They did their own laundry, they studied continuously, and ate enormously. Their rewards were in terms that collegians understood: song fests, picnics, baseball games, dances with Navy men also in the ROC program.

From conversations with the trainees at both the beginning and the conclusion of their course, I definitely sensed that something happened to them. According to Vice Admiral Laurance DeBose, chief of the Bureau of Personnel, "You can't beat the ROC training for making fine WAVE officers, because it means a college girl grows up Navy-minded." "Ninety-five percent seem to absorb the Navy through every pore," was the evaluation given by the officer-in-charge of the school, Lieutenant Commander Katherine Curtis, USNR, who in civilian life was a guidance counselor from Newtonville, Massachusetts. Assisting her in the administration of the program were seventeen reserve officers and seven rated women—all educational and professional women temporarily recalled to active duty.

The Bureau of Naval Personnel had, by July 1950, established an unofficial strength goal of 12,000 women, based largely on the results of a survey of housing facilities available in the continental United States and overseas.

Early in 1951 the Assistant Secretary of Defense (Man-Power and Personnel) Anna Rosenberg, reasoned that to meet the overall manpower needs the services of 125,000 women should be visualized. The Navy's portion of that number was 15,000 and to furnish this number quotas for enlisted women were increased to approximately 500 per month, and those for officers were set at 240 per year. During this "stepped up" program the Navy continued, successfully, to stress quality instead of quantity.

As a step toward reaching the overall 125,000 goal there was created in July 1951, the Defense Advisory Committee for Women in the Services DACOWITS). The committee was composed of fifty women drawn from all sections of the United States, each appointed for a two-year term. The members were outstanding representatives of various fields of endeavor: the professions, education, politics, (local, state, and national), community service, business, banking, and the arts. One of the committee's missions was to interpret to the public, particularly to the parents of young women, the need for the services of women in peacetime, the opportunities available, and the conditions under which the young women would live and be trained.

Twice a year, this committee met in the Pentagon to be briefed on all phases of military service for women. Their indoctrination consisted of visits to the installations of each of the services to observe the women at work. The committee, divided into subcommittees, studied particular aspects and reported the results to the whole committee. Their briefings at the Pentagon consisted of lectures by male representatives of all the services as well as by the directors of the nine women's components.

The nine service components with which **DACOWITS** was involved were as follows:

Nurse Corps	Medical Service Corps	General Service
Army	Army	WAC
Navy	Air Force	WAVE
Air Force	* Navy	Women Marines
		WAF

* The men and women in the Navy's medical service are not a separate corps as in the Army and Air Force.

In all the services, the members of the committee were concerned with housing, educational requirements, and promotional oportunities for women. They were also concerned with the areas of assignments, types of work and training, facts which had to be known to all members of DACOWITS if they were to be in a position to explain and encourage the young women in their areas to join one of the military services. For example, where they found differences in housing standards between the services, they were asked, by Mrs. Anna Rosenberg, to point out any undesirable feature they observed and make recommendations for improvement to her. Mrs. Rosenberg, in turn, would bring the matter to the attention of the appropriate service.

These women contributed to the services a wealth of experience, knowledge, and enthusiasm as well as great skill in dealing with the general public. The many activities they sponsored in their own states, involving great numbers of civic organizations with which they were personally and professionaly connected, helped to promote a better understanding of what the life of women in the military services meant and what it had to offer. These women helped to bring to public attention the need for women in the service, their consistently fine performance and the career possibilities for them.

In bringing women in the armed services into favor with and understanding by the public, Mrs. Rosenberg actually set the pace. At each meeting of the committee, she planned a special event. One of the most successful was the presentation of a new postage stamp honoring the women in the armed services, to each of the directors of the nine components of service women. President Harry S. Truman made the presentation at the White House, assisted by the Postmaster General. The event was made impressive by the honor guards of women, bands, the presence of high officials, and the attendance of all the members of DACOWITS. For such a scene, press coverage was assured.

Another event I vividly recollect took place on the grounds of the Pentagon in September 1951 as a tribute and farewell to General George C. Marshall, the retiring Secretary of Defense, and a salute to the incoming Secretary of Defense, the Honorable Robert A. Lovett. The Army, Navy, Marine Corps, and Air Force were each represented by fifty enlisted women. While the WAC band played some favorite songs of General Marshall, the two hundred women executed precision drills, then marched to the upper level of the grounds to form two lines and stand at hand salute as the new Secretary of Defense, the retiring Secretary of Defense, Mrs. Rosenberg, the directors of the women services, and the members of DACOWITS marched through.

It was my privilege to escort Secretary Lovett, who headed the procession. As we came to the top of the steps from the lower level, we paused to permit those following to fall into formation. As we stood there looking down the corridor formed by the service women, who never looked sharper in their smart uniforms, my pride in being a part of it all sent the unfailing chills up and down my spine and brought a lump to my throat. At that moment, Secretary Lovett remarked, "What an amazing spectacle!" Though finding it difficult to reply, I did manage to say, "I'm afraid, Mr. Secretary, that this sight is one which makes me very emotional." He replied, "There is indeed room in such scenes for emotion."

As we walked the length of the Pentagon approach and through the doors of the building, I knew that I had had an experience I would never forget.

Colonel Mary A. Hallaren, Director of the WAC, and Captain Hancock, Director of the WAVES, on an inspection tour of European installations where WAC were serving in 1949. Just after an audience with the Pope, they were photographed in Rome (*above*) with Sergeant Mary Lever, WAC, and Chief Yeoman Wilma Marchal, USN.

The two directors (*right*) are cordially received by General Lucius D. Clay, U.S. Army, while on their European tour.

Chief Wilma Marchal (*far right*), the yeoman who accompanied Captain Hancock on the tour, finds a friend at the Frankfurt, Germany, zoo.

European
Inspection Tour

$\mathcal{A}$T no time did I enjoy the prestige that came with my
assignment as Director, WAVES, more than during
a fact-finding tour of western Europe and England, to determine the practicability and need of assigning WAVES to
naval activities in those areas. The assignment had hitherto
been denied our women by the restrictive legislation under
which the program had been conducted during the war years.
I had considered the necessity of such a venture, but had not
yet embarked on implementing it when, on a social occasion,
the opportunity was presented. I seized it.

Colonel Mary Hallaren, my opposite number in the Woman's
Army Corps, my chief, Admiral Denfeld, and I were talking at

a reception, when Colonel Hallaren mentioned that she was preparing shortly to go to Europe on one of her periodic inspection tours. It seemed a good time for me to mention that I too had in mind a trip to western Europe to look into the possible billets and facilities available for the WAVES.

"Why not go along with me and see how the WAC live and the jobs they do?" Mary Hallaren asked.

As I turned to Admiral Denfeld, he said at once, "That sounds like a fine invitation—a good idea."

No more was needed to plunge me into the process of getting official authorization and transportation. I arranged also to take my yeoman, Chief Wilma Marchal. Such an expedition would require careful reporting and a day-to-day journal. In going to five countries in six weeks, I would have little time for this work, and a clerical assistant would make my mission more meaningful. I had never before, on my many inspection trips, had the services of a yeoman. But efficiency was not my only reason for taking Chief Marchal. I knew she would not only represent the enlisted WAVES handsomely, in every sense of the word, but she would also be able to give me, firsthand, the reaction of an enlisted WAVE to all we would see of the work of military women overseas.

Colonel Hallaren was also accompanied by an enlisted woman, Sergeant Mary Lever, and this arrangement had many advantages. When Colonel Hallaren and I were attending official receptions, the two girls were free to join enlisted Army women in their activities.

We arrived in England 6 April 1949. For the first week Colonel Hallaren was on her own schedule while I fulfilled the obligations arranged by the British Admiralty at the request of the U.S. Commander in Chief, Near East, Atlantic and Mediterranean (CinCNELM). My first day began immediately after an official call on Admiral R. L. Connolly (CinCNELM) and Admiral George Henderson at the U.S. Naval Headquarters, London.

Each day was filled with appointments and, since the first day is typical, it well serves as an example of the days and weeks following:

10:30: A call on the director of the Women's Reserve, Naval Service, Commodore Joyce Woollcombe, CBE, ADC, at Queen Anne's Mansions, where I met the ten members of her staff.

11:00: Press conference.

11:45: A call on Second Sea Lord of the Admiralty, Admiral Harcourt, who was of the unqualified opinion that the recent step to include women in the permanent British establishment was both wise and farsighted.

12:15: A two-hour conference with Commodore Woollcombe regarding all phases of administration of WRNS: training, discipline, utilization, uniforming, recruiting, pay and allowances, and various other considerations.

3:00 P.M.: Departure by train for Portsmouth accompanied by First Officer B. M. Hooppell, WRNS.

5:20 P.M.: Arrival at Portsmouth where I was taken at once to a reception followed by a dinner party given by Commodore and Mrs. D. P. Evans. Mrs. Evans, an American by birth, had served in the WRNS during World War II.

In Portsmouth I made a full tour of the WRNS facilities, saw the women at work and their quarters, both enlisted and officer. While naval life in England had some similarities to our own, there were great differences. In the manual labor and domestic categories, the British women were doing many tasks which had not even been studied as to suitability for WAVES. Creature comforts which we had taken for granted were either nonexistent or in short supply. For example, the WRNS had no central heating; small coal grates were lighted only after working hours. Only a short time earlier, showers had been installed for the women, but these had not proved popular, for they were of the overhead type used by men, with no movable shower heads, and, since shower caps were virtually impossible to come by, the showers soaked the WRNS' hair. Thus in many ways life was more rugged for the WRNS than for the WAVES, but this also was true of British civilian life. However, the peacetime barracks were a great improvement over what the WRNS had adapted themselves to during the war.

We lunched with the Commander in Chief Naval Forces in that historic vessel, HMS *Victory*, the ship on which Lord Horatio Nelson had died. The commanding officer pointed out to me that if I had noticed the meager stock of cannon balls there was a reason. During the war when many American ships were in the harbor, it had been customary to invite U.S. sailors, when the weather was bad, to await their liberty boats aboard *Victory*. Apparently the cannon balls had served as unique souvenirs.

247

Three days later, at Chatham, I was invited to take the "March Past" of the Women Royal Marines, and conduct personnel inspection. The review and inspection confirmed that the alert and trim appearance of the women reflected their total dedication to the ideals of excellence which they inherited from the male Marines.

During a visit to the Royal Naval Hospital I learned, in talking with the chief surgeon, Rear Admiral K. A. I. MacKensie, and the chief nurse, that the civilian nursing organization in England was accepting three years of service by "sick berth attendants" (the counterpart of our hospital corpsmen) as approximately one and one-half to two years credit toward a degree in nursing. This plan was devised to make available to the country more trained nurses, particularly to the Royal Navy Nurse Corps in which they would be commissioned. This information I was able to use to advantage later as I discussed with Captain Winifred Gibson, director of the U.S. Navy Nurse Corps, her proposal to initiate a program to interest WAVE hospital corpsmen in qualifying for commissions as Navy nurses.

During my last few days in London, I talked with the personnel officer at Naval Headquarters, Captain Warren, about the possibilities of assigning WAVES there. Our discussions were interspersed with radio broadcasts, press conferences, and visits to the British WRAC activities with Colonel Hallaren. We did not end our conversations; we delayed any definitive action until I should return to England. It was later decided that since staff personnel in the event of an emergency must be prepared to go to sea, there could only be a limited assignment of women. I was quite prepared to encounter a slow acceptance of the services of women in an activity which had not yet had their services. But it was satisfactory to be able to note that women, both officers and enlisted, were not long afterward assigned, living in the apartment arrangements we had surveyed, and filling the billets we had discussed.

Our next stop was Holland where, as elsewhere, we talked with the country's military representatives who were eager to learn about the experiences of women in the U.S. military services.

Each day Colonel Hallaren and I went our separate ways, she to visit the Dutch Army facilities and I to tour the MARVAS (women in Holland's navy), accompanied by Mafrau van Slooten, who was director of the MARVAS and who in World War II was an outstanding worker in the Dutch underground.

The MARVAS was not set up as a part of the regular navy, and the small organization was merely a nucleus since women in the service were strongly opposed by the general public and the churches, an opposition engendered primarily by what had been observed of German service women during the war. The German women, serving in Holland with the military, were of two distinct types, Mafrau van Slooten said; those who were sincerely trying to do their assigned work and were therefore infrequently seen in public, and those whose social and often immoral behavior created a highly unfavorable impression. Mafrau van Slooten, who believed sincerely in the worth of women's service and its future usefulness, was faced with the almost unsurmountable task of overcoming public opposition in establishing and maintaining the small nucleus permitted. She said that it was almost necessary to include parents in the training courses and encourage frequent visits to their daughters who were on duty in order to convince them of the decency and value of the program.

Our tour took us then to West Germany and Frankfurt, Heidelberg, Garmisch, Berlin, Munich, Berchtesgaden, Oberammergau, Bremerhaven, Vienna, Salzburg, Weisbaden, Paris, and Rome before returning to London. Accompanying Colonel Hallaren as she made her inspections enabled me to see how the Army women lived, their assignments, living quarters, mess facilities, recreational outlets, and civic activities in various youth programs. I was extremely impressed with the amount of effort the WAC were expending in their volunteer work with various civic and charitable organizations. Without exception, the commanding officers praised their work and conduct, requesting at the same time additional assignments of women to their commands.

In going to West Berlin, I was joined by Lieutenant Margaret Carver, who was assigned to the Navy's Air Transport Squadron One, one of the squadrons playing its part in the Berlin air lift. In one of VR-1's transports, we flew to the beleaguered city. The instructions, usually only for wartime, "If taken into custody, give only your name, rank and serial number," were grim. I clutched that small bit of notepaper throughout the flight, just in case we had a forced landing en route. However, the flight was uneventful, even when we made that always perilous approach through the chimneys around Templehof airport.

During the Berlin visit we attended a staff meeting of area commanders presided over by General Lucius Clay, America's High Commissioner. Later in the day, I reported to Headquarters, U.S. Naval Forces Germany, where I met the commander and members of his staff to discuss possible assignments of WAVES to his command. While expressing his desire to have WAVES assigned he thought it would be better, because of the tense political situation, to wait a year before making an official request. And I was not discouraged, for here the WAVES were wanted. It would just be a matter of time.

Berlin appalled us with the endless rubble on all sides, the evidence of the war bombings. We visited two hospitals where the buildings, equipment, and maintenance were in deplorable condition. The underground bomb shelters were being used to house the transients traveling from one sector of Germany to another. The transients were permitted only to sleep in these shelters and had to be out during the day, regardless of weather. Some of the people, their faces reflecting hopeless resignation, had been waiting for the necessary transfer approvals for as long as eleven or twelve weeks.

En route to Heidelberg, we visited various army installations in Austria and southern Germany. Our next destination was Bremerhaven where at the WAC mess hall a dinner party celebrated the birthday which Colonel Hallaren and I shared, 4 May. Colonel Hallaren departed early the next day for Frankfurt, but Chief Marchal and I stayed to inspect all possible accommodations in Bremerhaven which might be used if and when WAVES were assigned to that area. While in Bremerhaven I took personnel inspection of the men stationed there. While walking down one line, I recognized a petty officer whom I had known in the Bureau of Personnel. He also recognized me. I stopped for a few words of greeting and afterwards we had our picture taken together. Little moments like that make one feel elated.

That evening Chief Marchal and I departed for Frankfurt and traveled in a manner to which we had never had the opportunity to become accustomed. The train, now used by the American military government officials, and in no way changed from the condition in which it was taken over, had been designed for high Nazi military officials whose pomp and circumstances apparently dictated luxurious furnishings. Sunken marble bath tubs adjoined our bedrooms; the beds were fitted with linen sheets and silk covers; and we moved across deep pile rugs and read by the light of handsome bedside lamps. In the dining car, table silver and crystal vied with the furnishings. Incongruously against such a background I turned to the ordinary task of dictating material for my report. Chief Marchal and I hated to shorten our enjoyment of our extraordinary quarters by going to sleep. When we did finally retire, our beds had been turned down, the bedside lamps lighted and our baths drawn. The attendants aboard, all Germans in the pay of the United States, stood about waiting to fulfill our slightest wish. We were royalty for one night.

We managed with some difficulty the next day in Frankfurt to get back to our ordinary environments and hour-to-hour schedules. Accompanied by Lieutenant Margaret Carver, I inspected the living facilities of the WAVES who were serving as flight orderlies in the Navy's Transport Squadron Three, operating between the United States and Germany. Everything —security, quartering and supervision—was satisfactory, and the WAVES described themselves as fortunate to have such exciting duty. (I later found the same satisfactory condition existing in the Azores, a stopover point on the U.S.—Germany run, where Lieutenant Margaret Randall was the Navy's transportation officer.)

During a brief interlude in Paris, I met, through the good offices of our U.S. naval attaché, Captain Henri Smith-Hutton, the assistant director of Femmes de la Flotte, Madame Justin Thierry. The skeleton organization of the women in the French navy followed the wartime pattern, but there were very few women participating (18 officers and 150 enlisted women plus 200 nurses and nurses' aides), and all on a volunteer basis. No plans were in the making to establish the program permanently. It was interesting to note, however, that the few women who were performing this volunteer duty were still wearing the same type of uniform given to the French government during the war, that is, WAVE uniforms.

On 12 May, Chief Marchal and I were back in Frankfurt in time to attend a dinner at the Rhine Main Officers' Club to celebrate the lifting of the Berlin blockade. The entire operation, from beginning to end, had proved to be a marvelous exhibition of aeronautical skill on the part of the U.S. Navy's Air Transport Squadrons Six and Eight of the command, in that it had established an outstanding record for safety under exceedingly hazardous conditions. Their offices, which I visited, were crude shacks near the end of the runways—out in the boondocks, as the Navy men put it. In bad weather, the pilots wore rubber boots and trudged to and from their planes. Only small, pot-bellied stoves furnished heat. Loading cargoes of coal and food was a triumph over unsatisfactory conditions, but the squadrons had carried out their missions on time and to the letter.

But there remained on my schedule three unusual occasions, and for the first we joined Colonel Hallaren in Rome where she had arranged, through the office of the Honorable Myron Taylor, American delegate to the Vatican, for our party of four to have an audience with Pope Pius XII. Since Colonel Hallaren and Chief Marchal were Catholics and Sergeant Lever and I were Protestants, I assumed, as it turned out incorrectly, that I would be an observer. Later I learned that the Pope was particularly interested in all things naval. He directed his questions to me. I had not been instructed as to what to do during the audience and I had planned just to follow the lead of Colonel Hallaren.

As the Pope entered the audience room, I was struck with the fraility and serenity of his appearance, his ethereal appearance suggesting the delicacy of a bas relief in alabaster. His long robes of white were accentuated against the vivid colors of the uniforms of the Swiss Guards and the scarlet robes of his assistants. As he extended his hand to me I instinctively knelt and, remembering from somewhere the appropriate salute, I kissed the papal ring, only then to be shocked to note a slight touch of lipstick I had left just above the ring. I rose and faced him to see again only the tranquility of his expression. He questioned me about the employment and training of women in our Navy and asked whether or not the women in America had volunteered in sufficient numbers to meet requirements. He terminated the audience by saying, "Never forget this great responsibility which you carry. I desire to bless your work and to bless all the families of the women under your guidance."

I was deeply impressed by his apparent understanding of the contribution of the WAVES and his interest in them. Later, back in the States, I described this audience, on many occasions and at many places, to the WAVES.

The second occasion occurred in London near the close of my tour, when I was presented to King George and Queen Elizabeth at Buckingham Palace at an afternoon reception attended by approximately two thousand guests. Planned as a garden party, the function took place in the palace owing to a heavy rain, and their Royal Highnesses proceeded through the reception rooms bowing to the assembled guests.

While awaiting them to come to the central reception hall, I was presented to the Lord Chamberlain and the Princess Royal, Princess Mary. In meeting the princess, she seemed not a stranger, for in childhood I had collected many pictures published of the royal family where she was the only girl in the group. Princess Mary expressed great interest in the work which the women in the U.S. Navy were performing in peacetime and was impressed by the variety.

When the King and Queen appeared at the great entrance to the central reception room, I was escorted by a lady in waiting up the aisle between the guests to meet them. This again was a "first" which I had to play by ear, an assignment made extremely simple by the genuine graciousness of the King and Queen. On being presented I merely bowed since I believed that any attempt to make a curtsy by a woman in uniform would appear ridiculous.

The King immediately started to question me—I had been told that he would do so—about the uniform, the reason for its various features, and particularly about our new evening uniform which had appeared in the London papers the evening before, and about the designer. I answered his questions, and upon further questioning assured him that the designer, Mainbocher, was an American. He said he thought the uniform so smart that he would like to have had the credit for such a magnificent piece of work. Turning to the Queen he said, "With the exception of your own bonnet, I think that Captain Hancock is wearing the smartest hat at the party today."

The Queen then talked with me for several minutes about the WAVE program and asked if WAVES were to be assigned to London and, if so, when they would arrive. She extended to me her personal welcome to London and her hope that the WAVES and the women of the British military services would come to know one another well. I was personally gratified by the recognition accorded the WAVES and the knowledge of their honorable reputation.

The third occasion came at the end of the same day when I proceeded with Commodore Joyce Woollcombe to the Naval College, Greenwich, for dinner in the Painted Hall as guest of Captain Browning, commanding officer of the college. At the close of dinner, Captain Browning offered a toast to the President of the United States, and I, as senior American naval officer present, was asked to propose the toast to the King.

As I looked down the vast dining hall at those four hundred officers in military dinner clothes, the scene made brilliant with ancient silver and crystal reflecting the candlelight, I marveled how, despite the adversities of war, not only the silver and crystal, but also, more important, ancient British traditions survived. With my heart gladdened that this was so, I offered the toast "Ladies and Gentlemen, His Majesty King George VI." All rose to their feet, raised their glasses, and said, "The King, the King."

Captain Browning then said to the assembly, "This is the first occasion in the history of the Naval College, Greenwich, that a woman has proposed the official toast to the King, and it shall be so recorded in the annals of the college."

Possibly it was another case of the contrasts life always seems to offer after an exalted moment, but it did seem incongruous that the next event of the evening was to go to the bowling alleys with the commanding officer and his staff. With no question as to whether or not I played, I was assigned to a team. (It had been twenty years since I had bowled.) The alleys were a bit warped "due to neglect during the war, you know," but enthusiasm ran high. Probably only the warped condition of the alleys made my total of two strikes possible, or else Providence stood by me so that I might make a good account of myself for the WAVES.

The following morning Commodore Woollcombe and I proceeded to Burfield, Reading, to visit HMTS *Dauntless* where all WRNS recruits were trained. Upon arrival, a WRNS guard of honor stationed at the Top Gate greeted us. The Top Gate, I was informed, had been used for entrance by women on only two other occasions; the visit of Queen Elizabeth (now the Queen Mother) and the Duchess of Kent, who held the honorary rank of commodore in the WRNS.

My trip abroad was drawing to a close and, with my official report current, Chief Marchal and I departed on 28 May on a Navy plane for the United States via Port Lyauty, Africa, the Azores, Argentia in Newfoundland, then Westover, Massachusetts. Both Chief Marchal and I, though weary, agreed that the six weeks had been crowded with experiences which could never be duplicated.

At top, as the wife of Admiral Ralph A. Ofstie, Commander of the Sixth Fleet, Joy Bright Ofstie meets the King and Queen of Greece. Left to right: Princess Sophie, Prince Constantine, King Paul, Mrs. Ofstie, Admiral Ofstie, and Queen Frederika aboard the USS *Newport News*, in the port of Piraeus, Greece.

Above, the Directors of the Women's Components of the Armed Forces. Left to right, standing: Colonel Ruby Bryant, Army Nurse Corps; Colonel Miram E. Perry, Air Force Women's Medical Specialist Corps; Captain Winifred Gibson, Navy Nurse Corps; Colonel Emma Vogel, Army Women's Medical Specialist Corps; Colonel Derena M. Zeller, Air Force Nurse Corps. Left to right, seated: Captain Joy Bright Hancock, Director, WAVES; Colonel Mary Hallaren, Director, WAC; Colonel Katherine Towle, Director, Women Marines; and Colonel Mary Jo Shelly, Director, WAF.

It was not until November 1967 that the bill which removed the restrictions of rank for all women in the armed services was signed by President Lyndon B. Johnson. *Opposite*, Captain Hancock is presented to President Johnson.

Summing Up

As the day of mandatory retirement approached, upon reaching the age of fifty-five in May 1953, I submitted to the Chief of Naval Personnel an accounting of my stewardship. In writing this report, and making certain recommendations, I was somewhat amazed and certainly pleased by what had been accomplished just prior to and following the passage of the Women's Armed Services Integration Act, Public Law 625.

From 1948 until 1953, one of the principal goals had been accomplished: the integration of women in the regular Navy. Now that the naval planners were taking into active consideration this relatively new component, women officers, line and staff, were eligible to attend all appropriate postgraduate schools, and their interchangeability with male officers in billets was recognized. For the enlisted women, twenty-eight of the existing rating fields were available, and opportunities for commissioned status were fully established under the "Integration Program."

In anticipation of the passage of P.L. 625, plans had been made and approved, during 1946, 1947, and 1948, for its implementation. A strength figure of from approximately 4,500 to 5,000 enlisted women and approximately 500 officers was visualized. At the time of the passage of the legislation, there were on active duty only 1,510 enlisted women and 416 officers. The quota imputs established were very low and at the end of the first two years of the program there were on active duty in the regular Navy only 2,610 enlisted and 348 officers.

The Korean War necessitated the voluntary and involuntary recall of reservists to active duty, both men and women, and a naval expansion program got under way.

This program, which called for a 300 percent on-board increase of enlisted women, created certain problems in the enlisted structure, the greatest being the ratio of petty officers to nonrated women—17.5 percent to 82.5 percent, respectively. This problem was increased by the need to assign petty officers to recruiting, leadership school quotas, communications and hospitals. Of the 1,345 women on hand, 605 were assigned to these activities. In consequence, at activities to which large numbers of nonrated women were assigned, an undesirable lack, of close supervision prevailed. Furthermore, commanding officers were reluctant to assign trained clerical and technical petty officers to duties of administering barracks, even on the basis of a six-month rotation, for these women could hardly be spared from the tasks for which they were trained. They had, for the most part, never served outside the duties of their ratings and often lacked the necessary qualities for successfully supervising personnel. Thus we were faced with the neccessity, in some instances, of using seamen fresh from recruit school as masters-at-arms in the barracks.

To alleviate this problem, the Petty Officers Leadership Schools opened in February 1953 at San Diego, California, and Bainbridge, Maryland. The four-week courses, for which the quotas were 25 per month on a returnable basis (the students returned to their stations of origin), were designed to demonstrate and develop leadership. Time alone would produce the desired number, but the opening of the schools was a necessity if we were to have some of the supervisory staff so much needed.

Another reason for establishing the leadership program was to strengthen the possibility of having the right kind of training available for potential warrant officers. At the time WAVES were transferring to the regular Navy in 1948, two women who were lieutenants (junior grade) USNR accepted transfer in the warrant grade. However, it was not until 1949 that consideration was given to enlisted women with six years of service. Until March 1953, only two enlisted women were selected for warrant grade, and one of these failed to qualify physically. One woman was appointed a warrant officer by presidential request; this brought the total to four. One reason more were not selected was that, while women might be entirely qualified in the technical aspects of their ratings, they did not possess as wide backgrounds as the men or as varied experience in the military factors of their ratings.

Another recommendation I made dealt with the opportunities for advancement for enlisted personnel in connection with the limited duty officer (LDO) category. Public Law 381, which established the category, did not include women nor was that inclusion visualized by the legislators at the time of the passage of Public Law 625, but the language of the earlier law did not bar women from making application for such appointment. However, until 1951, the minimum age for enlistment of women was twenty years, and therefore no woman could be eligible for the LDO category until 1961, and then only those who had enlisted at the age of eighteen or nineteen. I urged that study be made to determine the feasibility of lowering the active naval service requirement from ten to eight years in order that at least some of our enlisted women—and men, too—might be eligible to apply. Another reason for this request was that we needed to increase the officer base in the lower grades in order to secure the additional numbers needed with which to bring into balance the existing structure on which officer promotion was based. This recommendation, when studied as a part of the overall personnel plans of the Navy, did not warrant adoption.

In framing Public Law 625, the Navy carefully considered the rank structure and the opportunities for future selection of women officers. The top permanent rank of commander, the percentage of 20 percent for lieutenant commanders and 10 percent for commanders, as well as the number of opportunities for consideration for selection (taking into account the mandatory retirement ages for women) were deemed satisfactory. However, by 1953, there arose an unforeseen situation; promotion from lieutenant to lieutenant commander was an almost impossible hurdle to clear because of the lack of input into the regular Navy in the grades of lieutenant (junior grade) and ensign on which the percentages for the higher ranks were based. This. I believe, was not due to any unsoundness in the basic law, but rather, to our inability to interest young women in a naval career without the incentive or impetus of war.

Another problem was housing. With the decrease in the numbers of women in the Navy following World War II, the barracks, originally modified for WAVES, were in good condition and more attractive, with their cubicles, than the open-bay barracks. As a consequence, these barracks were taken over in many instances by male chief petty officers and lower grade petty officers. In 1952 a survey revealed that housing was available for approximately 7,500 enlisted women and there was an on-board total of 8,488. At some locations the services of women could not be utilized in sufficient numbers to fill available housing; at others, the women exceeded the housing facilities. I recommended that more accurate housing reports be made by shore activities and thus women could be assigned to locations where adequate housing was available, and peacemeal submission of housing projects need not be turned down for lack of budgeted funds.

Another of my final recommendations had to do with rotation and reenlistment of women: In September 1948 when the first women were enlisted in the regular Navy, two, three, four and six-year enlistments were authorized. A year later, in September 1949, the two and three-year enlistments were suspended. In 1952, it was found that of the 413 women who were discharged by reason of expiration of enlistment during an eighteen-month period, 235 of them reenlisted. Although this was considered a good rate, we were not securing the desired number of recruits. I felt that a four or six-year commitment was formidable for an 18 to 20-year old. Rarely is a girl in this age bracket career-minded, so I recommended a restudy of the shorter terms of enlistment. This was done, and found to be unacceptable, and rightly so, from the standpoint of cost. Taking into account three months in recruit training and additional service school training, the Navy could not derive sufficient return in service.

As one of my last official acts before retirement, I participated, as reviewing officer, in the recruit review and graduation exercises of the men and women at the U.S. Naval Training Center, Bainbridge, Maryland, on 23 May 1953, at the invitation of Captain Frederick Wolsieffer, the commanding officer of the Recruit Training Command. For me it was a day filled with emotion as well as great pride. My mother, my brother Ward and his wife, and several friends of the family were on hand to witness the brilliant scene characteristic of graduations.

I had, on several occasions, served as reviewing officer, but this review was to be the last. Before me on the field, in whites, the men and women of the Navy were drawn up in company formation. The women were only a small part of the assembled recruits, of which there were well over fifteen hundred, but they were the living symbol of what we had hoped to accomplish in the program for women in the Navy— an integral part of the service. Their training as recruits paralleled that of the men. In advanced and specialized training they would attend schools with the men and compete with them for class standing. In qualifying for promotions, they would be governed by the same criteria of performance. Any breach of naval regulations was covered by the same code of discipline. All this so that the women's contributions would be as valuable as that of the men. To use an old expression, they must pull their own weight in the boat if they would be accepted without question.

At this ninety-seventh graduation review, both the WAVE and male recruit drill teams performed in front of the reviewing stand. Both were excellent, but I remember feeling somewhat smug because that sense of rhythm possessed by women seemed to give them a slight edge in performance. Or could it be that I was not entirely objective in judging the performances that day?

In introducing me to the assembled troops, Captain Wolsieffer ended his remarks by saying:

"And now, it is with distinct honor and great pleasure that I introduce to you my esteemed friend and colleague, the Assistant Chief of Naval Personnel for Women, the First Lady of the Navy, Captain Joy Bright Hancock."

At the end of the ceremonies, I formally departed the reviewing stand, accompanied by Captain Wolsieffer and Lieutanant Commander Jean Stewart, officer in charge of WAVE recruit training. WAVE personnel of the ship's company lined the walkway and rendered a farewell salute.

But there was still another memorable occasion. On 29 May 1953, the Secretary of the Navy, the Honorable Robert B. Anderson, in his office in the Pentagon, awarded me the Legion of Merit. At the ceremony, the secretary's aide read the citation and Secretary Anderson pinned the medal on my uniform in the presence of officers who had gathered to wish me well. The citation read:

"For exceptionally meritorious conduct in the performance of outstanding services to the Government of the United States as Director of the Women's Reserve of the Naval Reserve from July 1946 to October 1948, and as Assistant Chief of Naval Personnel for Women from October 1948 to June 1953. Exercising organizational and administrative ability of the highest caliber, Captain Hancock served with distinction throughout the transition period in which women became a regular component of the United States Navy, and was eminently successful in initiating the basic plans and in overcoming the many varied and complex problems which confronted her during the inaugural stages incident to establishing the women as an integral part of the naval service. A resourceful and inspiring leader, she was directly instrumental in the formation of plans and policies affecting the selection and training of the women, together with their utilization, administration, welfare and housing. Skillfully welding the personnel under her leadership into a highly efficient unit, she maintained a coordinated and effective command and contributed immeasurably to the success achieved by women in the various fields to which they were assigned throughout the naval service. Her outstanding professional skill, sound judgment and unswerving devotion to duty reflect the highest credit upon Captain Hancock and the United States Naval Service."

And how I dreaded the final orders which would place me on the retired rolls of the Navy. Yet even that circumstance was softened for me by a letter from the Secretary of the Navy:

"On the occasion of your retirement, I wish to take this opportunity to express my sincere appreciation for your distinguished service to our Nation.

"During your career including service in both World Wars I and II you have witnessed many advancements in the morale, strength, and efficiency of the Navy. You have contributed materially to the accomplishments of these results by the skillful direction, sound judgment, and determination you have applied to the tasks assigned you. Your record reflects your excellent service reputation for ability in planning and administration. You were commended by the Secretary of the Navy for your outstanding performance of duty from October 24, 1942 to October 23, 1945. Your subsequent service as Assistant Chief of Naval Personnel for Women has been of the same high level of performance. More than any one individual you are responsible for the establishment of the WAVES as a component of the Navy. Your ideals, energy, and enthusiasm are continually reflected in the integration of women into the regular Navy. The standards of leadership and performance you have maintained have had an incalculable effect upon the training and shaping the career of the numerous officers and enlisted personnel with whom you have been in contact. Your loyalty and devotion to duty throughout has reflected the highest credit upon you and the Naval service. I know that the Navy can depend upon your loyal support during the years to come.

"I sincerely regret your separation from active service and wish you continued success and many years of happiness."

I could not visualize what my life would be like without the compelling demands of a Navy schedule. All I knew was that I deeply regretted having to retire from the naval service, for the Navy had been the basis of my life for decades and within it I had formed lasting friendships. I had enjoyed carrying out varied tasks and missions and had known the rewards of accomplishment.

Since I was no Joshua and could not hold time back, the crucial day, 1 June 1953, arrived on schedule. The farewell parties and receptions, the many letters of congratulation received from the highest ranking officers in the Navy and Marine Corps and members of Congress, as well as from my WAVE colleagues, could not but give me a deep feeling of satisfaction and happiness.

With my retirement home on St. Croix in the Virgin Islands ready and my home in Virginia sold I departed, bag and baggage, to begin a new life in which I hoped to find time to write, paint, and travel. It was not by chance that I left Washington quickly. I felt strongly that I should not stay in the area lest I be tempted to look over the shoulder of my successor. I had seen too many cases where unsolicited suggestions hindered rather than helped, and I had resolved never to be guilty of this offense.

That first year of retirement yielded no time for the activities I had planned. Instead, since the "finished" house on St. Croix was far from ready, I was at once plunged into doing a succession of chores and consigned by necessity to manual labor. I learned to operate a tractor and small bulldozer so as to cut and keep open the roads to, from, and around my property.

Because everything grew rapidly, landscaping was bound to be successful. Transplanting varieties of cacti, palms, papaya and banana trees was strenuous work but worth it, for overnight they flourished.

And then the rains came. The cisterns were filled to overflowing; the banana and papaya trees were already as tall as I. But while the plants flourished, I wilted and needed a vacation. So I left for my home in New Jersey.

Among the friends who had come to visit me on St. Croix —WAVES from San Juan, relatives and friends from the mainland—was my old friend, Ralph Ofstie, now a vice admiral. Since he was to play so significant a role in my first retirement years, I need at this point to tell something of our long-standing friendship.

I had first known of him in October 1925 when I attended the Schneider Cup Race near Baltimore, escorted by Commander Richard Evelyn Byrd and Lieutenant Elmer F. Stone, U.S. Coast Guard, the latter having been a member of the crew of the Navy's NC-4 flying boat which made the first transatlantic crossing. Lieutenant Ofstie, who in 1924 had established three world speed records for seaplanes, piloted an R3C-2, the engine of which failed, to his great disgust, on the final lap. Two years later I actually met him in the lobby of the world-famed Shepheard's Hotel in Cairo, when I was on a Mediterranean cruise, and he was attached to the USS *Detroit* as senior aviation officer.

During the following years, Ralph Ofstie was to become one of our most decorated naval officers. Included in his twenty-three awards were the Navy Cross, two Distinguished Service Medals, and four Legions of Merit. These reflected his combat record in the Pacific in World War II, his service as Senior Delegate to the United Nations Commission for the military armistice negotiations in Korea, and his membership on the Military Liaison Committee to the Atomic Energy Commission.

Now, in 1954, as I spent the summer in Wildwood, New Jersey, my relationship to Admiral Ofstie was to enter a new phase. It was during this vacation that Ralph Ofstie and I agreed that St. Croix would be a fine place for both of us to spend part of each year following his retirement, which he had already planned to take place at the end of his current tour of duty as Deputy Chief of Naval Operations for Air. With this in prospect, we were married in August.

But the lure of just one more tour of duty overcame his plans to retire when he was offered the post of Commander, Sixth Fleet, operating in the Mediterranean. He found it no problem to convince me of the advantages of accepting the assignment, so in 1955 we went to Europe to enjoy the most exhilarating and fabulous year either of us had ever known. Retirement had not separated me from the Navy.

Beginning with our arrival in London and continuing throughout the year, I met again and again the WAVES stationed there and in Paris, Naples, and Frankfurt. The many get-togethers were reunions. On one occasion, some twenty WAVES serving at the Supreme Headquarters Allied Powers, in Paris, invited me to a luncheon at the Enlisted Club. At the U-shaped table which permitted easy "Do you remember?" conversation, I found I had known practically every one of the WAVES who had served at naval activities in the United States. Such was the fruit of my years as director of the WAVES when I had on inspection trips made it a practice to have "barracks meetings" at which the enlisted women and I had discussed freely matters of concern to them.

Still an earlier chapter in my life was a basis for my role as wife of the Commander of the Sixth Fleet. In the early 1920s, I had been, ever so briefly, a Navy wife, though, of course the duties of a wife of a junior officer were infinitesimal compared with those expected of the wife of a vice admiral, particularly on foreign duty. The social responsibilities as we traveled from port to port were sometimes physically wearisome but always rewarding.

Day by day, Ralph and I found the activities absorbing as he played his diplomatic role in port after port. So much was crowded into that year in the Mediterranean that it went all too fast.

In the spring of 1956, Ralph became ill. We flew to the Army Hospital at Landstuhl, Germany, where it was determined that surgery was indicated. And so we returned to the United States and to the Naval Hospital at Bethesda, Maryland.

Before his death several months later, there proved to be time to discuss, relive, and enjoy the events of that full and exciting year with the Sixth Fleet.

On 21 May 1959 I attended, as sponsor, an impressive ceremony held in Puerto Rico, when Ofstie Field was dedicated to the memory of my husband. Its strategic location at the Naval Station, Roosevelt Roads, where its facilities are in the furtherance of the operational units of the Atlantic Fleet, makes its name highly appropriate.

Within this book I have tried to tell the story as I saw it of the program for women in the Navy, from its beginning until I retired in 1953.

Although there were in the Navy at the beginning of World War II those who did not visualize the need for or possible utilization of womanpower within the service there were, fortunately, others whose foresight, interest, and confidence inspired them to make plans for the possible future need of this source. Such plans were realistic in that they were based largely on the reports being received of the accomplishments demonstrated by women in the British armed services and by civilian women in the United States already working in large numbers in aircraft plants and other wartime production industries.

And so, when legislation was finally enacted, a call for women's services was issued. There was no draft or conscription involved, but the women came forward, eagerly and proudly, to contribute their talents and skills. Their capacity to learn and to perform tasks in fields of work heretofore unknown to them brought high praise even from those men who had not been able to recognize their potential worth. Such praise did not cause the women to lose their sense of proportion, for they realized that what they did could not compare, in terms of sacrifice, to the work of the fighting men. They struck no heroic attitudes. Instead, they quietly demonstrated their qualifications and won the respect of the men of the Navy. They also demonstrated their devotion to and respect for the traditions of the organization of which they had become a part. While there continued to be a few naval men who doubted the necessity of having women in the Navy, once the war was over, this attitude appeared to be largely held by the few who felt that their own careers might be jeopardized by the competition with women. But the view did not prevail, and the women gradually achieved acceptance.

The women in the Navy, as did those in the other military services, by their successful performance of duties, contributed mightily to the sociological picture of women in the twentieth century. In fact, they created a new evaluation of the worth of womanpower.

However, it was not until November 1967, twenty-five years after the legislation authorizing women in the Naval Reserve, and almost twenty years after the legislation authorizing them in the regular Navy, that President Lyndon B. Johnson signed the bill which removed the restrictions of rank for all women in the armed services.

I admit to great pride in having had the privilege of being one of the leaders of an outstanding group of women, the WAVES. To them I shall always owe a debt of gratitude for they, by their performance, loyalty, and dedication, and their pride in the service, made our accomplishments possible.

Appendixes

CHRONOLOGY

30 July 1942: President Roosevelt signed legislation authorizing enlistment and commissioning of women in U.S. Naval
Reserve.

August 1942: Mildred McAfee, President of Wellesley College, sworn in as Director, Women's Reserve, with rank of
lieutenant commander.

August 1942: Advance class of probationary officers enters
Naval Reserve Midshipmen's School, Northampton, Massachusetts (Smith College) for indoctrination.

October 1942: First three enlisted schools open at Stillwater, Oklahoma (yeomen); Bloomington, Indiana (storekeepers); and Madison, Wisconsin (radio men).

November 1942: First officers and enlisted women from
training schools report for duty.

1 February 1943: Five aviation specialist schools opened to
women (coeducational).

February 1943: U.S. Naval Training School (WR) the Bronx
(Hunter College) commissioned formally for recruit training.

30 July 1943: First anniversary. 27,000 WAVES on duty in U.S.

November 1943: Act of Congress provided WAVES eligible
for all benefits and allowances available to Navy men.
Former restrictions on the number of women in each rank

269

were removed and provision was made for one officer to hold rank of captain, exclusive of women in Medical Department of the Navy.

November 1943: Director of Women's Reserve, Mildred McAfee, promoted to rank of Captain, USNR.

30 July 1944: Second anniversary. 72,350 women in naval service.

September 1944: Act of Congress permitted WAVES to volunteer for service outside continental U.S. in American area, Territory of Hawaii, and Alaska.

December 1944: Last class graduated from WR Midshipmen's school, Northampton. Over 9,000 women officers had been trained there.

30 July 1945: Third anniversary. 86,000 women on duty in U.S. and Hawaii.

August 1945: Navy announces its demobilization plan.

October 1945: Last class graduated from recruit school, the Bronx.

February 1946: Commander Jean Palmer becomes Director of Women's Reserve.

February 1946: Commander Hancock appointed Assistant Director of Women's Reserve (Plans).

27 March 1946: Legislation introduced in the Congress regarding women in peacetime Navy.

July 1946: Commander Hancock appointed Director of WR with rank of Captain, USNR.

12 June 1948: Women's Armed Services Act, PL 625, authorizing regular Navy participation, approved.

September 1948: Establishment of recruit training—regular Navy, Great Lakes Training Center, Illinois.

1 January 1949: Establishment of Officer Indoctrination Training—regular Navy, at Newport, Rhode Island.

July 1950: Establishment of Reserve Officer Candidate (ROC) training.

July 1948: First enlisted women sworn into regular Navy.

October 1948: First women officers sworn into regular Navy.

June 1953: Captain Joy Bright Hancock retires from the Navy.

8 November 1967: Legislation signed by President Johnson removing rank restriction from women in the Armed Forces.

OFFICER BILLETS HELD BY WOMEN

(As of 12/11/46)

Aviation
Aerological engineering
Aeronautical engineering
Air combat information
Air navigation gunnery instructor
Air transportation
Assembly and repair vocational training
Celestial navigation (air navigation)
Editor—Navy publications
Flight desk
Flight records
Link training
Photographic interpretation
Recognition
Recognition and gunnery
Radio-radar (administration)
Schedules
Special devices
Traffic control

Civil Engineering Corps
Design and maintenance
Sanitary engineer

Communications
Censorship (cable, postal, and telephone)
Coding
Communications (including CWO)
Courier
Cryptanalyst
Issuing
Postal
Radio
Registered publications
Telephone operations
Teletype operations

Intelligence
Area specialists
Language specialists
Publications research

Supply Corps
Accounting
Commissary
Contract termination
Disbursing
Incoming stores
Inventory control
Marketing (foods and provisions)
Nutritional research
Outgoing stores
Purchasing (material and equipment)
Ship's service
Statistical
Stock control
Storage
Supply
Transportation
Travel claims
War bonds

Legal
Claims attorney
Legal assistance

Legislative counsel assistant
Legislative liaison
Naval Courts and Boards rewrite specialists
Regulations consultant

Medical Service
Bacteriologist
Hematologist
Hygienist (dental)
Medical illustrator
Medical research
Occupational therapist
Parasitologist
Physiotherapist
Physiologist
Psychologist
Serologist

Medical Corps
Medical doctors (general and specialists)

General Line
Administrative assistant
Billet analyst
Cartographer
Chemical
Civil readjustment
Classification
Commissioned officer's mess
Demobilization
Education training
Educational services
Historical officer
Housing
Hydrographic
Insurance
Material (public works)
Machine record installation (IBM)
Navy Relief
Operations (ship movement, plotting, and routing)
Personnel (civilian and military)
Physical training
Public information
Security
Statistical

Technical editor and writer
Visual aids
Welfare and recreation

Dental Corps
Dentists

Engineering and electronics
Electronics instructors
Project engineers
Radar technicians
Radio-radar material
Sonar technicians

RATINGS HELD BY ENLISTED WOMEN

(As of 12/11/46)

Seaman
Hospital apprentice
Pharmacist's mate
Aerographer's mate
Aviation machinist's mate
Aviation machinist's mate (instrument)
Aviation metalsmith
Parachute rigger
Radioman
Electrician's mate
Telegrapher
Storekeeper
Storekeeper D (disbursing)
Storekeeper T (technical)
Storekeeper V (aviation)
Yeoman
Electronic technician's mate
Aviation electronic technician's mate
Ship's cook
Ship's cook B (butcher)
Baker

Printer
Printer M (offset duplicating process)
Ship's serviceman L (laundryman)
Ship's serviceman T (tailor)
Ship's serviceman B (barber)
Aviation ordinanceman
Mailman
Specialist (C), classification interviewer
Specialist (E), recreation and welfare
Specialist (G), aviation free gunnery instructor
Specialist (I), punched card accounting machine operator
Specialist (P), photographic specialist
Specialist (P) (ACR), aviation camera repairman
Specialist (Q), communications
Specialist (R), recruiter
Specialist (S), personnel supervisor-barracks administration
Specialist (T), teacher
Specialist (T) (LT), instructor-navigational aids
Specialist (T) (LCNT), instructor in celestial navigation aids
Specialist (W), chaplain's assistant
Specialist (X), pigeon trainer
Specialist (Y), control tower operator
Specialist (V), transport airman

HOSPITAL CORPS BILLETS ASSIGNED TO WAVES

(As of 12/11/46)

General ward duty (care of sick and injured personnel)

Operating room technician (care of operating room and instruments, assist doctor in operations, work in central dressing room, preparation of materials and solutions)

Laboratory technician (work in blood bank or in pathology, hematology, blood chemistry, bacteriology, serology, and parasitology laboratories)

X-ray technician (give treatments, take and process X-rays, assist doctors during fluoroscopic examinations)

Electrocardiograph technician

Dental technician (general dental assistant or prosthetic technician)

Technician in neuropsychiatry (care of neuropsychiatric patients)

Assistant in neuropsychiatric clerical procedures (filing, preparation of cases and forms)

Pharmacist

Assistant in clinics

Occupational therapy assistant

Physical therapy assistant

Teacher of deaf

Teacher of blind

Teacher of orthopedically handicapped
Medical illustrator
Medical artist for plastic eyes
Medical photographer
Sound motion-picture technician
Commissary and diet kitchen worker
Assistant in low-pressure chamber (work in altitude training program for aviators, operation of chamber, repair of oxygen equipment)
Telephone operator, typist, file clerk, property and accounting clerk, ship's service clerk, general office assistant, librarian

SEAMAN BILLETS IN THE WAVES

Bookkeeper
Typist
File clerk
Key-punch operator
Comptometer operator
Mechanical draftsman
Statistical draftsman
Statistical clerk
Cartographer
Research assistant
Librarian
Receptionist
Escort and messengers
Teletype operator
Switchboard operator
Elevator operator
Mimeograph operator
Multilith operator
Offset press operator
Assistant printer
Photostat operator
Developer of negatives

Photograph printer
Copy-camera operator
Photograph enlarger
Musical copyist
Hairdresser
Barber
Assistant master-at-arms in barracks
Line assistant
Laboratory technician
Chauffeur
Laundry worker
Commercial artist
Electrical draftsman
Accountant
Film projectionist
Linotype operator
Publications assembly worker
General office worker
Photographer
Varitypist
Ship's service clerk
Strikers for various petty officer ratings open to women

Index

Babine, Slc Mary, 204
Baldwin, Alice M., 60, 124
Baldwin, Raymond E., 227-28, 229
Ball, Comdr. Beatrice, 226
Ballentine, Lt. Elizabeth, 123
Bassett, 168, 169
Beard, Ens. Rachel A., 88
Beaulieu, Ens. Evelyn H., 88
Bogue, Lt. (jg.) Jane, 62
Bowman, Lt. Mary, 211
Bradburn, P01c Mary, 211
Bright, Comdr. Cooper B., 166, 202
Bright, Eloise, 16, 19, 33, 40
Bright, Henry, 5, 9, 12
Bright, Mary M., 5
Bright, Priscilla B., 7-8, 10, 33, 171, 228, 261
Bright, Comdr. Ward H., 96, 135, 228, 261
Bright, William Henry, 5, 12-13, 15-16, 17-18, 19; marriage, 8; occupation 6, 9
British Admiralty, 246
Brown, John Nicholas, 158
Brown, Mrs. John Nicholas, 157, 158
Brown, Lt. (jg.) Mary Elizabeth, 88
Browning, Capt., Royal Navy, 253, 254
Buck, Amandus, 8
Buck, Flora, 8
Buck, Louisa, 8
Buckingham Palace, 252
Bullis, Lt. Comdr. William A., 77
Bureau of Aeronautics, 37, 51-52, 54, 88, 89; early planning, 48-49, 185; issues on housing, 177-78; overseas billets, 197-98; requests WAVES, 61
Bureau of the Budget, 53
Bureau of Medicine and Surgery, 51, 84, 211
Bureau of Naval Personnel, 49, 52, 54, 55, 65, 101, 211; early planning, 61; organizational problems, 66-68, 70, 177-78; re-commends women's reserve, 53
Bureau of Ordnance, 51, 81-83
Bureau of Ships, 51, 83, 120
Bureau of Supplies and Accounts, 51, 81
Bureau of Yards and Docks, 51
Byrd, Comdr. Richard Evelyn, 264
Byron, John, 179

C-5 (airship), 31-32
Camera repairman, 136-37
Cape May Court House, 12, 13
Carlin, Lt. (jg.) Virginia, 62
Carof, Ens. Zelda, 88
Carver, Lt. Margaret, 249, 251
Cassity, P02c Aloha M., 205
Castlereagh, 7, 16
Champion, Mr. (bicycle shop owner), 14
Cheney, Lt. Mary Grace, 62
Chief of Naval Operations, 51, 52, 54
Chung, Margaret, 54
Clay, Gen. Lucius, 250
Cochrane, Rear Adm. E. L., 83
Collett, 165
Communications school, 79
Comstock, Ada, 60
Connolly, Adm. R. L., 246
Control tower operators, 133-34, 191-93, 212
Cook, Rear Adm. A. B., 49
Cook and baker ratings, 144
Coolidge, Mrs. Calvin, 39
Cooper, Capt. George, 23
Crandall, Lt. Elizabeth Borland, 62, 71, 77, 79
Cranmore, Lt. Doris, 238
Curtis, Lt. Comdr. Katherine, 241

DACOWITS, 241, 242, 243
Daily, Lt. Comdr. Mary, 62, 71
Daniels, Josephus, 22, 28, 48
Darden, Capt. Thomas, 230
Dauntless, HMS, 37

Dauntless, HMTS, 254
Davis, Ens. B. M., 96
Davison, Rear Adm. Ralph, 114
Day, Lt. Col. Carl S., 138
DeBose, Vice Adm. Laurence, 240
Defenderfer, Lt.(jg.) Doris A., 238
Defense Advisory Committee for Women. *See* DACOWITS
de Florez, Capt. Luis, 105
Demobilization, 211-15
Denby, Mrs., 38
Denfeld, Vice Adm. Louis, 216, 223, 245, 246
Dente, Ens. Virginia M., 83
Detroit, 264
Devaney, Frances R., 235
DeWitt, Capt. Nellie Jane, 157
Dimelow, Lt. Grace C., 71
Director's responsibilities, 65, 66-67, 70
Disert, Lt. Margaret C., 62, 79
Dougherty, Lt. Comdr. Kathryn, 71, 237
Driscoll, Alfred E., 171
Dryden, Maj. Marian, 200
Duncan, Vice Adm. Donald B., 231
Dunn, Lt. Bess A., 71
Durette, Lt. Comdr. Eleanor, 71
Dyer, Capt. James, 96

Earle B. Hall, 168
Educational Advisory Council, 191
Eisenhower, Gen. Dwight D., 229, 230, 231
Electronic schools, 128
Elizabeth (queen of England), 252, 253, 254
Ellinwood, Lt.(jg.) Estelle, 88
Elliott, Harriet, 56, 60
Elloughton-Brough, Yorkshire, England, 33, 34, 36
Enlisted training, 108, 127-49, 237
Erben, 165
Erickson, P01c Lief, 204

Evans, Commodore D. P., Royal Navy, 247
Evans, Mrs. D. P., 247

Femmes de la Flotte, 251
Finnigan, Ens. Margaret M., 88
Flora, Ruth, 235
Ford, Lt. Ellen, 238
Foreign Service Preparatory School, 16
Forrestal, James V., 121, 214, 225, 230
Forrestal, Mrs. James V., 152
Forsman, Lt. Comdr. Nancy V., 71
Foster, Ens. Dorothy, 62
Foster, Vice Adm. Dorsey, 171

Gabe, Mr. (blacksmith), 13
Gates, Mrs. Thomas, 60, 124
George VI (king of England), 252, 253
Georgia State College for Women, 102
Ghormley, Adm. Robert L., 201
Gibson, Capt. Winifred, 248
Gies, Ens. Edwina L., 118
Gilbreth, Lillian, 60
Gildersleeve, Virginia C., 49, 59-60, 124, 210
Glass, Meta, 60, 124
Graham, Mrs. Malbone W., 60, 124
Grant, Lt. Comdr. Sybil A., 239
Gross, Lt.(jg.) Rebecca F., 119
Ground Controlled Approach, 221
Gunnery instructors, 138, 140-42

Hale, Ens. Katherine M., 88
Hallaren, Col. Mary, 226, 245, 246, 248, 249, 250, 252
Hammerstein, Oscar, II, 179, 180
Hancock, Capt. Joy Bright: birth, 4, 9; at Bureau of Aeronautics, 37, 42, 45, 52, 63, 96,

Naval Auxiliary Air Station, Green Cove Springs, 141
Naval Aviation Training School, Hollywood, Fla., 90, 181
Naval Base, Newport, 239
Naval College, Greenwich, 253-54
Naval Convalescent Hospital, Sun Valley, 146
Naval Forces Germany, Headquarters, 250
Naval Headquarters, London, 246, 248
Naval Medical Center, Bethesda, 145
Naval Reserve Act of 1916, 48
Naval Reserve Act of 1925, 48
Naval Reserve Act of 1938, 48, 53, 55, 223
Naval Reserve Midshipmen's School, Northampton, 62, 65, 75-80, 211; curricula, 78; enrollment, 79
Naval School, Officer Indoctrination, Newport, 240
Naval Station, Green Cove Springs, 168-69
Naval Station, Roosevelt Roads, 266
Naval Training Center, Bainbridge, 4, 237, 240, 261
Naval Training Center, Great Lakes, 142, 145, 212, 237, 239
Naval Training Center (Women's Reserve), the Bronx. See Hunter College
Naval Training and Distribution Center, Camp Shoemaker, 204
Naval Training School, Communications, 79
Naval Training School, Sampson, 143
Naval War College, 16
Navy Nurse Corps, 248
NC-4 (flying boat), 27-28, 31, 264
Newman, Ens. Margaret, 88
New York Shipbuilding Corporation, Camden, 23, 24
Nicholson, Capt., 166

Nimitz, Adm. Chester W., 50, 52, 121, 201, 229, 230; on legislation, 231-32
Northampton. See Naval Reserve Midshipmen's School
Notenstein, Mrs. Wallace, 124
Nunn, Capt. Ira, 223, 224

Oddie, Tasker L., 48
Officer indoctrination courses, 113
Officer Indoctrination Unit (W), Newport, 239
Officer rank structure, 259
Officer training, 75-85, 239
Ofstie Field, Puerto Rico, 265
Ofstie, Vice Adm. Ralph A., 41, 49, 264-65
Ohio State University, 93
Oklahoma A & M, 102
Ordnance officers, 82-83
Overseas assignment, 197-206

Palmer, Comdr. Jean, 199, 200, 202; as Director, 219
Pappan, CPO Rubinie, 136
Parachute rigger, 131-32
Parker, Lt. Harriet Felton, 62
Parrick, Ens. Evelyn, 88
Pearson, Ens. Louisa, 120
Pensylvania Dutch, 7
Perrill, Ens. Martha E. C., 88
Personnel supervisor, 114
Pete (church janitor), 13
Peters, Paul, 179
Petersen, Lt. Tova L., 62
Petty Officers Leadership School, 258
Philadelphia, 14, 23, 24
Phillips, Sidney, 179
Photo interpretation officers, 93
Pigeonman, 137-38
Pius XII (pope), 252
Plane captains, 189-91
Pryor, Ens. Lucille, 120
Public Law 38, 78th Congress, 1st Session, 84, 85
Public Law 381, 259

Stone, Lt. Elmer F., 264
Storekeepers, 102
Stratton, Capt. Dorothy, 80, 200
Streeter, Col. Ruth, 200
Sullivan, John 236, 237
Supply Corps School, Cambridge, 80
Supply officers, 80
Surgeon General, office of, 226
Swanson, Adm., 227
Sweeney, Lt. Virginia R., 71

Taylor, Myron, 252
Tennant, Lt. (jg.) Betty Rae, 238
Terletzky, Lt. Serepta B., 62, 71
Terry, Lt. (jg.) Henrietta P., 88
Thierry, Madame Justin, 251
Towers, Rear Adm. John H., 49, 186, 189, 201
Towle, Col. Katherine, 226
Truman, President Harry S., 243
Turnbull, Ens. Esther M., 88
Twelfth Naval District, 111-12

Underwood, Frances, 80
Underwood, Capt., H. W., 77, 79, 80, 212
Uniforms, 152-55
United Nations Conference for International Organization, 210, 211
University of California at Los Angeles, 88, 89
University of Chicago, 88
University of Indiana, 102
University of Wisconsin, 102

V-9 designator, 78
Vance, John, 6
Vandergrift, Gen. A. A., 231, 232
van Straten, Ens. Florence W., 88
Victoria Hotel, Boston, 102
Victory, HMS, 247
Vinson, Carl, 223, 224, 230

WAAC, 50, 226, 231
WAC, 242, 245, 249
Wardsworth, Senator, 48
WAF, 226, 242
Waller, Gen. Beresford, 201
Walsh. David I., 55, 56
Wann, Flight Lt. Archibald H., Royal Air Force, 33, 37
War Manpower Commission, 49
Warrant officer selection, 259
Warren, Capt., 248
WAVES: acronym, 61; billet assignment criteria, 83-84, 111-13, 115-16, 118, 123, 147-48; discipline, 116-17; early planning and guidelines, 48-49, 50, 62, 113-14; enlisted training, 108, 127-49, 237; in Hawaii, 203-06, 232; housing problems, 173, 201, 260; nutrition, 119; officer qualifications, 76, 188; officer training, 75-85, 239; opposition to, 51, 65, 66-68, 114-15, 120; overseas limitations, 68, 198-99; permanent status, 119, 221, 236; recreation, 178, 201; recruit training, 101-09; specialized duties, 72, 188; statistical data, 151-52, 209-11, 241, 258; transfer policy, 69, 97; uniforms, 152-55
WAVES in Naval Aviation (pamphlet), 114
Westcott, Lt. Comdr. Doris T., 71
Weyerbacher, Comdr. Ralph D., 37
White, Lt. Eunice, 64
Wick, Lt. Zeno, 38
Wiederman, WAVE, 191
Wildwood, 6, 8, 12, 16, 170, 264
Wiley, Lt. Tova P., 123
Wilk, Jake, 179
Willis, Raymond E., 54
Willoughby, Lt. Comdr. Frances L., 238
Wilson, President Woodrow, 21 32
Winston, 166
Wohl, Lt. Comdr. Harry, 79

Wolsieffer, Capt. Frederick, 4, 261

Women Accepted for Volunteer Emergency Service. *See* WAVES

Women in the French navy, 251

Women in Holland's navy (MARVAS), 248

Women Marines, 80, 108, 128, 130, 131, 133, 139, 142, 187, 200, 223, 226, 232, 242

Women Royal Marines (British), 248

Women's Air Force. *See* WAF

Women's Armed Services Integration Act, 232, 235

Women's Army Corps. *See* WAC

Women's Auxiliary Army Corps. *See* WAAC

Women's Reserve, Naval Service (British), 246. *See also* WRNS

Wood, Capt. Elmer, 23

Woodruff, Lt. Helen M., 71

Wollcombe, Commodore Joyce, WRNS, 246, 247, 253, 254

Worden, Ens. Margaret E., 88

World War I, 21

WRNS, 247, 254

Yeoman (F), 21, 22, 23-24, 25, 28

Yeomen, 102

Yorktown, 202

Young, Edna E., 235

ZR-1 (airship), 37, 38-39. *See also Shenandoah*

ZR-2 (airship), 32-33, 36

ZR-3 (airship), 39

Composed in nine-point Aster with two points of leading by Tinker N. A. Corporation, New York, New York.

Printed offset on sixty-pound Deeplake Offset. Spine bound in Columbia Fictionette and front and back covers in Kivar Kidskin. Printed and bound by NAPCO Graphic Arts, Incorporated, Milwaukee, Wisconsin.